Following Nimishoomis

The Trout Lake History of
Dedibaayaanimanook
Sarah Keesick Olsen

Copyright © 2008 Helen Agger
Library and Archives Canada Cataloguing in Publication

Agger, Helen, 1946-
Following Nimishoomis : the oral history of Dedibaayaanimanook
Sarah Keesick Olsen / Helen Agger.

Includes bibliographical references and index.
ISBN 978-1-894778-60-2

1. Olsen, Dedibaayaanimanook Sarah Keesick, 1922-. 2. Lac Seul First
Nation--History. 3. Ojibwa Indians--Ontario--Lac Seul Region--History.
4. Ojibwa women--Ontario--Lac Seul Region--Biography. 5. Lac Seul Region
(Ont.)--Biography. 6. Oral history. 7. Oral biography. I. Title.

E99.C6D44 2008   971.3'112004973330092   C2008-903822-3

Printed in Canada

Printed on Ancient Forest Friendly 100% post consumer fibre paper.

Credits
Cover photo of Dedibaayaanimanook courtesy of John Richthammer.
Cover photo of Namegosibiing courtesy of Helen Agger

www.theytus.com
In Canada: Theytus Books, Green Mountain Rd., Lot 45, RR#2, Site 50, Comp. 8
Penticton, BC ,V2A 6J7, Tel: 250-493-7181
In the USA: Theytus Books, P.O. Box 2890, Oroville, Washington, 98844

  Patrimoine Canadian
canadien Heritage

 Canada Council Conseil des Arts
for the Arts du Canada

 BRITISH COLUMBIA
ARTS COUNCIL
Supported by the Province of British Columbia

*On Behalf of Theytus Books, we acknowledge the financial support of the Government
of Canada through the Book Publishing Industry Development Program (BPIDP) for our
publishing activities. We acknowledge the support of the Canada Council for the Arts
which last year invested $20.1 million in writing and publishing throughout Canada.
Nous remercions de son soutien le Conseil des Arts du Canada, qui a investi 20,1 millions
de dollars l'an dernier dans les lettres et l'édition à travers le Canada.We acknowledge the
support of the Province of British Columbia through the British Columbia Arts Council.*

Following Nimishoomis

The Trout Lake History of
Dedibaayaanimanook
Sarah Keesick Olsen

HELEN AGGER

Theytus Books

For my dear mother,
Dedibaayaanimanook Sarah Keesick Olsen.

Foreword

This important text documents a unique life as experienced by an Anishinaabe woman in what is now called Northwestern Ontario. The oral narrations of Dedibaayaanimanook and her people, derived from life experiences directly on the land inhabited by her ancestors since time forever passed, have largely been ignored by the Canadian historical community. This history gives a voice to Dedibaayaanimanook and indeed, to all Indigenous groups and individuals who continue to be silenced by dominant Eurocentric historical traditions.

Many in the more recent Anishinaabe generations do not speak the Old Languages, nor do they understand ancient traditions that are embedded within those languages. Helen Agger's writing retains the oral records of Dedibaayanimanook, Senior Knowledge Keeper and Elder of the Namegosibiing Anishinaabeg for both the present and future generations.

Agger's writing safeguards the accuracy of the details of land-based traditions, activities and practices, including those that are no longer in use. It protects the history of the Anishinaabe community of Namegosibiing from inaccurate and fabricated versions that arise from many different sources. As well, it sets an example to other communities in generating respect for their most Senior Knowledge Keepers and Elders and in seeking out, recording and reproducing the ancient truths they hold.

Elijah Harper
Ottawa, ON

Contents

ACKNOWLEDGEMENTS

Foremost, Dedibaayaanimanook Sarah Keesick Olsen's patience, generosity and willingness to share made this oral story possible. To her, my dearest mother, I am grateful. I also acknowledge the following individuals (in alphabetical order) who provided encouragement, support, critique and comment during the long process of putting Dedibaayaanimanook's story together: Garth Agger, my husband; Leslie Agger, my daughter; Professor Jennifer S.H. Brown, Department of History, Canada Research Chair & Centre for Rupert's Land Studies Director, University of Winnipeg, who generously took time to read through the manuscript, not only once but twice; Renate Eigenbrod, of the University of Manitoba who was my editor and mentor; Anita Harper, my sister, who helped to research Giigooyikewinini's history; John and Marion Neufeld, supportive friends for many years; John Richthammer, archivist, who so willingly shared information, contacts and photographs throughout the process; R. Paul Rogers (architectural designer in Sweden), a close family friend who remained enthusiastic about the project from the beginning; Gregory Scofield, who was Writer in Residence at the University of Manitoba; Theytus Books, Ltd. staff and review Committee, who saw potential in the submitted manuscript; and Peggy Venables, whose continual faith in the do-ability of this story was a constant inspiration. Without their support, this story would not have reached a successful completion.

Map 1—Namegosibiing Trout Lake

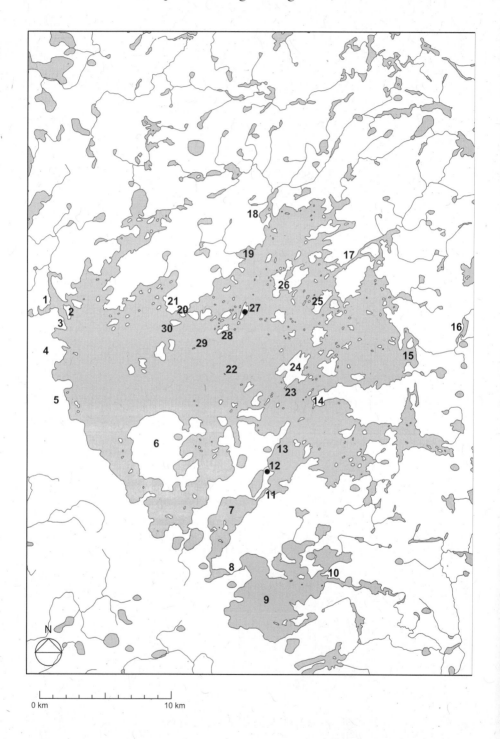

0 km   10 km

Map 1 — Legend

1. Mako'Odaaminike (Where the Black Bear Feasts on Spawning Fish)
2. Jiiiyaani Minis (Jiiyaan Island)
3. Ningaabii'anong (The West)
4. Oshedinaa (Trout Lake Ridge)
5. Binesiwajiing (Where the Thunderers Nested)
6. Bizhiwi Minis (Lynx Island, now known as Cat Island)
7. Aanziko Zaa'igan (Merganser Lake, now known as Otter Lake)
8. Waabashkiigaang
9. Namegosibii Shishiing (Little Trout Lake)
10. The Place Where Namegosi Ziibi (Trout Lake River) Begins
11. Gojijiwaawangaang
12. Sandy Beach Lodge
13. Mikinaako Minisan (Snapping Turtle Islands)
14. Gete Waakaa'iganing
   (Place of the Old Building, now known as Hudson's Bay Point)
15. Gaaminitigwashkiigaag (now known as Keesick Bay)
16. Manoonini Zaa'igan (Rice Lake)
17. Biinjidawaabikideng (now known as Long Channel)
18. Jiibayi Zaagiing (now known as Jackfish Bay)
19. Gweyeshikaang (Gweyesh's Place, now known as Minnow Bay)
20. Namebinibagida'waagan
   (Where Sucker Nets Were Set, now known as Alice Beach)
21. Gaazhimikwamiiwaagamig (Where the Water is Icy Cold, now known as Helen Beach and/or "Anton Beach")
22. Manidoo Minis (Spirit Island, now known as Seagull Island)
23. Negiishkensikaang (Where the Cedars Grow Along the Shore)
24. Ma'iingani Minis (Wolf Island)
25. Waagoshi Minis (Fox Island)
26. Adikamego Minis (Whitefish Island)
27. Trout Lake Lodge
28. Camp Island
29. Zhiishiibi Minis (Duck Island)
30. Aanizi Minis (Alice Island)

Map 2 — Traditional Use Territory of Dedibaayaanimanook's People

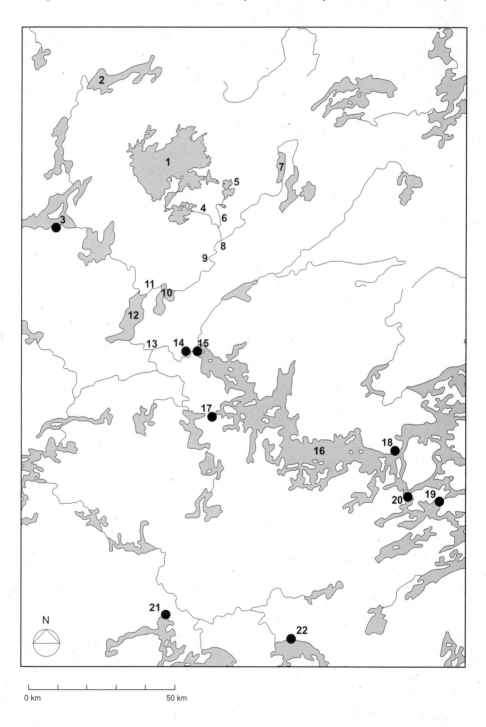

Map 2 — Legend

1. Namegosibiing (Trout Waters, now known as Trout Lake)
2. Oshkaandagaawi Zaa'igan (now known as Nungesser Lake)
3. Wanamani Zaa'igan (the town of Red Lake)
4. Namegosi Ziibi (Trout River)
5. Wazhashko Zaa'igan (Muskrat Lake, now known as Joyce Lake)
6. Wazhashko Maadaawaang
7. Ikwewi Zaa'igan (Woman Lake)
8. Apisaabiko Maadaawaang
9. Gaaodooskwanigamaag (The Elbow Place)
10. Baagwaashi Zaa'iganiins (Little Shallow Lake, now known as Bruce Lake)
11. Namegosi Zaagiing
12. Baagwaashi Zaa'igan (Shallow Lake, now known as Pakwash Lake)
13. Maadaawaang
14. Otawagi Baawitig (Ear Falls)
15. Gojijiing (now known as Goldpines)
16. Obizhigokaawi Zaa'igan (Lac Seul Lake)
17. Wabauskaang First Nation
18. Obizhigokaang (now known as the Lac Seul First Nation community of Kejick Bay)
19. Waaninaawangaang (Sioux Lookout)
20. Baakwaayshtigwaan (Lac Seul First Nation community of Frenchman's Head)
21. Vermilion Bay
22. Bigwaakoshebi Baawitig (now known as Dryden)

Map 3 — South East Manitoba and South East Ontario

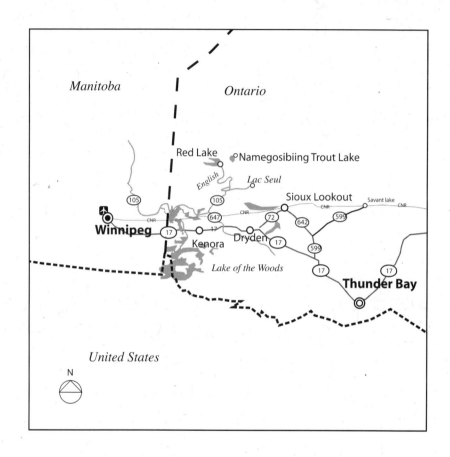

INTRODUCTION

Recounting the details of trips to Namegosibiing[1] made me think about the reasons why our visits were so special. It was because my mother, Dedibaayaanimanook Sarah Keesick Olsen, accompanied us. One outing that stood out as particularly memorable occurred during the summer of 2001 when my mother was 79 years old. Instead of taking a plane, she came along when my daughter and I set out for the hiking trail to Namegosibiing. We drove north on the Nungesser highway[2], then turned east onto a narrow logging road that came to an end at the beaver dam. With a small pack on her back and a walking stick to help with her balance, my mother was ready for the hour long hike.

The beaver dam, which has since been demolished by a logging company with the approval of the Ontario Ministry of Natural Resources (OMNR), required us to tread carefully. A few inches to the left were the murky waters of the beaver pond and immediately to our right were hundreds of smoothly de-barked logs in various lengths and thicknesses that made a solid footing all but impossible. Water immediately oozed from the places where our steps punctured the soggy structure. At one point, I lost my footing and very nearly toppled into the pond with all my equipment. The trail took us from the beaver dam for several kilometres up and down hills, in and out of spongy marshes, under windfalls, and—rain had just fallen the previous night—through gushing rivulets. In the densest regions of the forest where the wind is unable to penetrate, voracious mosquitoes and crawling black flies eagerly awaited our arrival. We stopped frequently for brief rests. As we examined the flora, my mother provided us with the names of various plants and explained their significance. She used her walking stick to point to the different types of trees, describing the role they play in the lives of birds and animals. She specified which animals associate themselves with which plants. During this time together on the hiking trail, my mother narrated only a small part of the forest floor story of which she was the expert decipherer.

A few days after our arrival at Camp Island[3] in Namegosibiing, we took our boat across the lake to the traditional Anishinaabe cemetery at Gojijiwaawangaang.[4] We stopped to view the graves and clear away the overgrowth. From there, we continued south to Aanziko Zaa'igan[5] and Namegosibii Shishiing[6] where my mother had not been since she and her parents passed through the region over 60 years earlier. She showed us different places where her family once camped, caught fish, collected firewood and carried out other similar activities as they journeyed to and from Namegosibiing. Having decided to build a fire and have lunch where my mother and her parents and relatives had stopped for the night three quarters of a century before, I began to realize that the entire region was well-known territory filled with memories for my mother, Dedibaayaanimanook. Later, she offered to drive home. I had previously tried to steer the 15-hp motor but soon discovered that I did not have the wrist strength to continue for very long. My daughter and I could not help but notice, on the other hand, the ease with which Dedibaayaanimanook was able to manoeuvre the boat at top speeds. Not only was she familiar with each and every island but she knew which ones allowed us to cut close and which ones required a wider berth. She skirted every reef expertly, while reading the distant horizon for Camp Island's exact location as we headed across the open expanse. When we reached our island and entered the bay, she swung the boat into a graceful arc that brought our journey to a smooth conclusion just inches from the dock.

Over the course of subsequent visits and conversations, it became apparent that many of my mother's grandchildren knew only a few details about her childhood. They had not heard the story of her experiences growing up in a traditional Anishinaabe family during the 1920s, 1930s and early 1940s. They were not familiar with the carefree little girl who grew up to become a young woman raising six children while providing much of the labour in a busy fishing operation. The story about the events of her life, her experiences and her insights needed to be gathered and written, and my mother, Dedibaayaanimanook Sarah Keesick Olsen, expressed interest in helping to do so. Accordingly,

I began taking notes of our conversations in 1997.[7] But there were certain limitations, provisos and parameters. She explained that one of the important Gichi Anishinaabeg[8] tenets she had learned from her parents was that talking about certain people and in some cases even mentioning their names was inappropriate if not completely proscribed once they were deceased. Since the Gichi Anishinaabeg of her childhood years upheld the teaching, there were instances when my mother did not know the names and events associated with individuals who had died before her birth or before the time she was old enough to remember her own first hand experiences with them. When we discussed that kind of information, Dedibaayaanimanook needed to decide to what degree she herself would set aside the sanction in order to clarify certain details relating to different individuals about whom she did have information. There were instances when she chose not to divulge specific names or discuss certain events in any detail. That was the type of limitation she clearly articulated. In addition, Dedibaayaanimanook reported only what she knew to be true, maintaining her silence on matters about which she was not certain. "Wiinge inzhiingendaan ji giiwanimoyaan!" She strongly emphasized her intent to be accurate to the best of her knowledge.

Not a lot of information based on sources other than Dedibaayaanimanook is included, but if incorporated, serves to situate her story within a broader historical context. It also enhances an appreciation for the extent to which some of Dedibaayaanimanook's people managed to hold onto traditional ways well into the 20th century, despite the events of a major gold rush in Wanamani Zaa'iganing[9] along with all its related activities, the pressures of a worldwide economic depression and other forms of encroachment. Additionally, the information serves to highlight the contrast between Anishinaabe world views and perspectives and those of the wemitigoozhiwag who were becoming more and more prominent within the people's traditional territories and homeland. In cases where her information may have proven to differ from that provided by others, my mother stressed that she had no wish to undermine either the credibility or veracity of others. Her most earnest desire was to be true to the telling of what only she could tell: *Her* story. With this narrative being based on what Dedibaayaanimanook shared with me, it is incomplete and/or limited only to the degree that I failed to record it completely and accurately.

The provisos are rooted in historical events. Until the 1950s, for example, no Treaty Anishinaabe person could legally access public places where alcohol was served. Dedibaayaanimanook heard of instances in which relatives jeopardized their Treaty rights when they were caught buying liquor for themselves or other Anishinaabeg. Subsequent changes in the Indian Act affected Namegosibii Anishinaabeg in very dramatic ways. "Amii 'i gii' biindige'aawindô Anishinaabeg." It was a common phrase that Dedibaayaanimanook remembered being spoken among people of Namegosibiing. Literally translated, Anishinaabeg were now being "brought in," that was to say, they too were now allowed certain rights, such as entering the local beer parlour and liquor outlet. These changes meant that it was no longer an act of crime for Anishinaabe people to access licensed premises; they no longer needed to fear punitive action. After that, however, rampant alcoholism and all its negative effects very rapidly led to the demise of many components of Namegosibii Anishinaabewiziwin.[10] Having said that, it is important to point out that no claim is made that the change to the Act in and of itself caused alcoholism. However, it set the stage for problems to begin playing out more freely in public and obvious ways. Pre-existing conditions, arising largely from the Act itself and the methods of its enforcement, were manifestly compounded. This resulted in a whole range of new but closely related problems.

Recently, a post card was available for sale at the coffee shop, the Mennonite bookstore and various other outlets in Red Lake. Produced from a photograph taken in 1949, the post card was a fascinating portrayal of a group of well dressed Anishinaabe men—both young and old—visiting together in front of the cafe in the centre of town. They looked relaxed and were obviously enjoying the informal gathering. Dedibaayaanimanook knew several of the individuals. Some were kin. After the Act was changed, that kind of street scenario vanished virtually overnight, to be replaced by another. Dedibaayaanimanook remembered once seeing two cousins, mere toddlers at the time, wandering hand in hand in the Lac Seul community while their parents and other adults were preoccupied with drink.

The sickness of alcoholism, along with all of its worst consequences, were daily realities for Namegosibii Anishinaabe people to some degree. Every member of the community was affected one way or another. Whether one lived in Namegosibiing, Red Lake or any other place, its effects were unimaginably brutal, physically and psychologically, spiritually and culturally. Many found the matter too painful to acknowledge, much less openly discuss. My mother spent all of her young and mid-adulthood in Namegosibiing, where their traditional lifestyle was somewhat protected, since alcohol was not as readily available as it was in town. Although she lived in the shelter of that relative isolation, she nonetheless heard the litany of tragic events that contrasted with the busy, peaceful and healthy lives her siblings, aunts, uncles and cousins had once led in Namegosibiing during the time of her childhood.

"Gaawiin niwii' dazhindanziin minikwewin." Dedibaayaanimanook stated categorically that she did not wish to talk about the subject of alcoholism and its effects in any detailed way. Out of a sense of respect for the memory of those who had passed on, and to honour the privacy of all individuals—whether they are still with us or not—there is very little mention of any alcohol related aspects of people's lives in this story. That subject is articulable when and only when other individuals themselves choose to tell their personal stories. These are the reasons why readers will not come across many descriptions of alcohol related events in Dedibaayaanimanook's life, even though their exclusion runs the risk of presenting an incomplete story. Readers are urged not to forget about the fact that the ubiquitous effects of alcoholism existed every day in people's lives, particularly as the narrative moves into the early 1950s.

Another historical force with enormous negative effects on people's lives was compulsory residential school attendance. Dedibaayaanimanook, who never attended school, did not discuss the brutal treatment of Anishinaabe children, in part because her nephews and nieces did not talk about all the details of the experiences they underwent while at boarding school. What my mother did mention more than once, however, was that most of the children returned from school "spoiled"—ruined—as a result of what they had undergone. With the use of that particular term, Dedibaayaanimanook meant that they had lost their desire to participate in any of their parents' activities. They had no ambition to hunt, fish or trap.

At least initially, the returnees seemed to prefer spending their time reading—in English. Comics were a particular favourite. In some cases, the youngsters appeared to forgot how to speak Anishinaabe. Most devastating for their parents, it seemed as though the children were ashamed to be Anishinaabe. They scorned their culture and their heritage. Parents were heartsick to see those of the next generation giving up their ability to live off the land and practise the old ways. They were at a loss as to how to deal with their children, who no longer appeared interested in Anishinaabewiziwin. From their own experiences, adults were familiar enough with the wemitigoozhii way of thinking that they saw little room for their children in the foreigners' world. They had long noted that Anishinaabeg were rarely able to "get ahead" with wemitigoozhiwag in terms of better paid work or anything beyond manual physical labour, for example. People were neither welcomed, invited nor encouraged to live among the wemitigoozhiwag whenever employment drew them into town. Some of Dedibaayaanimanook's younger nieces and nephews, therefore, returned to their homeland in Namegosibiing and lived, as best they could, a mixture of the old and the foreign.

These issues—the extremely negative effects upon the psyche of the young boarding school survivors—are not mentioned in any depth in Dedibaayaanimanook's oral story because her own situation allowed her to believe in the history and heritage of her people and to hold onto her faith in the validity of their teachings. Since her circumstances of comparative isolation served to protect her earlier life experiences as culturally intact and comparatively free from outside influences, her story may help to mend the fractures brought upon the community by those influences. For the rest of us of the Namegosibiing community, the act of researching, listening to and reading about the old ways allows us to capture a glimpse of the Gichi Anishinaabe wisdom from which people once received direction. It also helps us to develop a sense of value for this kind of knowledge about the history of the community and the forebears in order to (re)claim its ownership and do with it as we deem will be the best way for honouring the memory of those who preceded us. At the same time, Dedibaayaanimanook's story will assist in correcting misconceptions that the homelands were tracts of "wilderness" devoid of human history, when in fact, every square centimetre of this continent was someone's traditional homeland.

Those who understand about such things will notice that some of the subject matter discussed in Dedibaayaanimanook's narrative is of a sensitive nature. Inclusion of this kind of material draws the story into a sacred place that will be readily recognizable to the perceptive reader. Moreover, a note of explanation relates to how traditional narratives were told. They frequently contained information for which no explanations were given because it was understood that the astute listener-learners would eventually find the answers for themselves, if they were sufficiently interested. For example, the story of Mrs. Sapay's wolf dog in Chapter 5 serves to illustrate the fact that any event or circumstance containing a strong supernatural element came with no natural explanation. It was considered highly imprudent to probe for further details when none were provided during the telling of such an event. To refrain generally from asking questions was a form of respect that Anishinaabe people exemplified because it was understood that over the course of time, life itself would provide listeners with answers, and as a result, they too would one day be in a position to share their stories. In this way, the telling of stories served not only to share information and even to entertain, but on another level, to impart young listeners with patience, respect and trust for their elders. Along a parallel vein, therefore, Dedibaayaanimanook's narrative contains the occasional Anishinaabe statement in quotations, the meaning of which is not always in the form of a word-for-word translation. Rather, it is embedded within the remainder of the paragraph.

By way of further explanation, it is important to note that the process by which Dedibaayaanimanook's oral story evolved into the written word was for me to jot down bits of information as she spoke in Anishinaabe and I replied in English, carrying on our conversations over the course of 10 years, and then my arranging the information into a coherent sequence. As well, it is worth mentioning that the inclusion of some Anishinaabe terms is intended to remind readers of the narrative's original language. This story, it is hoped, will prove to be as meaningful an experience to read as it was to write.

1. Namegosibiing is Trout Lake, Dedibaayaanimanook's homeland and place of birth.

2. Nungesser highway leads past Nungesser Lake, which was known as Oshkaandagaawi Zaa'igan among Dedibaayaanimanook's people. Much of the homelands have been decimated by logging activities on both sides of this highway and elsewhere.

3. Camp Island in Namegosibiing is where Dedibaayaanimanook spent much of her adult life.

4. The Namegosibiing traditional cemetery is located along the west side of the narrows known as Gojijiwaawangaang.

5. Aanziko Zaa'igan, which translates to Merganser Lake, is a small lake connected to Namegosibiing in the south by Gojijiwaawangaang. Today Aanziko Zaa'igan is known as Otter Lake.

6. Namegosibii Shishiing has been correctly translated to Little Trout Lake.

7. At the outset, Dedibaayaanimanook expressed a strong aversion to having her voice recorded. Her sensibilities in this regard are related to a certain spirituality people of old associated with one's voice when certain matters were under discussion. Therefore, out of respect for those wishes, I never attempted to use recording devices during our conversations. If any recordings of her voice exist, they would without doubt have been made under some form or degree of dishonesty or even psychological pressure.

8. The Gichi Anishinaabeg were those elderly people of the community with the knowledge and life experiences necessary to serve as senior knowledge custodians, teachers, advisors and leaders. As for the term *Anishinaabe*, Dedibaayaanimanook used it in two ways, specifically to denote the Ojibwe people, and generally, for all Indigenous peoples.

9. Wanamani Zaa'iganing is (at, in, of, etc.) Red Lake, the gold mining community in northwest Ontario.

10. Namegosibii Anishinaabewiziwin refers to those essential attributes, qualities, traits, practices and beliefs that set the Anishinaabe people of Namegosibiing apart from other Anishinaabeg.

CHAPTER 1

Dedibaayaanimanook Izhinikaazo

~

"Her Name Is Dedibaayaanimanook"

The second decade of the twentieth century was already into its second year. Canada's Department of Indian Affairs had been established some forty-two years previously, and forty-nine years had gone by since the signing of the great and historic Treaty No. 3. Four years after the War to end all wars was ended, ships of the world's merchant marines were once again free to ply the oceans of the globe in safety. The people of Namegosibiing Trout Lake[1] had, of course, heard about such events. They knew of at least two men—one a relative and the other an acquaintance—who had gone to war. But it was the sequence of events confirming spring's arrival that was uppermost on their minds.

"Aazha ani bepegwajizhaagigamiiwan," was how Gaamadweyaashiik Emma Strang Angeconeb Keesick described in precise terms the ice conditions she observed as open water began to appear along the south facing shoreline of sounds and inlets that year in Namegosibiing Trout Lake. Winter's demise was clearly in evidence even during the morning's earliest hours. The next day, in fact, people reported a small amount of rain had fallen around midnight. It was bound to hasten the transformation of Namegosibiing's dense blanket of ice into the fragile honeycombs so characteristic of that part of the season.

Gaamadweyaashiik Emma and Dedibayaash William Keesick's daughter was born during the pre-dawn hours that spring morning. Dedibayaash himself was away at Jiibayi Zaagiing[2] on a trapping expedition, but Nookom, Gookomens and Gweyesh Annie were with Gaamadweyaashiik, watching her closely. The two elder women had many years of experience as senior midwives, and even though she was just beginning her training, Gweyesh Annie was ready to help in whatever way they required. Yet despite the women's care and attention, Gaamadweyaashiik was suddenly in great distress. Immediately the women sent for Giizhik Sam Keesick, widely recognized to have the gifts of Gizhe Manidoo. Giizhik arrived from his tent, then seated himself close to his daughter-in-law and blew across her forehead. Gaamadweyaashiik began to stir, and over the next several hours her condition steadily improved.

"Dibikigiizis gii' oshkagoojin," she later told others by way of referring to the wispy sliver of silver in the shape of a reverse C that came into view through a small tear in the tent while she rested. It was the first quarter of the moon known as the Loon Moon. Later on, Indian Affairs would record the date of the Keesicks' daughter's arrival as the 29th of April, 1922. The precise place of her birth was their camp situated a short distance from the beach Gaaminitigwashkiigaag[3] on the eastern main shore of the lake. Both of her parents were now in their mid 40s.

Gaamadweyaashiik recovered fully, but it was apparent that all was not well with their little girl. When autumn arrived and Dedibayaash and his stepson Jiins had to leave Namegosibiing for the remote regions of their trapline, family members agreed they needed to remain together. The entire household travelled the many miles to Memegweshi Zaa'igan[4] and upon arriving, they held a special ceremony to confirm the name that Giizhik Sam Keesick had given his granddaughter in a formal rite of celebration. That name was Dedibaayaanimanook, the feminine form of Dedibayaash. Indicating how deeply she was loved, Dedibaayaanimanook received two other names. From her father she received Zhaabonowebiik, a reference to the winds that blow through the forests and across the sky. From her uncle Jiiyaan Donald came the name Ekwaabanook. It refers to the first light of dawn that disperses night's darkness and brightens the eastern skies. Each name came accompanied with a special song providing an explanation of its meaning. Later on, Dedibaayaanimanook would hear her uncle Jiiyaan singing her naming song and she learned it, but although she too, as recipient, could sing or recite it, she was bound not to share it with anyone else. Name giving was an expression of affection in the highest order and because it was the sharing of one's spiritual essence, the gift created a special, lasting bond between the two individuals.

During their stay at Memegwesh, Dedibaayaanimanook developed a high fever. Her mother and her half-sister (Gichi Jôj, George Trout's mother) took turns holding her, listening as she breathed and keeping her safe. Dedibayaash was away trapping, but as soon as he returned and observed his daughter's condition, he immediately set out across the darkness for an all-night journey to Ikwewi Zaa'igan, Woman Lake, where he sought out an individual knowledgeable in the use of traditional medicine. Gaadadakokaadej John Angeconeb—a relative of Gaamadweyaashiik's late husband—agreed to accompany Dedibayaash back to Memegwesh. By the time they arrived back, Dedibayaash had been on the trail for over thirty-six hours, but he was unaware of his physical exhaustion as Gaadadakokaadej instructed Gaamadweyaashiik to boil a small quantity of plant substance. Dedibaayaanimanook swallowed some of the medicine from a small spoon, then her mother placed a number of drops on her forehead. Her fever broke.

It was still early winter, but Christmas was rapidly approaching. The Keesicks wanted to be home in order to begin preparing for the celebrations. Now customary among Namegosibii Anishinaabeg, these feasts were a manifestation of wemitigoozhii influence. Little Dedibaayaanimanook peered up from her cradleboard, well secured to the tiny sled her father had made to match its dimensions exactly, as the family set out on their two nights' journey. Her teenage brother, Jiins, had the responsibility of guiding the dog that pulled her sled. Although dogs were in use for hauling toboggans, each person also pulled a sled or toboggan in addition to carrying a backpack. The Keesicks were well into the first day of their journey when they came to a tight bend in the trail. Dedibaayaanimanook's sled brushed against the tip of a low hanging evergreen branch. Jiins stopped immediately, but his sister's tiny face was already covered over with a dusting of snow. The shocking realization of what might have happened dampened his momentary sense of amusement.

Even though Dedibaayaanimanook survived her illness at Meme-gwesh, she continued to be unwell. Pressure from within the upper part of her head began to push outward, and once again her parents turned to Giizhik. While Dedibaayaanimanook slept fitfully in her cradleboard, her grandfather watched her intently. Just as he had done for his daughter-in-law several months before, Giizhik drew a breath and blew into his granddaughter's face. He took careful note as she gasped.

"Dabimaadizi Dedibaayaanimanook," he reassured Gaamadwey-aashiik and Dedibayaash. Having received the information from a powerful dream that their daughter would live, he was able to calm their fears. The Dedibayaashes were rejuvenated with new optimism, and they resolved anew to provide her with whatever care and pro-tection she needed for as long as they had the ability to do so. Only after Dedibaayaanimanook was old enough to begin talking did they realize that she suffered from a severe form of headache. The sickness would continue to plague her intermittently throughout the rest of her life.

"Onzaawizhooniyaawasin gii' mikiganiwi!" Right around the time when Dedibaayaanimanook was born, her parents heard that yellow moneyrock had been discovered in Wanamani Zaa'iganing Red Lake.[5] The unsettling news reverberated throughout the homelands as wemiti-goozhiwag began to pour over the landscape in numbers that numbed the imagination. Spilling in all directions, they were like a disturbed anthill erupting into dark, stinging masses. The people of Namegosi-biing felt the threat to everyday life, and they were deeply concerned about the effects of so sudden and so large a confluence. They wondered what would become of the earth, plants and animals they depended on for survival. It was almost too difficult to fathom what could possibly be the ultimate outcome of so much careless trampling and destruc-tion. Over the course of time, other Anishinaabe people's lands had felt the effects of the wemitigoozhi's mindset and seeming inability to understand their reciprocal relationship with the earth. Now, with the Namegosibiing traditional homelands about to suffer the same fate, Dedibaayaanimanook's people could feel the impending collision. But as others had been doing in other places ever since wemitigoozhiwag first appeared on the landscape, they realized that the new realities taking shape were permanent. They too needed to find ways to best deal with the emerging order, and they searched through the annals of the ancient teachings. Giizhik Sam Keesick was their repository of sacred knowledge, and they probed the wisdom of his teachings to guide them.

Not only did Dedibaayaanimanook's grandfather have an immediate influence on her life when he foresaw her survival and then blessed her with a special name, he also directed her life's course in another significant way. She was still in her cradleboard when he informed her parents that she would one day marry—a wemitigoozhi. A few years after that pronouncement, Giizhik and his wife Nookom Mary finished their work. Other members of the community had been helping to see to their needs, but when the end of their lives drew near, Dedibaayaanimanook's parents and her sister Gweyesh Annie Keesick Angeconeb took on the task of caring for them. Dedibaayaanimanook's elderly grandfather died when she was around seven and a half years old.[6] Even though she had developed an abiding sense of connection with him, only a few images withstood the passage of time. One of her visual memories included the Métis-style sash he occasionally wore around his waist as an accessory. She also remembered how fond she was of sitting on his lap and running her finger over a bump on his forehead. But the most enduring of her memories was his hand holding hers protectively as they canoed up Namegosi Ziibi[7] on his last journey home. Just as he had taken hold of her hand, Dedibaayaanimanook would hold onto his teachings throughout the rest of her life.

The Keesicks, in a similar manner, resolved to retain their power to choose traditional ways and to continue to uphold the world view of the forebears as relevant and worthwhile. In that manner, they succeeded in forestalling the profit-driven, increasingly invasive influences throughout Dedibaayaanimanook's early childhood. Rather than settle on the reserve, for example, they held onto Namegosibiing Trout Lake as their homeland, and even though they kept an open mind about anything the newcomers might offer by way of novelty or apparently benign improvement, they opted to skirt around the wemitigoozhi's milieu. These decisions helped to keep them relatively sheltered from the disturbances, and they were able to maintain—albeit for only a while longer—the old lifestyle, values and customs which included the annual journeys. Themselves encompassing so many aspects of those old ways, the journeys were worthy of a detailed recollection.

With physical mobility characterizing the lifestyle of Dedibaayaanimanook's people, travel was one of life's central features. It continued to be an integral and natural part of their activities, just as it had been for as far back as memory served. Distance, along with the time it took to traverse it, was neither an obstacle nor an inconvenience, so people did not expend time and energy in finding ways to overcome, circumvent or expedite travel. In fact, moving from place to place was not simply an acceptable part of every day living, it was embraced with its various features as a positive and beneficial component of existence even though wemitigoozhiwag were moving into the traditional homelands in massive numbers. Since most everyone had, by this time, acquired some degree of firsthand familiarity with the newcomers' way of thought, people were aware of what seemed to be their inclination to judge Anishinaabe ways exclusively from their own point of view. An example was that the newcomers often showed disdain toward Anishinaabeg for not using the wheel, whether to facilitate travel or make work easier. There was, at best, an attitude of disinterest about the people and about the reasons they lived as they did. Beyond that, there was a prevailing lack of appreciation for a world view in which the wheel—and any other such intrusive aberration—was regarded as a device that not only disconnected people from their land but left the land gouged in ruts. Dedibaayaanimanook's people had to accept that Anishinaabe ideas were not usually respected, and until the displacement of their lifeways was complete, they rejected the newcomers' ways.

Accordingly, Dedibaayaanimanook's family and relatives followed the patterns of the predecessors by taking two great journeys every year. One took place in spring, the other in autumn. Consisting of stages, they were an enduring tradition, a microcosm of how people lived their lives. In fact, these journeys were so intertwined with how people thought about themselves that they were an essential part of their self-identity and lived memories—in the same way that people travelled physically across their homelands, the memories of their journeys were a part of the stories that travelled temporally across the generations. Dedibaayaanimanook herself began to accumulate such memories from the time she was old enough to remember, and they would become a central part of her oral story to which she would continually refer back. Beginning as a small child, for example, she soon recognized the phrase niwii'madaawa'aamin as the first of the two yearly journeys that began during the latter part of spring after lakes and rivers had all opened. She became accustomed to the routine of leaving their homes in Namegosibiing and following the old canoe route south to the Anishinaabe community of Lac Seul in order to spend time with friends and kin and to pursue various forms of work. Even though she did not realize it until she was older, Dedibaayaanimanook and her people were in fact fulfilling the terms of Treaty 3 when they joined with the others of the Lac Seul First Nation at Treaty Point to claim their annual payments.

Long before starting their down river travels, however, family members anticipated the earliest signs of spring's arrival in Namegosibiing. Dedibaayaanimanook learned the names that captured the essential characteristics for each facet of the seasons. These terms indicated not only how closely people watched the changes taking place around them, but how intimately they retained connection to the natural environment. With the first half of spring beginning with the milder weather and terminating with break-up, and the second half opening with the appearance of new plant growth, the people of Namegosibiing actually recognized the existence of five seasons per year. This first warm period, known as ziigwan, was the time of year when large flakes of feathery textured snow occasionally floated down from the sky. It was the beginning of the Bald Eagle Moon. Dedibaayaanima-nook knew that if she looked upward she would soon spot the very first migratory bird of the season. The bald eagle came soaring upon lofty currents above Namegosibiing, scanning the landscape for signs of food. The crows, on the other hand, would not be filling the air with their animated calls for another several weeks, but in the meantime, the sun began to turn the snow's top layers into coarse, gritty granules that reminded Dedibaayaanimanook of white sugar crystals. Those who walked on the lake observed the strong winds of March molding what was left of the snow into heaps that looked very much like gulls from a distance. For that reason, people referred to such mounds as giyaashkwajishin.

"Aazha wii' biindige—giba'an ishkôndem!" Dedibaayaanimanook's mother urged her to close the door quickly one cold spring morning in order that the nameless being who brought cold weather—it may have been the Anishinaabe version of Old Man Winter to which Gaamadw-eyaashiik was making reference—could not enter the house and delay spring's progress. Dedibaayaanimanook had just put on her parka and mittens and was setting out to check rabbit snares. When she stepped outdoors and noticed that she could walk on top of the snow without falling through, a feeling of freedom sent her scampering across the hard crust. She enjoyed this final farewell gesture from the nameless being of winter's cold weather.

When the Keesicks were still at Jiibayi Zaagiing one spring, the comfortable routine of Dedibaayaanimanook's mid-childhood was interrupted by a conversation in which she overheard her parents discussing the subject of her upcoming vision quest. It was around the time of her ninth birthday, about two years after her grandfather had passed on. Immediately, the details of her father's spiritual journey came to mind. She had sat down and listened closely as he began the story of his experiences. Going on such a quest, he explained, was a purely spiritual pilgrimage for the purpose of finding ones's life's path. It was intended only for pre-adolescents—never adults—and only for those who were not fearful. He also explained that, long before he himself was born, his own father, Giizhik, had gone to seek out the being known as Gizhe Manidoo, the Loving Spirit. As she listened, Dedibaayaanimanook tried to imagine what it must have been like to visit Manidoo Minis,[8] the tiny rock-laced island which sits solitary near the middle of Namegosibiing. She wondered how it felt to be left alone for all those days without food or drink, long enough for the mundane cares of everyday life to no longer matter. Her father went on to depict nights filled with strange and terrible sounds designed to weaken his resolve as his physical strength faded with each passing day. But he also explained that, at the same time, it had become increasingly apparent to him that Gizhe Manidoo would give him courage to persevere. Finally, on the sixth day, his father, Giizhik, arrived from Ma'iingani Minis—Wolf Island—where the family had relocated during his absence. Dedibayaash gathered what physical strength he had left to begin their homeward journey. Although his efforts to keep pace were laboured and he yearned to rest on the sled, his father would not allow him to ride. Hours later, his mother stood waiting for them at Negiishkensikaang,[9] on Ma'iingani Minis. The cup she handed him contained a tiny quantity of water.

On the eve of her own departure for Manidoo Minis, Dedibaaya-animanook recalled the details her father had told her, and with mixed feelings she wondered what might be in store for her. How would she survive being left alone for so long on the enigmatic island of dark shadows and terrifying noises? What about the torment of her hunger and thirst? Importantly, what if Gizhe Manidoo failed to provide her with the vision of her life's purpose? But then Dedibaayaanimanook remembered the peace her father had spoken about when Gizhe Manidoo finally came to him, and her worries began to subside.

"Gego izhiwinaakeg Dedibaayaanimanook Manidoo Minisikaang!" were the clearly spoken words of Dedibaayaanimanook's grandfather the night before she and her father were set to leave for Manidoo Minis. Out of concern for her health, Giizhik appeared in a vivid dream and instructed her father not to take her to Spirit Island. Her journey did not take place, and all the worrisome questions did not need to be answered. Not having taken such a journey, Dedibaayaanimanook would never be able to give ceremonial names, but she would realize in the years to come that Gizhe Manidoo's gifts came in other forms. The dream quests of her siblings would assure spiritual content in the ceremonies of the community and in the daily lives of her people for a few more years. With Dedibaayaanimanook not visiting Manidoo Minis, it turned out to be a routine spring for her that year.

Part of the daily routine was to take careful note as upper layers of snow cover began to dissolve into water that froze overnight into slippery, uneven surfaces. The word zhoonzhaakwaa described this condition, with a more specific term, jiichiingwaaskwadin, depicting the actual process of freezing. Knowing that the ice was extremely treacherous during the early hours of the morning, people needed to ensure that the sharp ice formations did not cut the dogs' paws. Dedibaayaanimanook recalled that one of her aunts made leather slippers to protect her animals from those kinds of injuries. They proceeded under precarious conditions from Jiibayi Zaagiing to Negi-ishkensikaang on Ma'iingani Minis with much caution. Being at least ten miles, it was the longest one-day stretch of the entire journey. When Dedibaayaanimanook first walked the distance as a child, she felt so stiff and sore the next morning that she was barely able to move. Fortunately, spring break-up restricted people's mobility for up to ten days or longer, so their stop-over at Negiishkensikaang allowed her to recover.

When the usual routine for food management during such events as the family's seasonal travels was interrupted, it was necessary to develop various eating alternatives. Before leaving their campsite at Jiibayi Zaagiing, for example, Dedibaayaanimanook's mother prepared a special treat by cooking rabbit stomachs stuffed with rabbit livers. Storing the protein-rich packets in a rabbit skin sack kept them warm overnight, and the next morning, Dedibaayaanimanook enjoyed a nutritious breakfast, which she held in one hand as she hurried to keep pace with the others. The travel season had another effect on food supplies. Since everyone concurred that no meal, whether it was roasted rabbit, partridge, grouse or anything else, was ever complete without a piece of bannock, people took extra care to ensure that they had sufficient flour to last through those times when ice conditions brought mobility to a temporary standstill. But despite their best efforts, there were rare occasions, such as if a break-up or freeze-up was unexpectedly long, when the Dedibayaashes found that the unthinkable had happened and they were completely out of flour.

"Bakwezhigan niwii amô!" Dedibaayaanimanook had just taken on the task of watching over Gichi Jôj and little Gwekabiikwe Annie while Gwekabiikwe's mother, Naakojiiz, who was Dedibaayaanimanook's niece who married her cousin Gikinô'amaagewinini, was out cutting wood one afternoon. When she heard Gichi Jôj howling as though he were in pain, she ran to investigate the reason for his distress. Gichi Jôj had already finished his meal, but without a piece of bannock, he was not satiated. In fact, his feeling of hungriness had become so intolerable that he began to cry. Thinking how she might remedy his discomfort, one of Dedibaayaanimanook's aunts flaked a small portion of dried pickerel, a fish that was easily caught throughout the year, with a fork, and shaped it into the form of bannock. She soon discovered, however, that her attempts failed completely to distract Gichi Jôj and his playmates from their desire for real bannock.

Even though Dedibaayaanimanook's family had run short of flour, the people were not starving because traditional sources for basic foods were still secure. Their traditional use territories were still able to provide plants and animals in sufficient quantities to meet their needs, and her father and brothers were expert fishers, trappers and hunters. Dedibaayaanimanook's father, for example, caught trout year round for the family. Dedibayaash knew precisely where the fish would be during the various seasons. He also knew that the flavor of trout changed very noticeably, depending on the depth of the water where the fish lived. The fish's habitat, in turn, depended upon the season of the year. Eating trout during the summer when they were in deep water where temperatures were comparatively low was therefore a different experience from having the same meal during seasons when trout were moving into shallower regions of the lake. Although not to the same degree, this phenomenon was evident with other fish species as well. In terms of how he caught the fish, Dedibayaash's method was to go onto the ice a suitable distance from shore, and using an axe, chop a small hole. He finished tying a series of lines onto a sturdy pole which he secured to one side of the ice hole, then he baited the hooks with a piece of sucker's tail and dropped them into the water.

One evening just before sundown, he gave directions for Dedibaayaanimanook and Gichi Jôj to check the lines. The children set out. After finding the site without difficulty, Dedibaayaanimanook knelt by the edge of the water hole and took hold of the pole. She drew the lines up as her nephew hovered closely, squinting into the hole for the first sign of a fish. But when each hook came up empty, the children's enthusiasm turned to disappointment. Dedibaayaanimanook half-heartedly began to return them all into the water as her father had instructed.

"Aaniin wiin i'i!" She was completely caught off guard by a sudden jerk that yanked the lines from her hands. As the entire assemblage disappeared irretrievably into the blackness beneath, she wondered aloud how such a thing could have possibly happened. She knew that her father would be annoyed because the unfortunate incident meant that someone would have to make a whole new set of fish hooks from scratch. Dedibaayaanimanook tried to explain the accident to her father, but her lack of carefulness sounded too blamable for a sympathetic ear. Later that evening when her father sat working, he gave the matter further thought. The flashing bits of metal must have attracted the attention of a fish lurking in the vicinity and, at precisely the most critical moment, the fish grabbed onto a hook. The fish that should have been in the family's cooking pot was undoubtedly swimming—as though on a fishing expedition of its own—with a set of hooks in tow somewhere in the depths of Namegosibiing.

Other species of fish were available for the family's consumption whenever the Keesicks spent break-up east of Namegosibiing at Manoomini Zaa'igan, Rice Lake, or even further east at Gichi Onigaming.[10] These were the two small lakes where Dedibaayaanimanook's father caught pickerel, jackfish, tulibee and suckers with a gill net. At the same time, Dedibayaash trapped muskrats in the swampy regions of the area, where he was close enough to Ikwewi Zaa'igan, Woman Lake, to obtain groceries and other supplies with his bundle of spring furs. Dedibaayaanimanook remembered that the whole family visited George Swain's post at the northeastern end of the lake on two different occasions.

"Wiinge gii'maanaadan!" Dedibaayaanimanook once informed her friends, after they had returned home. She alluded to the dreary look-ing tools, sacks and boxes of foodstuff she and her nephew saw at the trading post. They were a stark contrast to the colorful fabric, ribbons and buttons she had anticipated seeing.

With most of the snow cover melted by this time, family members took turns going down to the shorelines and taking notes on what changes were taking place. The receding ice meant that canoe pas-sage was soon possible. When Dedibaayaanimanook was old enough to have her own paddle, she imitated her parents by pushing her weight into the paddle and dipping it deep into the water. "Aazha waazooskodewa'am indaanisens!" her father exclaimed with obvious affection and pride as he observed her arms beginning to move in rhythm to the canoe's forward surges.

The ice was said to have "lifted" after it detached itself from the shoreline and took on a distinctively dark appearance. Another term, biinjskwajiwan, described the upper layers of ice as they melted into tiny pools of water that trickled down into the lower layers like mil-lions of miniscule rivulets. Warming temperatures soon reduced the once formidable ice masses into little more than a weak latticework of crystal spikes barely adhering together. This phase in the ice's demise was known as ogichizigwaa, a visual warning that the decay was at an advanced stage and all ice travel was at an end. Warm winds began to blow from the south. Sweeping relentlessly across the unstable surface, these winds generated tremendous upward pressures that eventually reached a critical point. The ice succumbed to these forces, disintegrating into chunks of sharp, translucent crystals that grated and ground against each other when the newly liberated waves tossed them to and fro. Dedibaayaanimanook acquired knowledge about these types of minute details about the lake from the time of her childhood.

"Amii' gii'zhaagigamiiwang!" was the common expression for announcing that break-up had finally occurred and people were once again at liberty to travel. Dedibaayaanimanook's father, ever concerned about the family's food supply, was eager to resume his hunting activities as quickly as possible. If they were at their camp site near Jiiyaani Minis,[11] he launched his canoe and headed toward a creek that ran into Mako'Odaaminike,[12] where black bears denned and hibernated before awakening to gorge on pickerel and suckers, the fish species that spawned in spring. Dedibaayaanimanook was fond of listening to the stories her father told her of his many hunting trips, and she heard about the particular time he went to the little creek and settled into a low position with his rifle and pocket watch at the ready. Having been there to hunt bears many times before, Dedibayaash focussed his attention on the bear's mound, knowing when the animal would be most likely to make an appearance. The bear, however, failed to show itself as expected. Instead, a tiny dark object protruded from the far side of the mound. Dedibayaash waited motionless and silent for several long moments when the object—just barely perceptible—seemed to make a slight movement. As soon as he observed a black bear rising for a swipe at the water, he realized he had been watching the beast flicking an ear for the slightest sounds while it, too, sat waiting for food to appear. The unsuspecting animal thus gave Dedibayaash the clear shot he needed, and once again, his hunter's patience was rewarded. This location, however, was not the only place he visited during this time of year. For example, he often went to where the muskrats lived. As a little girl eager for adventure, Dedibaayaanimanook was scarcely able to contain her excitement whenever her mother gave her permission to accompany her father on one of his shorter outings.

"Agaawaago ingii'zaagikweb!" On one of her very first trips, she climbed to the front of the canoe, where she hoped for the best view.

But being a small child, she was barely able to peer over the top. At other times, Dedibaayaanimanook needed to stay home with her mother. Gaamadweyaashiik kept her occupied with small tasks, but as soon as her father returned, she rushed down to the shore to help him carry the muskrats. One day she raced back to her mother empty handed. "Binesiwag obiinaa' indede!" Her eyes wide with wonderment and barely able to catch her breath, she informed her mother that her father had captured the Thunderer—she had just seen it lying in his canoe! A few moments after her breathless announcement, however, Dedibayaash appeared, not with the Thunder Bird as Dedibaayaani-manook thought, but a fully grown bald eagle. He had once caught a golden eagle at Maadaawaang,[13] but in keeping with a personal taboo, Dedibaayaanimanook's mother avoided eating either bald or golden eagles.

By this time of year—when the ice had just finished breaking up—the winds persisted with enormous force, churning the water into powerful waves that piled ice fragments into massive white heaps along the shores of Namegosibiing and the islands. Agwaashkaa mik-wam was the phrase to characterize this piling-up phenomenon that remained visible from great distances across the lake for as long as two weeks after break-up. This early phase of spring then faded away to be replaced by minookamiing, that part of spring which commenced when the earth and all its uncountable creatures arose from months of frozen slumber. When Dedibaayaanimanook was around ten years old, an interesting phenomenon occurred during the Keesicks' stop-over at Ma'iingani Minis at this time of year. The sap had already begun to flow, and as each day lengthened, the poplar buds swelled up until they burst through their casings to take the shape of tiny leaves. The driving winds no longer blew, and during brief periods when tranquility reigned over the waterscape, the lake's surface was a liquid mirror. It was perfect for Dedibaayaanimanook's brother Jiins and one of her male cousins to canoe to the main shore to hunt.

"Giga bitamaa manijoosh!" As he crouched by the edge of the shoreline for a handful of water, Jiins was startled by the sound of his mother's voice cautioning him about swallowing water bugs.[14] He and his cousin were both amazed and mystified because they knew that Gaamadweyaashiik was miles away at Ma'iingani Minis. They had to wait until they returned home later in the day to learn that the lake had been sufficiently tranquil to transmit Gaamadweyaashiik's voice undistorted across the distance. They also learned that Gaamadweyaashiik had actually been speaking to Gichi Jôj, who by great coincidence, was grabbing some water for himself at precisely the same moment that Jiins was about to swallow his handful. The lake had made it posssible for Dedibaayaanimanook's mother to caution them both with one sentence! It was during such times of calmness, moreover, that thunder-like sounds rumbled over the water's surface from Manidoo Minis as a reminder of the Island's sacredness.

Late spring was also that time of year when Dedibaayaanimanook accompanied her mother to collect tree sap. Spruce, jack pine, birch, but especially the white poplars, produced a delicious, nutritious sap that usually began to run from mid-May through to early June. In order to harvest the liquid, Dedibaayaanimanook's mother used a sharp knife to slice through the bark in a 'v' shape, then she hung a tin pail beneath a spout she had formed from a piece of folded birch bark. She boiled the sap into syrup. Boiled birch sap was the color of molasses and the thickness of commercially made table syrup. But for more immediate consumption, Gaamadweyaashiik scored the tree bark using an axe and peeled away a small section. She scraped the exposed surface with an upward motion and collected the candy-sweet pulp laden with a flavor that reminded Dedibaayaanimanook of her great-aunt Gichi Gookom (also known as Zaaging Gookom). During a *Midewin* gathering at Zaagiing[15] in Lac Seul, Dedibaayaanimanook and Gichi Jôj once saw the elderly woman going from tree to tree gathering poplar bark and eating the sugary substance.

The term minookamiing also encompassed that time of year when the songs of sparrows, robins and warblers began to resonate in the forest. Whiskey jacks joined their voices with the blue jays and gulls to create a cacophonous chorus upon arriving. Dedibaayaanimanook began to notice that certain species of birds seemed to keep company with one another. For example, the loons arrived with the kingfishers during the month of the Loon Moon, and the nuthatches and chickadees remained within close proximity of each other. This was when Dedibaayaanimanook's family continued with their journey south. Following their usual routine, they proceeded from Negiishkensikaang on Ma'iingani Minis, over a stretch of water, then toward a large point of land on the right that comprised part of the Namegosibiing main shore known as Gichi Neyaashiing.[16] The point, situated almost directly opposite Gete Waakaa'iganing,[17] formed a gentle embrace for two tiny islands known as Mikinaako Minisan.[18] It was on the sandy shores of the bay formed by Gichi Neyaashiing's long extension of land that Dedibaayaanimanook's aunt Omashkiigookwe once stayed for several hours alone. While she waited for the choppy waters to subside, she looked toward the north and noticed several gigantic snapping turtles emerging from the two islands. The awesome reptiles dived into the foaming waves and disappeared. Today, most wemitiogoozhiwag who visit Namegosibiing are not aware that the two islands, Mikinaako Minisan, are sacred to Dedibaayaanimanook's people.

One spring, after Dedibaayaanimanook and her family arrived at Gojijiwaawangaang,[19] her cousin, Maashkizhiigan George Ashen Keesick, along with his wife and two children, decided to stop at Gwiigwiishiwanii Minis[20] for the night. Also on their way south, the Maashkizhiigans had just joined the others at Gojijiwaawangaang the next morning when someone noticed a billow of smoke rising in the direction of Gwiigwiishiwanii Minis. A forest fire in Namegosibiing Trout Lake was a rare occurrence, but one that resulted from a camp fire was practically unheard of because people knew about the impact that fire can have on even the smallest of living organisms. Hence, they used fire with care. Alarmed by the sight of smoke curling skyward, Dedibaayaanimanook's cousins canoed back to the island and doused the flames. People later concluded that an ember inadvertently left glowing had caused the fire.

Gojijiwaawangaang was a shallow passageway that connected Name-gosibiing and Aanziko Zaa'igan.[21] Its name alluded to the sandy nature of the area, although Dedibaayaanimanook's mother preferred to use the name Namegosibii Gojijiing, because it was the first point of exit for Namegosibiing's discharging waters. The people's travel route took them across Aanziko Zaa'igan in a southerly direction where sedges, reeds and grasses rose from the water in great abundance to indicate the shallow depth of the lake. As they canoed through the crooked channel between Aanziko Zaa'igan and Namegosibii Shishiing,[22] the travellers paused long enough for the children to listen as their voices reverberated in hollow echoes between the towering evergreens that stood on either shoreline. Flocks of mergansers, fluttering into the air and protesting the intrusion in gutteral croaks, were a familiar sight along this segment of the journey.

A narrow section where rocks protruded near shore was where the Dedibayaash family made a practice of stopping for at least one night's rest, whether they were returning from or going to Lac Seul. It was known as Waabashkiigaang.[23] When her father and brother Jiins returned from trapping excursions into the area during early winter, Dedibaayaanimanook often heard them talk about finding the frozen carcass of yet another moose that had drowned after falling through the ice just after freeze-up. From here, the Dedibayaashes continued to Namegosibii Shishiing across which canoe travel ideally took place when the winds blew softly. Otherwise, there were too few islands to block prevailing winds, and waves turned the stretch of water into a treacherous passage. The travellers also needed to know the precise direction to the source of the south flowing Namegosi Ziibi in order to avoid being drawn off course by the lake's irregular shoreline. But Kee-sick family members, including Dedibaayaanimanook herself when she began to take such notice, were thoroughly familiarized with the details of these potential hazards. On reaching the eastern shores of Namego-sibii Shishiing, the travellers completed the initial stage of their down river journey to Lac Seul, which they referred to as "Nimidaawa'aamin."

1. Although the non-Anishinaabe name of the lake is Trout Lake, Anishinaabe people refer to it as Namegosib. Since the prepositional suffix —*iing* imparts the meaning of in, into, on, at, by, for, above, of, etc., to the name, the lake is referred to as Namegosibiing for the sake of simplicity. Literally, however, Namegosib is trout waters, or, waters where the trout live.

2. Jiibayi Zaagiing is now called Jackfish Bay. *Jiibay* is the word for ghost; *zaagiing* is the mouth of a river.

3. Gaaminitigwashkiigaag is a term that refers to the swampy nature of the area. The bay is now called Keesick Bay.

4. Memegweshi Zaa'igan has become angicized to Mamakwash Lake. It is characterized by rock cliffs that slice perpendicular lines into the lake at various places along the shoreline. A clue of how its name came about is found in the form of ancient rock paintings that were drawn by either those who lived there, the *Memegweshiwag*, or the Anishinaabeg who witnessed the spirit-like beings. Many years later, when she visited Memegweshi Zaa'igan with her son Gwiiwizens (Harald), Dedibayaash and Gaamadweyaashiik's daughter would express amazement at the artists' ability to produce drawings that continued to remain intact after so many years of exposure to the elements.

5. Wanamani Zaa'igan is, literally, Red Ochre Lake, but wemitigoozhiwag have referred to Wanamani Zaa'igan as Red Lake since they first arrived in the area. See Note 9 of the Introduction.

6. A family friend, J. Richthammer, provided copies of the provincial certificate of death for Giizhik Sam Keesick and his spouse. They indicate that Giizhik died on October 10th, 1929 of old age. His birth year being registered as 1830, he would have been approximately 100 years old, depending on what month in 1830 he was born. Giizhik's occupation was listed as "trapper." Nookomiban's *wemitigoozhi* name was Mary. She too was listed as having died of old age; the record correctly stated that her date of death was exactly one year after Giizhik's. Nookomiban was a "Homemaker."

7. Namegosi Ziibi is now Trout (Lake) River.

8. Manidoo Minis, translated as Spirit Island, and is now known as Seagull Island among non-Anishinaabe speakers.

9. Negiishkensikaang, on the southwestern shore of Ma'iingani Minis Wolf Island, is where the Dedibayaash family lived for brief periods during spring and autumn.

10. Gichi Onigaming (now called Stiff Lake) is just east of Manoomini Zaa'igan Rice Lake.

11. Jiiyaani Minis (Jiiyaan Island) is located in the northwest quadrant of Namegosibiing; Dedibaayaanimanook's uncle Jiiyaan Donald and his family often camped on the island.

12. Mako' Odaaminike is near Black Bear Lake; a creek runs from the lake into an irregular shaped bay on the northwest main shore of Namegosibiing.

13. Maadaawaang is where Chukuni River meets English River.

14. Children had to be careful not to swallow insects when they drank water directly from the lake, especially during spring when bugs often appeared in water holes. Due to their painful bite, the odazheboyesiwag (water boatmen) and similar aquatic insects were especially to be avoided.

15. Zaagiing was not far from a large sand escarpment where Dedibaayaanimanook and her siblings once made a game of trying to climb up the steep incline during a *Midewin* gathering.

16. Gichi Neyaashiing translates to Big Point.

17. Gete Waakaa'iganing is the Place of the Old Building, now referred to as Hudson's Bay Point.

18. Mikinaako Minisan are the Islands of the Snapping Turtles.

19. Gojijiwaawangaang is where the traditional cemetery in Namegosibiing is located.

20. Gwiigwiishiwanii Minis is Whiskey Jack Island.

21. Aanziko Zaa'igan, Merganser Lake, is now called Otter Lake.

22. Namegosibii Shishiing is (correctly translated as) Little Trout Lake.

23. Waabashkiigaang is a term that refers to the narrow width of the passageway and physical makeup of the immediate area.

CHAPTER 2

Nimadaawa'aaminaaban

~

As We Travelled Down the River

Dedibaayaanimanook became conversant with the details of their river journey early on. As a child, for example, she counted up to nine rapids making it necessary to use portage trails between the source of Namegosi Ziibi at Namegosibii Shishiing and Adikamegwaaminikaaning.[1] She knew that Manidoo Baawitig[2] was the first set of rapids and she was familiar with its distance from the source. She also knew that the next set followed closely, and that in order to circumvent the third rapids, they needed to use a portage trail. Flanked on either side by tall standing jack pines, it was known as Gaagakiiwekikawemog.[3] The trail was fairly long, but family members were prepared for the challenging task of making several trips back and forth to haul their goods. Dedibaayaanimanook's mother found the trek easier to manage by using an apicaneyaab. This was a leather strap she positioned across her forehead to carry her backpack. Dedibaayaanimanook's father, on the other hand, transported their two (store bought) canoes by carrying them, one at a time, right side up across his left shoulder. The canoes built by wemitigoozhiwag were much heavier than the traditional crafts of years earlier.

Birch bark canoes were sturdy and easy to maneuver, yet they were also relatively lightweight. If handled correctly and given proper maintenance and care, they lasted through several summers. When the wazooskodewan period of spring was at an advanced stage and openings along the shoreline had expanded several feet in width, people exercised a great deal of caution in order to avoid scraping their canoes against the jagged ice edges. They also nudged their crafts gently onto shore, away from protruding rocks and other potential hazards. Dedibaayaanimanook's mother told her about how she travelled with her parents in birchbark canoes of their own making. Gaamadweyaashiik Emma Strang Angeconeb Keesick's family and relatives were from Pikangikum, a community northwest of Namegosibiing, but they relocated to the Wabauskang[4] region at some time in her early childhood. During the summer season, long before industrial activities of the wemitigoozhiwag altered and polluted the rivers, she and her parents journeyed even further south than Lac Seul in their birchbark canoes. They followed along the waterways that connect with Wabigoon River[5] as far as the Dryden area. When Gaamadweyaashiik Emma married Gichimookomaan George Angeconeb and left her family to join her husband's, she had to transfer her treaty membership to the Lac Seul band.[6] In order to take part in the regional *Midewin*, she and Gichimookomaan brought their little son Jiins with them on canoe trips along the Wabigoon and Eagle River systems through Bigwaakoshebi Baawitig Dryden. In fact, Gaamadweyaashiik's preference was to attend the gatherings at Eagle Lake because she enjoyed the travel even though the Lac Seul community held its own *Midewin* events. The opportunity to travel throughout these territories allowed her to become knowledgeable about the rivers and lakes of the region.

During a journey to a *Midewin* celebration, the Angeconebs were passing by a place called Getemiikanaang[7] near an old abandoned railway. It was where Gaamadweyaashiik witnessed a scene that disturbed her so profoundly that one day, years later, she would be compelled to share its story with Dedibaayaanimanook. Ravaged by the sickness of alcoholism and no longer with homes to live in, local Anishinaabeg had apparently attempted to assemble dwellings to shelter themselves. However, they were only able to find enough material for what were essentially little more than lean-tos. Considering Gaamadweyaashiik was an Anishinaabe woman who continued to enjoy the old luxury of choosing to live in a home that she and her family themselves fashioned from hides, bark and poles that their homeland still provided with generosity, and considering that she and her family could still design their homes with care to accommodate their wants and needs while taking the variant seasonal conditions into account, for her to see that other Anishinaabe people—now completely surrounded by wemitigoozhiwag—were reduced to this meagre level of survival was both shocking and difficult to comprehend.

After Gichimookomaan George Angeconeb passed on and she met and married Dedibayaash, Dedibaayaanimanook's mother would adopt her new family's customs, including the Keesicks' usage of the Namegosibiing-Obizhigokaang Lac Seul travel routes. But Dedibaaya-animanook herself was not familiar with the more southern water routes beyond Lac Seul with which her mother was so well versed because the Dedibayaashes kept within the Keesick families' traditional territories. Other than trips to the Diitibisewinigamiing Hudson area to gather blueberries, Dedibaayaanimanook's primary travel experiences encompassed the canoe routes between Namegosibiing and Obizhigokaawi Zaa'igan Lac Seul Lake. These, of course, included the many portage trails.

Dedibaayaanimanook was accustomized to the use of hiking trails from childhood, and she was soon able to anticipate what lay beyond the next bend. Being responsible for her own bundle of belongings, she had to be sure to pack whatever she might need for the future. But, she also needed to ensure she was able to carry the weight of her possessions over the trails. As she hurried along and her back pack of belongings began to feel heavier one late afternoon, she recalled her father's story about two Anishinaabe men who were renowned for their exceptionally great physical strength. It was said that each was able to pack an amazing load of six 100 pound sacks of flour on his back! One of the men, Waaboozhwayaanag, a Trout, was not a particularly large man. The other, known as John Washkigwayaw, began to develop callouses on his shoulders and back due to the nature of his work. Eventually his upper spine became so distorted he was no longer able to straighten his neck. That kind of strenuous labour resulted in many serious and painful injuries. In fact, hernias, ruptured discs, torn ligaments and other crippling ailments occurred frequently. Yet, as Dedibaayaanimanook's father stated, the men received very low wages from the wemitigoozhiwag who employed them for the onerous work. Recalling the details of this story, Dedibaayaanimanook began to imagine that her own bundle had become at least five flour sacks heavy when they finally reached the end of the portage trail at the end of the day.

Further on, Namegosi Ziibi entered into a semi-marshy region where it became a winding course named Gaawaawaagoshkiikitigweyaag.[8] Waaboozo Baawitig[9] and Gookooko'oowi Baawitig[10] appeared immediately thereafter. It was at the latter set of rapids that Dedibaayaanimanook's mother once showed her a set of large indentations leading up a steep hill directly opposite the trail. She told her that they were the footprints of zaaskwaaj. Although very few people had ever actually encountered zaaskwaaj, the very idea of such a being's existence sent a shiver through Dedibaayaanimanook. Thankfully, there was never a need to linger at Gookooko'oowi Baawitig. Instead, they always proceeded on, just past Bizhiwininjiiwi Baawitig[11] to where a small river from Wazhashko Zaa'igan[12] merged into Namegosi Ziibi at Wazhashko Maadaawaang.[13] Dedibaayaanimanook's uncle Netawibiitam John and family usually spent the spring at Wazhashko Zaa'igan where they trapped for muskrats because the marsh dwelling rodents were not only plentiful, but fat and sleek by this time of year. As soon as the ice disappeared, the Netawibiitams left Wazhashko Zaa'igan and proceeded down the river to Wazhashko Maadaawaang from which location they all continued together. There were, at times, as many as four Keesick brothers with their families and their children who camped together at Wazhashko Maadaawaang. Dedibaayaanimanook's cousin Maashkizhiigan George Ashen and his family were always part of the assemblage.

Clumps of black poplars grew at another favored camp site. As afternoon turned into evening and another day of canoeing drew to a close,

Dedibaayaanimanook's father cut away a small clearing, releasing the spicy aroma of resin coated maanazaadii buds into the air. The fragrance was so distinctive that no matter where she was, Dedibaayaanimanook was always reminded of this special place where her family camped whenever she came across black poplar buds. In the evening, as soon as the meal was finished, her parents spread out a large canvas for a relaxing session of card games. The prize usually included several of the season's best muskrat pelts. Not being old enough to participate, Dedibaayaanimanook and her cousin Meniyaan Mary Anne, who was, in fact, a sibling according to the traditional relational system, played together. They embarked on a journey into the world of make-believe by acting out the various activities of their everyday lives on a miniature scale. Using whatever leaves were large enough, along with scraps of fabric from their mothers, they created imaginary families getting ready for a voyage similar to the one they themselves were on. Then they shaped strips of birch bark into canoes in which the tiny dolls and all their luggage could travel. With a long pole and a length of string, they guided their flotilla along the shoreline, and if a male sibling happened to be nearby—usually it was Meniyaan's brother Mazinigiizhig James—he had the task of making motor sounds to accompany the journeyers. These motor sounds were in fact a manifestation of the wemitigoozhi's influences, and even though the Keesicks themselves largely avoided such contrivances, the children were naturally fascinated by the novelty of an outboard motor. "Dagasa gibichiidaa—aazha indishkidoone!" Mazinigiizhig begged his play mates for time out because the effort it took to produce continual motor sounds with his mouth proved to be exhausting. With that, the make believe journey usually ended. The dolls were taken from their canoes and bedded down for the night on a mattress of balsam needles carefully put down inside a birch leaf dwelling.

Another source of entertainment for the youngsters was a game known as onaabiiginige. It contained a certain element of showmanship in that the performer had to produce intriguing designs by executing a series of complicated maneuvers with a length of string. Another game of skill involved a type of toy known as a naaba'ôgan. Dedibaayaani-manook's brother Jiins once made one for her. Starting with moose bones which he attached onto a length of sinew, he attached a piece of leather slashed with a set of parallel lines to one end of the string for the object's "tail." On the other end of the string he tied a long, needle shaped bone with which the player tried to catch as many of the moose bones as possible. An expert player could catch all of the bones as well as the tail. Before her brother gave her the gift, Dedibaayaanimanook and her nephew Gichi Jôj improvised by using evergreen boughs which they tied together into a bunch. Needless to say, it did not prove to be a very satisfactory substitute!

When it was time for bed, the parents did not usually allow the two girls to sleep together because their bedtime stories would have kept them up too late, and everyone needed to be up early the next morning, well rested and ready for another day at the paddle. From Wazhashko Maadaawaang the river journey continued along a rela-tively straight line south for approximately five miles to Apisaabiko Maadaawaang.[14] This was where Ikwewi Ziibi[15] from the northeast emptied into Namegosi Ziibi. While taking one of their exploratory excursions into the woods, Dedibaayaanimanook's male cousins once came upon pieces of flat crystalline rock that peeled off in layers like an onion. People referred to the curiosity as gaakaawaskwaabik. Feel-ing compelled to prove that they could find something just as unusual, Dedibaayaanimanook and Meniyaan went exploring in the woods but were disappointed when all they managed to find were some bits of decaying rock. It was here at Apisaabiko Maadaawaang that others on their way to Lac Seul often joined the Keesicks.

No matter how many times she saw the Oojiiwasawaan women's cradleboards, Dedibaayaanimanook's mother was amazed and fascin-nated by the way they were decorated. The mothers had collected, cleaned and buffed caribou hooves and porcupine breastbones to a glossy finish. By stringing the objects together like necklaces and draping them around the cradleboards, the women transformed them into muted chimes that lulled the children to sleep when they were rocked. The women also preserved mallard heads and the bills of geese and other waterfowl as visual stimuli for their infants. To someone as keenly perceptive as Gaamadweyaashiik, the patience, effort and attention to detail with which the work had been done was immediately evident.

The Oojiiwasawaans were kin, and the origin of their relationship with the Keesicks reached as far back as the generations contemporaneous with Dedibaayaanimanook's paternal great-grandfather, Jiiyaan, and beyond. In addition to the regions of Goshkwegaawinigam[16] and Ikwewi Zaa'igan Woman Lake, the Oojiiwasawaans' traditional use territories stretched to Niki Zaa'igan Goose Lake, Memegweshi Zaa'igan[17] and Gaamangadikamegokaang.[18] Dedibaayaanimanook's father and uncles visited these kinsfolk while they were in the area to obtain trade items from the trading posts, and the relatives reciprocated by coming to Namegosibiing for visits at various times during the winter. In earlier days, the Keesicks sold furs and purchased goods at the Hudson's Bay post, but when independent trader George Swain established one of his outlets on the northwestern shores of Mashkiigonigam,[19] his post became the preferred place of trade because he offered better trading terms than the Hudson's Bay Company. It was at Swain's post that Dedibayaash and Jiins once purchased yards of brightly patterned fabric for Dedibaayaanimanook and her mother to make skirts, blouses, bedding and whatever else they fancied.

From Apisaabiko Maadaawaang, these relatives of the regions to the east continued their journey to Lac Seul with Dedibaayaanimanook's family. The group reached a tight bend, known as Gaaodooskwanigamaag,[20] where the river banks dissolved into wetlands that produced an abundance of wild rice at the end of summer each year. Thick bunches of rushes and aquatic grasses were the domain of at least five kinds of damsel flies that never failed to catch Dedibaayaanimanook's attention. As they sat resting in the sun's warmth, their delicate wings shimmering in the sunlight, each of the ephemeral creatures seemed little more than a set of large eyes glued to the end of a stick. Dedibaayaanimanook wondered how they managed to find such regal shades of orange-brown, blue and metallic green for dressing themselves. The rushes, intermingled with sweet flag, were also the habitat of red-winged blackbirds. Hearing their fluid gurgles was another source of seasonal pleasure. Dedibaayaanimanook once joined her cousin Noosi, who was chasing countless dragonflies darting and diving in pursuit of mosquitoes. Later that evening, she was lying exhausted on her blankets, when she looked up at the opening above. She saw trees silhouetted against the faintly glowing dusk, but she was too sleepy to know whether she was dreaming or imagining the faces of her sister and her relatives that seemed to appear in ever changing patterns among the branches.

From the lower end of Gaaodooskwanigamaag, the river took them briefly back in a northeasterly direction before it once again resumed its southward flow toward Gichi Baawitig Big Falls. The final three rapids, situated immediately up the river from Gichi Baawitig, were too strong to ride, so the travellers were once again required to walk. This portage trail was approximately a mile in length. A little further ahead, a horse trail known as Gwaagwaazhiidinaawinigaam[21] ran parallel to the river for a distance of about four miles, all the way to Adikamegwaaminikaaning Whitefish Falls. Work-weary horses, housed in an old stable located at the northern end of the trail, pulled heavy loads of foodstuff that included fruit and other perishables destined for Swain Post before motorized vehicles were introduced into the region. One autumn when the Keesicks were returning from Lac Seul, they came upon a wooden crate that had apparently fallen off the wagon and broken up, leaving dozens of oranges to lie molding among the fallen leaves. During Dedibaayaanimanook's early childhood, an elderly man from across the ocean drove the horse drawn wagon.

People gave him the name Gaabaashkaabij when they noticed that he had lost the use of one eye, but whether he was the person known in the local wemitigoozhi circles as Jim Hayes is not known.

The journey continued on the river itself rather than the horse trail because there were no rapids between Gichi Baawitig and Adikamegwaaminikaaning to impede progress. Whenever they were a short distance south of Gichi Baawitig at the end of the day, the Dedibayaash Keesicks pitched camp at an especially flat place on the west bank of the river. This location was close to where Mina'igo Ziibiins[22] trickled leisurely into Namegosi Ziibi, across the river from where Dedibaayaanimanook's cousin Omooday Paul Keesick and his family began to spend their winters in order to stay close to Omooday's parents. Part of the reason Dedibaayaanimanook's eldest paternal uncle Mooniyaans Thomas and his wife Maajiigiizhigook Mary Keesick decided to stop in this area rather than proceed to Namegosibiing Trout Lake one autumn illustrates how mobility and travel normally served to protect the people's non-consumptive way of living. In order to remain full participants of a mobile society, people needed to guard against excess materialism, or they had to be willing to leave the nonessentials behind. In the case of the Mooniyaans Keesicks, it was due to the abundant quantity of their belongings combined with their advanced age that the journey for them proved impossible to continue beyond Mina'igo Ziibiins that autumn. This was despite the fact that they—having acquired the means to do so—had decided to purchase a kicker for their large canoe in the hope that it would help them to maintain their mobility while still taking their goods with them. Maajiigiizhigook Mary later described how it took nearly an hour before Mooniyaans was able to start the motor, but when he finally succeeded in getting it started, the sceptical onlookers were left in a state of amazement as the Mooniyaanses sped off into the distance. Dedibaayaanimanook's parents also had a cabin at Mina'igo Ziibiins. With the Mooniyaans Thomases only a short distance down the river, they spent an entire winter there one year when Dedibaayaanimanook was small. Other Anishinaabe travellers in the region were grateful to stop at the cabin for a night's rest at various times during the trapping season.

"Nimisenz,[23] nashke ezhinaagwak o'omaa!" The first time Dedibaayaanimanook was old enough to take such notice, she leaned over and pointed into the river where an interesting phenomenon presented itself immediately north of Adikamegwaaminikaaning. The water discharging from Namegosibiing changed abruptly from the clarity so characteristic of their lake to the turbid waters most commonly associated with rivers. The clear water on which they had been travelling remained a tangible connection to home, but from there on, they would need to wait until autumn to arrive at this precise location where the remarkable transformation took place and to experience once again this visual vestige of home. Adikamegwaaminikaaning itself was a short paddle down Namegosi Ziibi before the travellers reached Baagwaashi Zaa'iganiins Bruce Lake. Re-named Whitefish Falls by the wemitigoozhiwag, Adikamegwaaminikaaning contained a bed of fine clay and was where one of the family's dogs once feasted on whitefish it had, with much resourcefulness, caught for itself. It was also the place where a scow Dedibaayaanimanook's father was steering once hit a rock, shearing off a propeller blade and bending another. As he described the incident and talked about his fears of getting fired, Dedibaayaanimanook was saddened that her father would need to carry the burden of such worries. But the necessity of Dedibayaash's work exemplified the reality that her people were becoming increasingly drawn into the affairs of wemitigoozhiwag. Dedibayaash's summer job with a transport company, operated by a man named Bob Starratt, included a scow for hauling loads of food, gasoline and other goods from Otawagi Baawitig Ear Falls on the English River to Adikamegwaaminikaaning on Namegosi Ziibi and to Ginebigo Baawitig on Chukuni River. Dedibaayaanimanook's cousin, Jigoozhi Pat Keesick Kiiweyaasin, also worked for the company, as did an individual by the name of Daabiise David Bull. However, Daabiise, who was great-grandfather of Lac Seul Chief Clifford Bull, hauled goods to Otawagi Baawitig from the railway town Diitibisewinigami-ing Hudson.[24] A wemitogoozhi called Gaazhooshkozij owned another transportation company, but Dedibaayaanimanook's father said that he never hired Anishinaabe people. The man's English name was Wilfred Wright Sr. Dedibaayaanimanook's father also stated that relatives used to work as oarsmen on flat bottomed boats that brought supplies north from Hudson before the advent of motorized travel. Indicative of the harsh working conditions was the name by which her people referred to one of the rowers, Bakwaninjii, whose hands were often blistered and raw.

Adikamegwaaminikaaning was a relatively short distance north of a small lake known as Baagwaashi Zaa'iganiins, which literally means little shallow lake. As was their inclination to re-name the Anishinaabe homelands everywhere they went, the wemitigoozhiwag referred to Baagwaashi Zaa'iganiins as Bruce Lake, and this is the name by which it is known today among all except Dedibaayaanimanook's people. The Keesicks, including the widow and family of Dedibaayaanimanook's uncle Mooniyaans Thomas, stopped along the northern shores of Baagwaashi Zaa'iganiins as they journeyed to Lac Seul on a late afternoon that same year of Mooniyaans Thomas's death. Their camp was not far from where Namegosi Ziibi proceeded toward Baagwaashi Zaa'igan Pakwash Lake.[25] It was across the lake from the old traditonal cemetery. Immediately after a special conversation with her mother, Dedibaayaanimanook went to visit her widowed aunt. She entered the tent where she found Maajiigiïzhigook Mary lying quietly on her bed. She drew close and knelt beside her ancient aunt.

"Ganawenindizon, indoozhimens." Dedibaayaanimanook barely heard the faintly spoken words urging her to take good care of herself, and she barely felt the frail hand that reached out and touched her arm. Her aunt then gave her a kiss. Overcome with a deep sense of saddness, Dedibaayaanimanook sat quietly for a long time before returning to her parents. The next morning she learned that her aunt Maajiigiizhigook Mary Keesick died in her sleep. She was buried where her life's partner Mooniyaans Thomas and their grandson Imbedam were also at rest, across the lake from where she had said her last farewell to Dedibaayaanimanook.

Whenever they were in Baagwaashi Zaa'iganiins on their spring journey down the river, Dedibaayaanimanook's mother gathered eggs from the nests of a small species of gulls that lived on the lake. The whites of their eggs were translucent and their yolks a deep orange. Having an even richer flavor than the eggs her mother collected at Manidoo Minis in Namegosibiing, the gulls' eggs were a special spring treat for the family. The journey then continued along a relatively short, unimpeded stretch from Baagwaashi Zaa'iganiins to Namegosi Zaagiing, where the river emptied itself into Baagwaashi Zaa'igan Pakwash Lake. Many years later, in 1946, wemitigoozhiwag would build what came to be called Highway 105 through the homelands north from Vermilion Bay on the Trans-Canada Highway. It would stretch to Wanamani Zaa'igan Red Lake, crossing over Namegosi Ziibi approximately half a mile east of Namegosi Zaagiing.

Baagwaashi Zaa'igan, a relatively large body of water, was known among Anishinaabe people as hazardous due to its shallow depths. Waves behaving in unpredictable ways frequently caused canoes and boats to capsize. Many Anishinaabe people, including Keesick relatives, lost their lives in drowning accidents on this lake. When Dedibayaash was away working for the transport company, Dedibaayaanimanook, her mother and her nephew Gichi Jôj George Trout often spent time on Wiimbaashko Minis.[26] This island was prominently situated southwest of the long peninsula separating the mouth of Namegosi Ziibi and the Chukuni River at the upper basin of Baagwaashi Zaa'igan. It was a short distance south of Ginebigo Baawitig, where Dedibaayaanimanook's mother and others who studied and became learned in the harvesting and use of traditional medicines came to gather medicinal plants. More so than anywhere else along the entire river route, in fact, the Baagwaashi Zaa'igan region yielded bountiful varieties of medicine for Anishinaabe medical practitioners.

A particular, harrowing, incident that took place on one of the Keesicks' down river journeys indicates the extent to which their ways of living and world views were still rooted in and governed by the old traditions of the ancestors. The Keesick family had just arrived in the vicinity of Wiimbaashko Minis when Dedibaayaanimanook's mother became very ill. Her affliction had actually begun several days previously when they were still early into their travels on Namegosi Ziibi. As they were approaching the three rapids above Gichi Baawitig, Dedibaayaanimanook thought she noticed that her mother's facial expression appeared strangely different. Gaamadweyaashiik seemed to suffer from stroke-like symptoms, and over the next several days, a type of abscess began to develop around her mouth and neck. Her condition continued to worsen, and when they reached Wiimbaashko Minis, a sense of hopelessness and despair prevailed among family members. Dedibaayaanimanook did whatever she could think of to make her mother comfortable, but she avoided looking directly at her because she could not bear to see her suffering. When they first arrived at Baagwaashi Zaa'igan, Dedibayaash sent word to relatives in Lac Seul via the water traffic, and within a few days, Dedibaayaanimanook's sibling/cousin Niingaanaashiik Mary arrived with several types of medicine.

One evening just after Niingaanaashiik's arrival, Dedibaayaanimanook's father was out canoeing near the shoreline when an unearthly cry rent the quietude of dusk. Dedibayaash glanced up to where the sound originated and there on the branch of a tree he saw an owl. It looked as though its feathers had all been singed. Dedibayaash reached up with his paddle and knocked the bird from its perch, and when he saw only bones and feathers heaped on the ground, he knew that its presence was in some way connected to Gaamadweyaashiik's illness. Realizing that a curse had been placed on her, he drew upon his vision quest powers to fend off the attacker and "send him back." He then burned the creature's remains. In combination, the medicine from Niingaanaashiik Mary's mother Baswewe, his power to identify the cause of the illness and the actions he took, reversed Gaamadweyaashiik's condition. She made a complete recovery, and the Keesicks continued their journey in a mood of quiet jubilation. Later, relatives confirmed that an elderly man from Grassy Narrows known to use his personal gifts in malevolent ways had been the offender. [27]

As a small child, Dedibaayaanimanook was fascinated by the water traffic on Baagwaashi Zaa'igan. She was too young to realize it at the time, but to see the endless stream of wemitigoozhi crafts in all shapes and sizes flowing up and down the lake and along the Chukuni River system northward was to witness the homelands being inundated before her eyes. Countless numbers of these men hurried by Wiimbaashko Minis in whatever type of floatable vessels were available to them as they made their way toward Red Lake in pursuit of gold. Even the likes of a paddlewheel made its odd appearance. Ambling slowly past the island, it continually drew large sheets of water onto its rotating paddles. Dedibaayaanimanook and her mother were once on the lake when the craft came puffing into view. Aware of how it affected the water's behaviour, they paddled immediately toward the safety of shore. The craft was actually not much slower than the tugs and barges that came loaded down with supplies and equipment, but it was capable of turning the water into an amorphous beast ready to swallow their tiny craft in an instant.

Long before the appearance of wemitigoozhiwag in the region, Anishinaabe people were travelling the system of rivers and lakes north of Baagwaashi Zaa'igan. However, they had a different name for each segment, unlike the newcomers who reckoned the entire route consisted of just one river. Now known as Chukuni River, it continues to flow from just north of Wanamani Zaa'iganing Red Lake southward through Baagwaashi Zaa'igan to Maadaawaang where it merges with the English River near Manidoo Baawitig. A relatively small falls once referred to as Gaabimidaabikijiwang[28] by Anishinaabe travellers is located just up the Chukuni River from its mouth. After the rapids became Snake Falls in the language of the newcomers, people began referring to it as Ginebigo Baawitig. Dedibaayaanimanook, her parents and her brother Jiibwaat Edward Angeconeb, his wife Gweyesh Annie and their young children, once spent part of a winter at Ginebigo Baawitig, across the river from the Nels Andersons. At another time, she accompanied her father along the Chukuni River route to Wanamani Zaa'iganing in order to attend a funeral at the old Anishinaabe cemetery in Post Narrows. Her mother did not go with them, having decided to stay behind at Maadaawaang to prepare for the final thrust of the family's journey to Obizhigokaang Lac Seul.

A particular place along the Keesicks' travel route to and from Wanamini Zaa'iganing on Chukuni River is a short distance from where the river's waters flow out of the southeastern region of Red Lake. It is close to a set of rapids known as Aagimaako Baawitig, [29] not far from the bridge over which Highway 125 to Balmertown now crosses the river. Today, this location on the bank of Chukuni River is visible from the highway if one stands on the bridge and looks down. It is where Dedibaayaanimanook's family pitched camp before continuing on their journey. One afternoon while they were on a trip, family members were in the midst of their usual routine when a wemitigoozhi wielding a camera suddenly appeared from nowhere. The man began taking photographs as Dedibaayaanimanook, in her early teens at this time, took up a position near her seated mother and her young nephew Gichi Jôj, sharing his grandmother's seat, smiled accommodatingly at the stranger. Dedibaayaanimanook's sister Gweyesh Annie Angeconeb, remained standing near the tent entrance, holding her small infant as she looked unsmilingly at the intruder. Her two other children, Niiyoo Leo and Bejii Betsy were on her left. Little Niiyoo appeared somewhat doubtful, and Bejii registered a mildly inquisitive expression on her face. Dedibayaash had taken off his hat and it hung on an upright pole close to where he seated himself on the ground, waiting obligingly for the stranger to finish photographing his family. This type of abrupt, uninvited encounter was becoming an increasingly common experience in the lives of the Keesick families whether they were in Namegosibiing or on one of their travels.

When Dedibaayaanimanook's family and travelling companions reached the southern end of Baagwaashi Zaa'igan, their journey to

Lac Seul was approximately two thirds finished. Chukuni River continues to flow along a southeasterly course to merge with the English River at Maadaawaang. From there, the travellers paddled against the English River's current toward Otawagi Baawitig Ear Falls where Dedibaayaanimanook's brother Jiins and one of his mates once came to harvest a special leaf that was used in combination with the needles of an evergreen shrub.

"Ginebigobag osha wiin i'iwe!" Jiins had not quite pulled out a clump of leaves when his companion warned him that he was about to pick the wrong ferns. Being similar in appearance, the plant was easily mistaken for the medicinal variety, but his friend was an experienced practitioner who could distinguish the one from the other. After he finished his harvest, Jiins put down a small object to acknowledge the reciprocal relationship that existed between him, the human being, and the earth.[30]

At Otawagi Baawitig, the travellers portaged around the hydro electric dam that had begun to be built during the late 1920s. From there, it was a relatively short canoe journey to Gojijiing Gold-pines. People noted that this and other similar communities were typically divided into three separate neighborhoods. One was where Anishinaabe people lived together. In another part of the settlement resided the maadaawaawogimaag,[31] the wemitigoozhiwag with whom Anishinaabe women partnered and had children. These children were referred to as maadaawaawogimensag. Examples of mixed heritage families of the Otawagi Baawitig and Gojijiing regions were the Williamses, Andersons and Youngs. The Keesicks' friend Giishkinik of Maadaawaang was a maadaawaawogimens. The community's third neighborhood was where the wemitigoozhi folk lived among themselves. In the minds of Anishinaabe people, the notion of this type of community segmentation was not in and of itself a negative. It was acceptable and natural that everyone wanted to live with family and kin, those with whom they had the most in common.

Proceeding from Gojijiing, the travellers were now plying the waters of Obizhigokaawi Zaa'igan Lac Seul Lake. "Nashke nimaamaa—ganabaj madwe zakide!" Dedibaayaanimanook shouted excitedly at her mother one bright clear morning on the lake as she pointed to what appeared to be large billows of smoke swirling skyward in the distance ahead. When the canoeists drew near, thousands of lacy winged fish flies swarmed everywhere, creating a temporary nuisance. Dedibaaya-animanook waved her sweater in the air to swat them away but her efforts were futile. Being at the northern end of Lac Seul Lake, they would not reach the settlement of Obizhigokaang before several more hours of steady canoeing. The entire trip from Namegosibiing to Lac Seul could take as little as three and a half days, depending on what the activities were along the way, and since people were travelling with the river's current, the spring journey usually took less time and required less energy than the one in autumn. It was a distance of approximately one hundred-fifty miles. The Keesicks' second great journey would be their return to Namegosibiing toward the end of summer.

1. The name Adikamegwaaminikaaning refers to where the whitefish spawn. Today it is known as Whitefish Falls.

2. Manidoo Baawitig translates to Spirit Rapids.

3. Gaagakiiwekikawemog is Jack Pine Portage Trail; –*kik* refers to an *okik*, a jack pine.

4. Wabauskang is a First Nation community accessible from Highway 105.

5. Wabigoon River flows throughout the northwest Ontario region of Dryden.

6. Anishinaabe language scholar R. Roulette has stated that the structure of Anishinaabemowin, the Anishinaabe language, itself provides evidence that the practice of a woman's being adopted into her partner's family had already existed before the influences of wemitigoozhiwag prevailed.

7. Getemiikanaang translates to the Place of the Old Railroad.

8. The term Gaawaawaagoshkiikitigweyaag alludes to the zigzag pattern of the river at that location.

9. Waaboozo Baawitig is Rabbit Rapids.

10. Gookooko'oowi Baawitig translates to Owl Rapids.

11. Bizhiwininjiiwi Baawitig is Lynx Paw Rapids.

12. Wazhashko Zaa'igan, which translates to Muskrat Lake, is now referred to as Joyce Lake. The river which flows from this small lake did not have a name among Dedibaayaanimanook's people. It is now known as Joyce River.

13. Wazhashko Maadaawaang was the name of the location where Joyce River merges into Trout River.

14. Apisaabiko refers to a type of rock found in the area.

15. Ikwewi Ziibi has been correctly translated to Woman River.

16. Goshkwegaawinigam now goes by the name Swain Lake; Niki Zaa'igan is Goose Lake.

17. Memegweshi Zaa'igan now goes by the wemitigoozhi's pronunciation of Memegwesh and is therefore referred to as Mamakwash Lake.

18. Gaamangadikamegokaang is literally, Where the Large Whitefish Live. Dedibaayaanimanook did not know its English name.

19. Mashkiigonigam is an alternate name for Goshkwegaawinigam (Swain Lake); it is a reference to the swampy nature of the area.

20. Gaaodooskwanigamaag is the Elbow Place; the river resembles a bent elbow at this location.

21. The meaning of Gwaagwaazhiidinaawinigaam is unknown.

22. Dedibaayaanimanook was not certain as to the meaning of the word mina'igo as it applied to this name.

23. Dedibaayaanimanook referred to her cousin as her older sister, in accordance with the traditional custom which regarded cousins as siblings; it served to bond members together with a closer connection. To illustrate, the wemitigoozhi way would describe Dedibaayaanimanook as having no full siblings, but the Anishinaabe system provided her with numerous brothers and sisters. Each and every one of her cousins were siblings, even though she was her parents' only child together. Meniyaan Mary Ann Keesick, the daughter of her paternal uncle Netawibiitam John and his wife Minogaabawiik "Gookomens," was an example of such a sister, while Meniyaan's brother Mazinigiizhig James was one of Dedibaayaanimanook's brothers. There was another important function of the tradition, and that was to protect people from inherent risks associated with intermarriage. According to the old way, one did not marry a certain first degree cousin because one would not think of marrying a sister or brother.

24. Diitibisewinigamiing was known as Rolling Portage at one time. Today the village is called Hudson.

25. Baagwaashi Zaa'igan (literally, Shallow Lake), Pakwash Lake, is now a provincially regulated park.

26. Wiimbaashko Minis received this name because of the large quantities of wiimbaashkominan, a certain type of berry that grew on the island.

27. At that time, there were individuals with exceptional powers. Many chose to use their gift to help others, but there were those who were led by darker, more vindictive motives. In order to minimize the risk of giving offense and being cursed as a result, children were admonished by their parents not to laugh at or speak disrespectfully toward anyone, particularly a visitor. Furthermore, Dedibaayaanimanook was taught not to look directly at anyone because to do so was an affront to the person. Gichi Jii, who married one of Dedibaayaanimanook's cousins, was similarly taught as a child. She too held to the same beliefs all her life and conducted herself accordingly. With each day that passes and the Gichi Anishinaabeg become fewer in number, the extinction of such teachings, associated terms and practices becomes more real.

28. Gaabimidaabikijiwang refers to the water of a falls as it flows over its rocky ledges.

29. Aagimaako Baawitig is named after the black ash trees that once grew in abundance throughout the area.

30. Whenever people were without tobacco, they expressed appreciation for what they took from the land by the symbolic gesture of placing objects such as a knife or other tool, a spoon, cup, dish or even a piece of jewelry on the ground.

The custom manifested a value system in which people acquired a physical object for its usefulness rather than for the sake of material accumulation. The incident with Jiins embodies one of many reasons why de-colonization of Western archaeological practice is critical: It is vital that uninformed archaeologists and those who circumvent traditional, community developed protocols re-educate themselves in order to prevent defilement and disturbance of such sacred objects.

31. The term maadaawaawogimaag alludes to the fact that wemitigoozhiwag who married Anishinaabe women generally obtained jobs that came with some degree of authority, such as a foreman. That feature about their employment distinguished them from virtually all Anishinaabe workers.

CHAPTER 3

E'niibing

~

Summertime

"Obizhigokaang ingii' izhaamin e'niibing," was how Dedibaayaan-imanook's people expressed the tradition of going to Obizhigokaang Lac Seul for the summer. But they were using the Anishinaabe name for Lac Seul in a general way to apply to all the southern regions of their traditional territories where they spent eight to ten weeks each year. One of the reasons for these annual journeys was the need to vacate Namegosibiing in order to allow their homeland time to rejuvenate and rest from their occupation, in much the same way that farmers leave their fields fallow. In addition, they wanted to visit with friends and relatives living in Lac Seul, and they wanted to re-affirm their membership with the Anishinaabe First Nation. After Obizhigokaang Lac Seul signed the adhesion to Treaty 3, the people of Namegosibiing needed to take part in the yearly Treaty Time celebrations which they referred to as diba'amaadim. Then, from the turn of the twentieth century and thereafter, their stay increasingly included wemitigoozhi-related work.

Although people enjoyed socializing and otherwise interacting with the larger community, they were careful to maintain their own distinct identity. One way had to do with appearance, but there was a kind of hazard attached to using this method for establishing distinctiveness. "Bizhishig e'zenibaa wawezhi'owaaj Namegosibii Ikwewag!" was a comment family members overheard one summer when Dedibaayaan-imanook was a small child. A group of young Anishinaabe men, in the midst of discussing the clothing style of Namegosibiing's womenfolk,

expressed curiosity about their extensive use of ribbon for adorn-
ment. Upon hearing the conversation, one of Dedibaayaanimanook's
uncles used the opportunity to explain that the women, who valued
their identity, were simply honouring the instructions of their patriarch, Giizhik Sam Keesick, to use ribbons on their clothing by way
of symbolizing their membership with the Keesick clan. When the
people of Lac Seul generally spoke of Dedibaayaanimanook's people,
they referred to them as the Namegosibii Ininiwag and Namegosibii
Ikwewag, the Men and Women of Trout Lake. Some called them
the Oshekamigaa Ininiwag and Oshekamigaa Ikwewag, the Men and
Women of the Height of Land, with the shortened version Oshekamigaa Anishinaabeg, the People of the Height of Land. The origin of
this latter set of names originated from the well known fact that the
Keesicks came from regions where the land was of a higher elevation.

As for how the community of Lac Seul was once known, Dedibaayaanimanook's family retained knowledge about the original
Anishinaabe names for Lac Seul. For instance, the community of
Whitefish Bay was referred to as Gakiiweyaawangaang, in reference
to its predominantly sandy conditions. The original, pre-flood place
name for Lac Seul, moreover, was frequently mentioned in conversations among those who were acquainted with the region before
wemitigoozhiwag began building hydroelectric dams. By describing
the channel that existed near Kejick Bay, the old name Waabizhingwaakokaang was a direct allusion to the former geographic features
of the region. The Anishinaabe term waabiiyayaa referred to the
place where a channel forms, and since both land masses creating
the narrows were replete with zhingwaakwag (white pines), the
two words were combined into Waabizhingwaakokaang, a precise
physical description which translated to White Pines Channel.
Later on, however, when wemitigoozhiwag and the French began to
arrive in greater numbers, the original name changed as a result of
misunderstanding, translational/re-translational errors and incorrect
pronunciations. In their conversations, non-Anishinaabeg may have
thought they were hearing bezhig—which means "one"—rather than

the actual (waa)binzhing(waak). This then became the French "seul" [sole, single, lonely], and from that emerged the current non-Anishinaabe Lac Seul and the Anishinaabe Obizhigokaang, the latter being more than a slight distortion in the sound of the original name.

Alterations in place names that wemitigoozhiwag brought about were not benign in their consequences upon the psyche of the people, yet they exemplified the many peculiarities that Dedibaayaanimanook's people noticed about these newcomers. As alluded to previously, employment was one of the most important factors that brought people into closer physical proximity with them, helping to increase their understanding about their way of thinking. A set of events with far less neutral effects upon Anishinaabe people, whether they lived in Namegosibiing or Obizhigokaang, related to the fate of a place known historically as Neyaashiing. It was a point of land where members of Lac Seul First Nation assembled to collect their Treaty payments from the Indian agent. Not many years after Dedibaayaanimanook's birth, the newcomes began to construct dams. The one at Otawagi Baawitig Ear Falls turned Obizhigokaawi Zaa'igan Lac Seul Lake into a large reservoir. As a consequence, Neyaashiing—in addition to many acres of the Anishinaabe traditional homelands, which included sacred sites and cemeteries—immediately vanished beneath the risen waters. To this day, the land remains submerged several metres below the water's surface. Even though Dedibaayaanimanook's mother and travelling companions stopped briefly to watch the on-going construction whenever their travels took them through Otawagi Baawitig, no one from the wemitigoozhi community provided them with any information about how the structure was expected to affect their lives, much less asked whether they may have had concerns or opinions about the matter. This behaviour was very typical of the newcomers.

Beginning just after the time of Confederation in 1867, Treaty making, the Indian Act, and how the Act came to be implemented, formed other major wemitigoozhi influences in the affairs of Dedibaayaanimanook's people. From the very beginning, Canada had moved quickly to establish a monitor/control system in which

Indian agents—at various times, former employees of the Hudson's Bay Company—became street-level bureaucrats who arrived in the community, armed in some cases, and with the authority to exercise absolute control over the people. Anishinaabe people living on the reserve were especially at the mercy of these individuals' discretionary powers. But because Dedibaayaanimanook's people did not reside year round on the reserve, they were able to enjoy relative freedom from the Indian agent's direct interference, which often extended down into the minutiae of everyday life if he was so inclined. In the Keesicks' case, the agent's involvement was largely restricted to keeping records of their vital statistics, which he formally updated when they gathered annually at Lac Seul for Treaty Time.

Few single events on the people's yearly calender held the same degree of symbolism as the one they referred to as diba'amaadim. Treaty Time was therefore worthy of description. Although diba'-amaadim's literal meaning was a neutral reference to "everyone being paid," it was in fact, a tether that kept Anishinaabe people permanently bound to the wemitigoozhiwag, their institutions, systems and ways of doing things. Moreover, it was a reminder of the wemitigoozhi's gichi ogimaakwe,[1] who was purportedly so compassionate and caring that the specific terms of how Anishinaabe people would be allowed to live their lives were carried out through the authority of her name. The essence of how wemitigoozhiwag interpreted these terms became apparent during the transactions that typically took place outdoors. Perhaps the agent thought a more natural venue would help to lessen the risk of any scepticism that might surface and threaten to cause disruption. With this event being held out of doors, weather was an important factor in how well everything proceeded. The year Dedibaayaanimanook was ten years old, conditions continued to be sultry and humid for two days straight, the mercury reaching 88°F in the shade. The crowd of people waiting for the Indian agent to arrive felt the stickiness intensify as smoke from forest fires burning throughout the region cloaked the sky with a thick haze. Then, shortly after lunch, people observed the Lac Seul Hudson's Bay Company trading post manager making preparations to welcome the Dominion's Treaty agent whom they expected to appear at any moment.[2] He typically arrived by boat.

"Aazha biijibizo zhooniyaa ogimaa!" Dedibaayaanimanook and her friends felt an immediate surge of excitement when someone shouted that the Indian agent was motoring toward the Point. One year, when she was still a small child, she and her mates were frightened by loud shots that suddenly rang out. Nanaagaawibinesiik Mary, wife of Aman-isookaan David Angeconeb, happened to notice the children's fearful reaction and reassured them that the men deliberately fired their rifles into the air by way of welcoming the agent. Another memorable Treaty Time occurred when Dedibaayaanimanook was 16 years old. Unlike the rainy, foggy conditions of the day before, Thursday, June 16th was bright and warm. A fresh wind blew in from the east as the Dominion's Indian agent began to dispense the annuities at 9:00 a.m. sharp. That year, the weather was perfect and everything went according to schedule.

The men typically wore their finest clothes. One year, Dedibaay-aanimanook's father donned the sleevelets Gaamadweyaashiik made him specifically for the occasion. Considered as leaders in these types of matters, the men organized themselves into a group to accept cash allotments on behalf of their families. The entitlement of Treaty 3's people to collect five dollars from their nearest agency each year was intended to continue in perpetuity, even though the value of five dollars changed considerably since 1873. In addition to cash, the men received a set of goods that included shotgun shells and some flint. Dedibaayaanimanook would be helping her father fill the shells as soon as they returned home. The task was known as onashkinachigewin. In the meantime, the women of Lac Seul formed a group of their own. Before she joined the rest of the women one year, Dedibaayaanimanook's mother took the time to secure the family's paddles beneath their canoe. After inadvertently picking up the wrong one, she discovered that it was just as difficult to find the rightful owner as it was to try to become accustomed to using someone else's personalized paddle. Following what came to be the established convention, Gaamadweyaashiik and her fellow women sat down in a large circle. She had used a finely woven fabric known as zaa'wensiwegin to make the outfit she decided to wear. Namegosibii Anishinaabe women, in particular, preferred using this fabric because of its glossy, luxurious appearance and comfortable wear. Before too long, each of the women was handed a small box containing twelve balls of cotton twine with which they would make fish nets. It was just as well that Dedibaayaanimanook's mother never told the Indian agent about having a preference for ready-made nets since, somewhere far away, decision makers had long been preoccupied with their own concerns about Anishinaabe people, specifically, that they might become indolent if life was made too easy for them. From the beginning, it was a known fact that Canada's state officials had adopted a miserly attitude toward fulfilling the Dominion's Treaty obligations. By the time of Dedibaayaanimanook's birth in 1922, in fact, one MP could not help but make the observation that the department of Indian Affairs "carried its economy to the point of penuriousness"[3] during a debate about Treaty expenditures in the House of Commons.

Dedibaayaanimanook herself knew that her elders—her parents, aunts and uncles—understood that the Treaty agreement was not being upheld in an honourable manner. In terms of the material goods that the Indian agent brought along with him, for example, the Keesicks and others were well aware that the wares were consistently substandard, meagre in both quality and quantity. Some people even came to regard the Indian agent's merchandise as a kind of standing joke. Clearly, they would have made better choices themselves, but with no direct avenue to decision-makers, their sentiments remained among themselves. Others saw the entire Treaty Time notion as little more than a parody, but they regarded it as their obligation to participate in the annual activities.

Especially at proceedings as important as taking treaty or conducting certain ceremonies, Anishinaabe parents took great pains to make sure that their children were close at hand and under strict supervision, hence they did so during such official events as diba'amaadim and *Midewinaaniwan*. That did not preclude the children's freedom to play, although it sometimes took a while for Dedibaayaanimanook and her siblings to venture out and mingle with the other youngsters. A ball being tossed around was often enough to break the ice because everyone wanted to partake of anything that looked like fun. Predictably, however, it was when the children were enjoying themselves most that the Indian agent was most efficient at conducting his business. He typically stayed in the community for two days, then departed for the next Treaty 3 destination, which was Wabauskang, the band from which Dedibaayaanimanook's mother had transferred when she married Dedibayaash.

The Keesicks' registered membership with the Church of England was further evidence of wemigoozhi influence in their lives. Having considered the implications of such a relationship, and having decided in favor of its benefits, Dedibaayaanimanook's parents made a point of attending services the Sunday immediately following Treaty Time. Canon Sanderson came every year at that time to conduct services at the on-reserve mission house,[4] but once he left, people were free to attend to other matters. Local Anishinaabeg paid their bills at the Hudson's Bay Company store conveniently located close by, unlike Dedibaayaanimanook's father and uncles, who purchased goods with credit at trading posts further to the north. One year, a trader from Wazhashkonigamiing Kenora appeared on the scene with a wide assortment of goods for sale. With his prices much lower than those of the local trading post, the independent trader had no difficulty attracting attention, and since people now had ready cash, he was not obliged to accept furs for his merchandise. Dedibaayaanimanook's mother purchased ten yards of fabric for a dollar and a pair of sturdy leather soled shoes for twenty-five cents. Later, independent trader Ken McDougall arrived from Red Lake. The Lac Seul Hudson's Bay Company post manager was not amused by these invasions into his domain.[5]

After the bills were all paid and purchases made, community members began a series of social activities that served not only to commemorate their Treaty, but to reaffirm their membership with the Anishinaabe Nation and their relationship with one another. It was a time to enjoy the company of friends and relatives while participating in various social activities. Card games proved to be one of the most popular forms of recreation, especially the year that the grand prize heaped in the center of the circle of players consisted of merchandise the independent trader from Kenora had brought along for the occasion. Even Dedibaayaanimanook's mother participated in the occasional game. During one such contest, Gaamadweyaashiik found herself holding what appeared to be a very promising hand. She noted the demeanor of her fellow players as they took turns laying down their cards. With only one player left, she was on the verge of reaching for the lucrative pot. "Ishe!" Gaamadweyaashiik was taken completely aback by the last set of cards, but other than an exclamation of surprise, she accepted her disappointing loss without comment. When Dedibaayaanimanook was old enough to earn her own spending money by means of her beadwork, she too played once or twice. But as a young child, she enjoyed being with the other children while her parents were preoccupied with the card games.

"Dagasa gookooko'oowidaa!" She and her relatives, who included at different times Ginôk Eliza, Niksaandan George, Diike, Ishkwe, Moshish Mary and Gichi Jôj George Trout, began their games that required nothing more than an active imagination by pretending to be owls and other equally frightening creatures. "Giininaa Maangonini!" At other times, they pretended to Mide by mimicking Maangonini, the near-blind elderly gichi Midewinini from Frenchman's Head who often led the ceremonies.

Community dances, among the best attended of all the post-Treaty Time activities, and other similar events, took place in a cabin and were normally reserved only for adults. The exceptions were when Dedibaayaanimanook once received permission to attend with her cousin's wife Giizhoonj, then later, when she went with Niingaana-ashiik Mary. As children, therefore, Dedibaayaanimanook and her friends crept into the bushes that grew near the dance hall, and guided by the music and laughter from within, conjured up images of who might be dancing with whom. They shared exaggerated descriptions of what they fancifully imagined. One evening, Dedibaayaanimanook and her companions were suddenly discovered by a group of teen lads who had stepped out for some fresh air. One of the boys had stuffed his pockets and jacket with apples and oranges. The next day, Dedibaayaanimanook's mother mentioned someone had been complaining that the fruit he was selling to the dancers had mysteriously disappeared. When Dedibaayaanimanook became a teen, she too was able to attend the dances if she was accompanied by female cousins of a similar age or older. She discovered that the events were every bit as much fun as she had imagined.

"Awenen waa' baashka'igej?" The social began when someone shouted out by way of inquiring who among the participants was willing to open the dance. As soon as one of the men came to the front of the line of women, the music began. All dances were adaptations and variations of jigs, reels and square dances that people had learned from wemitigoozhiwag. Even though one was called the duck dance because dancers needed to duck under each other's extended arms, people named it Zhiishiibishimowin. Zhaaganaashii Nishôchiwag, Gaa'aazhideyaasing and Waakaashimowin were some of the other well known dances. Waaboozoshimowin, however, was without a doubt everyone's favourite, and the most entertaining of all the participants was Dedibaayaanimanook's cousin Debanaa. The crowd watched delightedly as Debanaa maneuvered adroitly among the other dancers, eluding the one waving a brightly colored handkerchief. Debanaa's performance reminded people of another lively dancer who had once contributed immensely to the popularity of the affairs with his amazing dexterity. But since Omiimiisi, who was from Grassy Narrows, died when Dedibaayaanimanook was a young child, she never saw his performances.

When Dedibaayaanimanook was around nine years old, the eldest daughter of her cousin Omooday Paul lost her life in a canoeing accident. People decided to organize a special square dance in attemps to lift the community's morale, and for the benefit of Dedibaayaanimanook's senior aunts who were particularly distraught by the enormity of their loss, Waakaashimowin was repeated several times. Being an exceptional dancer herself, Dedibaayaanimanook's mother joined the elderly women who formed a circle as the men stepped forward to give each grandmother a gentle twirl to the music. People were particularly gratified to see Maajiigiizhigook Mary, the grandmother of the deceased, enjoying a brief moment of laughter as she too took a turn on the dance floor.

Of all the musicians, Giishkinik was one of the most popular square dance callers. He had lost part of an arm during his service in the Great War, but his loss did not affect his ability to please the crowds with his amazing fiddle playing. A particularly amusing incident happened during one of the socials in which he was calling the dances and Dedibaayaanimanook's male cousin Imbedam was dancing with her sister Moshish Mary Keesick. "Ambe giin o'maa, Animoshish!" When Moshish momentarily lost her place among the swirling dancers, Imbedam intended to call her by name. Instead, he did something quite different. The Anishinaabe word for dog is animosh. Attaching the suffix -ish to a noun expresses a low opinion or negative criticism. With animosh, the word becomes animosh*ish*, meaning a dog that is considered despicable or undeserving in some way. By a slip of the tongue, Imbedam had inserted "ani" in front of Moshish's name, thus inadvertently referring to his dance partner as a contemptible dog! Dedibaayaanimanook and the others who heard Imbedam knew that his monumental blunder was the result of the excitement generated by Giishkinik's music. As for Moshish Mary, she too was amused by her partner's faux pas.

Maajiiyaashkaamewinig
Gidikwezensimiwaag
Ozho'igook
Gidikwezensimiwaag
Gizhibaawebinigook
Gidikwezensimiwaag! [6]

The music continued throughout the evening, and Giishkinik continued to delight Dedibaayaanimanook and her companions with his energetic performance.

As soon as the diba'amaadim celebrations drew to a close, people dispersed in order to pursue the rest of summer's variant activities. But the Dedibayaashes were not always the first to leave, so there were times when Dedibaayaanimanook and her sisters came across bits of fabric left behind by women who had already begun using their new fabric. Finding the colorful little scraps of cloth was akin to discovering treasure! The Keesicks then gathered their goods together and canoed to the Obizhigokaang community where families built houses in rows just the way the Indian agent had instructed. As they were making their way past Treaty Point one year, Dedibaayaanimanook noticed someone making a birch bark canoe. It was an activity most had long given up by that time and was therefore a very rare sight. Throughout the rest of the season, employment drew people to different places. Fighting forest fires was one form of work opportunity for those who were willing and able. Just after diba'amaadim in 1932, for example, a boat arrived in Lac Seul around dinner time to recruit Anishinaabe men for a large fire burning in the vicinity of Wapasu Lake north of the Hudson's Bay Company post. Several weeks later, a provincial forestry plane landed at Lac Seul in search of men for another large blaze, this one on the other side of Wanamani Zaa'iganing Red Lake. Stewart and Wilfred Vincent and Alex Lawson were among those who signed on for three weeks.[7] When Dedibaayaanimanook was a young girl, her father, her uncle Jiimis James and several cousins joined a crew gathered in Lac Seul to fight a blaze that had started somewhere to the north. Her eldest uncle, Mooniyaans Thomas, however, stayed home in order to help care for the children during their fathers' absence. Whether that was one of the fires mentioned in the Lac Seul Hudson's Bay Company post journal is not clear.

For many summers, Dedibaayaanimanook's father worked as a cook for the fire fighters. The work was not for anyone weak or indolent since it came with long hours and very low pay. Dedibayaash was away from his family throughout the entire forest fire season. However, the fact that he was given whatever food remained unused once the fire season was over helped to compensate for the low wages and for his long absence. "Aazha dagoshin indede!" When her father finally returned after many weeks in the bush, Dedibaayaanimanook was overjoyed, and when she saw his canoe laden with several pounds of butter, containers of canned food, jars of jam and peanut butter, packets of dried fruit and other similar goodies, she was overcome with delight. For the rest of the summer, Dedibayaash worked for a transport company steering scows back and forth from Ear Falls to Whitefish Falls on Namegosi Ziibi. Potentially, it was an extremely hazardous occupation because a drowning could—and did—result from one misstep, especially when cold weather encrusted the boat with ice.

With her father away working at these jobs, Dedibaayaanimanook and her mother travelled from place to place throughout the region. Obizhigokaang Lac Seul, Diitibisewinigamiing Hudson, Baagwaashi Zaa'igan, Otawagi Baawitig Ear Falls, Gojijiing Goldpines and points between were the places that made up their itinerary. One of the reasons why Dedibaayaanimanook's parents avoided staying in any one community for very long was their wish to protect her from the many untoward influences that now existed. The Keesicks were well aware that there were those who tried to impose their unwelcome presence on the community. Thoughtless, disrespectful, unpredictable, these characters were often drunk, disorderly and potentially very dangerous, particularly for the women and children. One time when the Keesicks were living near Ear Falls, a wemitigoozhi and his friend tried to induce Dedibaayaanimanook's aunt and her sister Gweyesh Annie to accept the alcohol the two had brought with them. But the women fled to Mooniyaans Thomas, who prevailed against the intruders by verbally shaming them before sending them on their way. Another reason for Dedibaayaanimanook's parents' mobility was their desire to continue with the custom of harvesting and using traditional foods. As well, her mother needed to be mobile in order to find temporary employment. Gaamadweyaashiik was not one to shirk physical labour, and from time to time she was able to find work with a wemitigoozhi woman who lived in Gojijiing Goldpines. Gaamadweyaashiik took the load of laundry to a little island on Lac Seul Lake just east of the settlement where she washed the clothes with a washboard. "Wiinge dash egii' gichi inendang e'anokiij." In fact, Dedibaayaanimanook's mother expressed her appreciation for having this kind of paid work because it allowed her a certain measure of independence and the opportunity to carry out her work in privacy, away from wemitigoozhiwag. Whenever she worked for the woman with two young daughters, Gaamadweyaashiik accepted used clothing for Dedibaayaanimanook in exchange for her labour.

Dedibaayaanimanook's mother ensured that they were always accompanied by various members of the extended family during their summer travels. While the arrangement provided for much appreciated companionship and greater safety, it also gave Dedibaayaanimanook learning opportunities by allowing her to observe the activities of their companions. Her aunt Maajiigiizhigook Mary, for example, collected birch bark for making boxes and spruce tree roots for sewing the seams together. Whenever a moose was killed and smoked, Maajiigiizhigook pounded the meat into a fine consistency called nooka'igan and stored it in her birch bark baskets. Dedibaayaanimanook's mother herself made birch bark containers which she used for the smoked pickerel, whitefish and trout that she and Dedibayaash caught and prepared before they left Namegosibiing in the spring. These boxes made it possible for the family to enjoy a protein rich diet during their down river journey and also to share it with various friends and relatives they met along the way. Smoked trout from Namegosibiing was a particularly special treat for the kinsfolk who lived in Obizhigokaang Lac Seul.

Dedibaayaanimanook also had opportunity to see some of the forms of artistic expression which people often incorporated into their everyday tasks. Before canvas was readily available, for example, one relative constructed a madogaan-type dwelling using birch bark. Midaasogiizhigook secured the segments into place, then gathered bark from a shrub found along the shoreline. After boiling the bark until it turned pumpkin orange, she set it aside to cool, then took handfuls and applied various bright designs along the lower edges of the house. Dedibaayaanimanook thus acquired knowledge about the dye and would one day teach others to dye birch bark using this method. Another one of Dedibaayaanimanook's observations related to Giizhoonj, who used deciduous branches and some cotton thread for making an object that resembled what we today refer to as a dream catcher. Attached to her child's cradleboard, the object was intended to protect against the type of air borne germs that often led to colds and other illnesses.[8] Other Anishinaabe women decorated their cradleboards with round pouches made from leather and beaded on one side. Each contained a small piece of umbilical cord from the child's birth. Both of Dedibaayaanimanook's cousins Moshish Mary and Moshishens Keesick used beaded designs, while others sewed fabric onto the lower edges of the leather bag. Because some women did not have the means to acquire beads, their decorative designs were less elabourate. Biiwidekwe, a woman who had lived in both Mishi Baawitig[9] and Miskwa'oowi Ziibi[10] before joining the Keesick clan, was one such person of more modest means.

While she and her mother were once in Obizhigokaang to attend a *Midewinaaniwan* gathering at the top of a gigantic sand precipice near Zaagiing Lac Seul, Dedibaayaanimanook saw a sample of the artistry executed by an elderly woman whose ceremonial name was Gaagige-binesiik. Many people in the community, however, preferred to call her Zaagiing Gookom, or simply Gookom. Dedibaayaanimanook's father referred to her as Indoozis because she was, in fact, one of his aunts. Although people once had good reason to mistrust Gaagige-binesiik—she and her father Godabaad had been associated with a type of spiritualism that placed the safety of others at risk—they put aside their suspicions during her latter years. An example of Zaagiing Gookom's artistic expression that Dedibaayaanimanook remembered was a series of connecting x's made from flattened porcupine quills that she sewed onto the vamp seams of her moccasins as a decorative detail. Sometimes Zaagiing Gookom even dyed her quills. Dedibaaya-animanook's mother, too, used quills for decorative purposes, and in addition, occasionally purchased packets of dyed horse hair that she whip-stitched over the seams of her moccasins. In another instance, Dedibaayaanimanook watched her cousin's wife Omoodayikwe smoking a moose hide, noting that she used willows for firewood.

As summer progressed, Dedibaayaanimanook and her mother visited with relatives at Wiimbaashko Minis[11] and other places along the northern basin of Baagwaashi Zaa'igan. Each of these visits was an opportunity for Dedibaayaanimanook to acquire new experiences and further knowledge about the geography of the traditional use territories. In so doing, she was adding to and shaping the oral history she would carry with her for the rest of her life. One year when the lake's water level was particularly low, Dedibaayaanimanook and her cousins heard that people were finding different objects along the shoreline. They decided immediately to join the hunt. Some of the items they came upon after several hours of searching included buttons of various shapes and sizes and old coins of which there were three different types of one cent pieces. At one point, their five cent pieces were redeemable for up to ten cents each. Then there were times when Dedibaayaanimanook's mother stopped at Nekobaang, a place located near Ginebigo Baawitig Snake Falls where willows and other types of shrubs grew profusely. Early on however, Nekobaang ceased to exist. "Gaawiin miina wiikaa awiya gii'izhidaasii i'imaa," is how Gaamadweyaashiik explained that no one since the time of Dedibaayaanimanook's early childhood was ever able to live at Nekobaang again. It disappeared into a watery grave when the area was flooded, so Dedibaayaanimanook was left with few memories about the ill-fated island. Their travels also provided for incidents that nudged her gently out of her world of childish naiveté. During one of their canoe trips on Obizhigikaawi Zaai'gan Lac Seul Lake, she and her mother were approaching Manidoowabaang. Although she had already been on the lake before, Dedibaayaanimanook looked ahead from her vantage point at the canoe's bow and noted for the first time how the water stretched endlessly into the distance.

"Giga daanginaamin ina wakwi, nimaamaa?" Pointing toward the far horizon where the sky and clouds dropped into the water, she wanted to know what the clouds would feel like. She had never heard anyone mention such an experience, so she asked her mother whether they would be able to reach out and touch the clouds when they finally arrived at the horizon. Her mother simply told her that she would find her answer when they arrived. In another instance, the workings of her young imagination became evident during a brief stop on a nearby island. Dedibaayaanimanook found a grassy spot by the shoreline, and when the warm sun began to make her drowsy, she lay down. Shading her eyes from the sun, she watched the wispy clouds that came drifting unhurriedly across the sky. A thought suddenly crossed her mind and she sat upright. "Gaawiin wiikaa niin niwii'nibosii!" She informed her mother with the force of a child's conviction that she had just decided that she would never die because she could not possibly endure the boredom of having to look up at the sky forever!

Something else the journeys did for Dedibaayaanimanook was to produce an on-going yearning to own a pet of her own. But what she imagined for herself was not the usual dogs of the others in her family. While gathering wood one afternoon during early summer, Dedibaayaanimanook stopped to find out what had caused the rustling sound beneath a clump of bushes. She crept toward the sound, and there in the plant growth was a tiny porcupine. Even though—or was it because—no one else had ever owned such a creature, she decided immediately to adopt the baby porcupine. "Biizhaanisa o'omaa!" she coaxed, trying to persuade the animal that it needed to come out. Instead, however, it swished its tail and rolled into a spiky ball. She waited patiently for a few moments and as it relaxed, she tried to grab its quill-less underbelly, but each time she reached out, the porcupine repeated its curl. After a while, Dedibaayaanimanook realized the futility of her efforts and returned home crestfallen. She carried only a few pieces of wood. "Nashke niin!" After hearing how the animal had outmaneuvered her, Gichi Jôj George Trout declared that he knew how to capture it, so with renewed hope, Dedibaayaanimanook led her nephew to where she had last seen the animal. It had not shuffled far, but Gichi Jôj was mistaken in thinking that he would succeed where she had failed. Dedibaayaanimanook now understood why no one owned a pet porcupine.

It was not long before Dedibaayaanimanook overcame her disappointment about the porcupine episode because she and her mates were never without ways for amusing themselves. Since they always lived close to the lake, for example, they spent a lot of time searching for tiny fish that swam close where the water was shallow. Sheltered places among the rocks where the sun's warmth attracted the fry were among the likeliest places to begin a search. Very slowly, they reached into the water and caught handfuls of little fish. Most of the fun came from daring each other to swallow what they had caught. As tiny fishlings wriggled down her throat, Dedibaayaanimanook could feel their tickly sensation. At other times, when they were briefly in the community of Obizhigokaang, Dedibaayaanimanook and her companions managed an occasional caper despite their parents' attentiveness. Her niece and cousin, Ginôk Eliza Ashen, was the mastermind behind a particular ruse which was based on their observation that grown-ups were always interested in socializing. Following Ginôk's formula, each of the friends approached her parents and casually mentioned that some of the grown-ups in the community were planning an evening of cards.

"Giwii'izhaam ina giinawaa?" They asked their parents whether they too wished to participate in the gathering. Having elicited the anticipated positive response, each offered to take the message back to the "hosts." Of course, the parents chosen to host the evening received a slightly different version of the planned event! Once the evening was underway and the parents were engrossed in their card games, Dedibaayaanimanook and the others were quite on their own—the objective of the entire operation. Under the cloak of darkness one summer, the girls crept away to spy on an eccentric old man who lived alone at the edge of the village. Their sense of danger as they made their way along the trail was magnified by the knowledge that their parents would have certainly disapproved. Soon they caught sight of the elderly man who was poking about in his garden by the dim light of a soot-laden lantern. As they watched his movements, one of them snapped a twig and giggled too loudly. The old man started. "Aweneniwiyan!" Hearing no reply to his query of who was out there, the old man muttered unintelligibly and resumed his work. At that point, the interlopers decided it best not to press their luck further. They scurried back along the trail, content to arrive home before their parents had time to notice their absence. The children's deception was relatively harmless, and it served to satisfy a periodic urge for risk taking. They, in fact, carried out their little subterfuge in various forms on more than one occasion, and to Dedibaayaanimanook's knowledge, their parents were never the wiser about how these spontaneous little socials had actually come about.

"Dagasa ando-mawadishiwedaa." Interspersing her pronouncements throughout the summer, Dedibaayaanimanook's mother made special trips to visit with family members not seen in months. One of the highlights of these get togethers was the exchange of homemade gifts carefully wrapped in bits of fabric or leaves. Dedibaayaanimanook could not help but be delighted by the cleverness that inspired these tokens of affection. Next, she and her companions made dolls from freshly picked birch leaves. Her mother had shown her how to fold a leaf several times until it formed a narrow rectangular shape for the figure's head, then use larger leaves to make a multi-tiered shawl that she secured into place with a leaf stem. By choosing leaves of different colors and sizes, it was possible to produce an endless assortment of figurines. Dedibaayaanimanook and Ginôk Eliza crafted enough to represent each member of their respective families, then they created fantastical stories that exaggerated the various events of their everyday lives. For as long as their families continued to get together, Dedibaayaanimanook and her friends enjoyed these recreations, even when they became teenagers.

One of Dedibaayaanimanook's favourite stops was Gojijiing Goldpines whenever their visits occurred on a weekend. Saturday night dances held at the small community were always filled with fun and laughter. In fact, they were equally as much fun as the ones at Treaty Time. The Youngs, Williamses and Smiths, all families of mixed heritage who lived in the Gojijiing region, were well known for their musical talent and were the ones who provided music for the gatherings. People from all throughout the region attended. Even John Paishk of Red Lake was frequently present.

"Aazha ganabaj miinikaadog." Toward mid-August, Dedibaayaanimanook's mother commented that the blueberries were probably ready to harvest. For Dedibaayaanimanook and her nephew Gichi Jôj George Trout, whose father was Gaagizhii and his grandfather, "Joozhimimaa," her pronouncement signalled another phase in their summer activities. Blueberry season was a time for carefree play and for eating whatever quantity of the berries they wanted. This tradition, in which the Keesicks and various relatives canoed southwest along a network of rivers and small lakes, then walked along trails toward the railway tracks to where the blueberry meadows lay, had persisted since long before Dedibaayaanimanook was ever born. The custom continued for some time, as was evident when the ever observant Lac

Seul Hudson's Bay Company post manager noted in late July, 1938, that the Anishinaabe people were "berry picking at Hudson."[12] Accordingly, the Keesicks set out on the trip, reaching the furthest limits of the waterway where they cached their canoes and continued on foot for a considerable distance along a hiking trail west of Diitibisewinigamiing Hudson. They arrived at Gaabaagoshkiwagaag to the berries that grew in greatest quantities on either side of the railway tracks beyond Minijing.[13] But before the harvest got under way, senior harvesters made an assessment for a cursory value of the season's growth. Then the work began. Dedibaayaanimanook's mother and other experienced harvesters knew from a glance which of the shrubs contained the largest fruit. They kept to a steady work pace, taking periodic breaks throughout the day. At dusk, they stopped for a meal, then reposed in the open air beneath their mosquito net canopies.

One late summer at Minijing, their group included Gweyesh Annie, her infant son Niiyoo Leo, who was in a cradleboard at the time, and her small daughter Bejii Betsy. Midaasogiizhigook as well as Soons and his family were also among the group. It was late in the afternoon after the activities had begun to wind down for the day. As the young Dedibaayaanimanook stood and watched Soons approaching the campsite, a shapeless form suddenly hovered before her. The pain she felt behind her eyes was so severe she became dizzy and nauseous. For many days, she remained bedridden and in constant pain. Only after a relative arrived with special medicine and suggested blocking out the light did her torment begin to subside and she was finally able to have a complete night's rest. Dedibaayaanimanook never forgot the incident. At another time while in the area, they noticed railway workers passing through in their quaint little carts. Was it possible that one of them was a young wemitigoozhi named Einar Olsen? If so, might he have seen a group of Anishinaabe children playing among the berry bushes near the tracks, and might he have even caught a glimpse of a particular little girl with long braided pony tails that bounced in the air as she darted hither and thither with her playmates? Perhaps! As soon as the berries were picked, Dedibaayaanimanook's parents put them in wooden boxes in which powdered milk was sold. Keeping them fresh and firm was important if they were to yield reasonable prices. Once all the boxes were filled, the harvest was over. Dedibaayaanimanook recalled that for a few years, the Giiwegaabowensag[14] helped her father transport their berries along the foot trail, while Ginôk Eliza and Nechaaw accompanied them back to the landing. Taking their canoes with them, Akandoo Matilda and some of the others took the train back to Hudson.

"Ambesh amii'iyaazha Namegosibiing izhaayeng!" Even though autumn was still a few weeks away one year, Dedibaayaanimanook and her cousins began voicing their wish to return to home. As each day passed, it became more difficult to contain their longing for Namegosibiing. "Aazhana giwii' giiwemin?" More than once, Dedibaayaanimanook inquired whether it was time to go home, and when her parents finally mentioned the word gopa'am—travel up river—she was euphoric. She hurried to pack her belongings, and in practically no time at all, she was ready for the journey. Her only hope was that the others would be equally as speedy! Most of summer's activities were now at an end, and her mother had already taken note that both the chokecherries and mountain ash berries were ripe. It was nature's way of signaling that the wild rice was ready to harvest. The Keesicks began to organize their belongings, deciding what to take with them and what to leave behind. Since travel was the basis of their way of life, people such as the Keesicks of Namegosibiing had to be very careful not to accumulate an overabundance of material goods. Each and every purchase was thought out in terms of how the item would potentially affect their mobility. It was usually necessary to leave some household items behind, even though leaving their houses at Lac Seul vacant meant facing the risk of break-ins, vandalism and theft. Then they decided on a specified time and place from which to begin their travels back to Namegosibiing.

While Dedibaayaanimanook's family and relatives made provisions for the journey, she recalled that friends and acquaintances who remained in Obizhigokaang Lac Seul year round prepared for another season of commercial fishing for a man they called Bowman. One September, the men of Lac Seul prepared to meet with a constable Gray to register their guns; approximately 100 were inventoried with the authorities that year.[15] The Dedibayaashes therewith departed for Gojijiing, at the northern end of Obizhigokaawi Zaa'igan, where they made their first stop for supplies at the Hudson's Bay Company outlet. In addition to a quantity of staple items, Dedibaayaanimanook's mother purchased one or two treats, including hens' eggs, candy and some chocolate to be savored periodically throughout the journey.

"Gii'manzina'igewag e'gopa'amowaaj." It was standard practise for them to procure a certain amount of goods on credit. As soon as trapping season was in full swing, harvesters would return to the post with enough furs to pay off their debts. The Keesicks then proceeded to Otawagi Baawitig Ear Falls. Before freeze-up in 1940, the gates regulating water levels on Obizhigokaawi Zaa'igan Lac Seul Lake had been lowered to "accommodate shipping to Red Lake, Ear Falls, etc."[16] Officials in charge of the dam and water regulation apparently anticipated that the lake level would need to be additionally altered to provide sufficient water for power generation at Otawagi Baawitig Ear Falls, so a type of guage had been installed to monitor the levels. From Otawagi Baawitig, the people's journey proceeded along the English River to Maadaawaang. Dedibaayaanimanook remembered the few times when her family took a side trip south, past Manidoo Baawitig,[17] to a place known as Gaaminisiwang.[18] Beyond that, the waters of the river eventually flowed into a lake called Manidoobaawi Zaa'igan,[19] somewhere toward the west. The Keesicks embarked on this segment of the journey in order to gather wild rice growing in the lake Gaaminisiwang. Being high in both protein and vitamins, wild rice was an important part of their diet.

The travellers held a special feast consisting of fresh fish and duck roasted over an open fire before they began the harvest. The primary purpose for the ceremony was to waangawike, that is, to appease the great Being(s) by their expressions of gratitude for their lives and their safety. Its purpose was also to confirm their commitment to live honourably, and also to seek help in the form of favorable weather conditions. Because moisture prevented the mature grains of wild rice from dropping easily from their stalks, the Keesicks asked for a delay in the rain and for mist free mornings. Finally, they requested continued safety as they carried out the many activities of their journey. There were times, however, when there was not enough wild rice in the region. Whenever that happened, the people of Namegosibiing needed to proceed to Zagadikwaning,[20] a connecting lake about a half day's canoe journey beyond Gaaminisiwang. There they were able to harvest the additional crop they needed. It was at Zagadikwaning that Dedibaayaanimanook's uncle Jiimis was once observed standing alone near a large dead poplar tree. One of Dedibaayaanimanook's young cousins had fallen ill, and Jiimis was seeking help on behalf of his daughter. When family members heard the dreaded sound of the old poplar crashing to the ground around midnight, they knew immediately that the child would not survive the illness. Indeed, she died not long after they left Maadaawaang. The Keesicks returned to Gojijiing and buried their little girl where graves of other departed friends and relatives were located. Soons Oojiiwasaswaan's younger sister Ena was one such person who was buried at Gojijiing. Dedibaayaanimanook and Ena had become close friends when their families were together one summer. The two young girls got along so well, in fact, that Ena began to think of Dedibaayaanimanook as her sister.

As soon as the wild rice harvest was finished, the travellers were ready to continue north. Some canoes were already laden to near capacity with provisions that would last them through the entire journey. The Dedibayaash family's 50 pound bag of wild rice, for example, was expected to keep them supplied until mid-winter. They re-traced their route along the Chukuni River past Maadaawaang to Baagwaashi Zaa'igan. Nekobaang, before the inudation, was where a box containing the family's personal possessions once went missing. Included among them was a medallion on a red silk ribbon that Dedibaayaanimanook's grandfather had received from a government official by way of acknowledging his leadership role among the Namegosibii

Anishinaabeg. Giizhik Sam Keesick was granted free passage to travel on the train anywhere in the country whenever he wore the medal, but since he had no desire to travel by train, he never took advantage of the arrangement. Another valued artifact that went missing at Nekobaang was a water drum that Dedibaayaanimanook's mother had hand crafted. Fortunately for the Dedibayaashes, Niingaanaashiik Mary found the box with its contents and, knowing their value, she returned them at once.

When Dedibaayaanimanook was in her teens, a side journey took the family beyond the Andersons' home at Ginebigo Baawitig Snake Falls. That family lived across Chukuni River from where Dedibaaya-animanook and her mother occasionally stopped for brief visits during their summer travels. Mrs. Anderson was Njôy Margaret Sapey, a young Anishinaabe woman whose husband was a Swede named Baka'aakwaan Nels Anderson. He operated the Hudson's Bay Company post at Ginebigo Baawitig, and prior to the arrival of Swain himself, he also managed the post at Swain Lake during winter's trapping season. Finding that Dedibaayaanimanook's presence filled the void she felt after the death of her young sister, Njôy developed a special fondness for Dedibaayaanimanook, and began to encourage her visits. Dedibaayaan-imanook herself was happy to spend time with the Andersons. Njôy's eldest son was Eric; her others were Lawrence, Paddy, Bill, Mike and the son who was born when Mike was twelve years old. Dedibaaya-animanook got along especially well with Eric, the one closest to her age. As the two entered their teens, it was Njôy's fondest wish for Dedibaayaanimanook to one day become her daughter-in-law, even though she probably knew in her heart that their relationship would never go beyond a brief friendship. Eric had been suffering from a chronic condition since early childhood, and over the course of time, his illness worsened. A series of operations resulted in a colostomy that eventually made physical activity all but impossible. When word reached the Keesicks a few years later that Eric Anderson had died, Dedibaayaanimanook grieved for her dear friend.

The Dedibayaashes canoed as far as Andersons' camp the autumn they were briefly in Ginebigo Baawitig Snake Falls, but they failed to see Njôy with the rest of her family. To their sorrow, they learned that she had died four months after giving birth. They left immediately, even as they mourned the passing of Njôy Margaret Anderson. After proceeding past Namegosi Zaagiing, they arrived at Baagwaashi Zaa'iganiins Bruce Lake where the Cromarty family of Ikwewi Zaa'igan Woman Lake joined the Keesicks since they too were returning to their winter home. Maagii and Eliza Cromarty were the granddaughters of Gebiyaaniman Joe Cromarty and his wife Giniikwe. Tall and slender, the two girls had inherited the physique of their grandfather, who was well known for his unique mannerisms and for the way in which he expressed himself. Whenever people heard him beginning to sniffle, for example, they knew that they were about to hear another of his off-handed remarks. However, they learned not to laugh too heartily, since no one was ever sure who would be the next subject of his forthright comments. People also knew not to take offense to anything Gebiyaaniman had to say. Occasionally, travelling the route with the Keesicks, was Naakojiiz and Gwejech's uncle Zhaawan, who was referred to by the term bigwaj Anishinaabe because he preferred to make his home in the woods, far from everyone else. In fact, solitude was so important to him that he sometimes embarked upon these river journeys alone. It was said that people never actually saw such a person as Zhaawan's wife because only he had the special ability to see her and know of her existence—she was real only to him.

For these seasonal travellers, Baagwaashi Zaa'iganiins Bruce Lake was a particularly bountiful source of food at that time of year. In fact, the lake made it possible for them to wait until they reached Namegosibiing and other destinations before commencing with big game hunting. "Wiinge gii'gichi initaagwan!" Dedibaayaanimanook recalled the air being filled with the din of honks, quacks and avian cries as hundreds of migrating water birds feasted on the lush aquatic vegetation that grew profusely in the marshy regions of the lake. Family members had no difficulty catching geese, ducks and even loons in whatever quantities they wanted. With jackfish and pickerel swimming the waters in such great numbers, her father was easily able to catch fish by dragging a length of string in the water as they canoed across the lake. The store bought lure he attached to the end of the string jerked forward with each stroke of his paddle. From the forests that surrounded Baagwaashi Zaa'iganiins, snowshoe partridges and rabbits were easily caught. The Keesicks enjoyed delicious traditional meals of rabbit, muskrat, fish, grouse, duck as well as geese, in combination with nuts, berries and wild rice, but as usual, Dedibaayaanimanook's father avoided beaver meat. Invariably accompanying each of their meals was the ever popular bannock, cooked by using the preferred method of twisting the dough around a pole and propping it over the open camp fire. As soon as it was puffy and golden, it was unwound from the pole and topped with fat.

"Niminopô e'apanjigeyaan." Dedibaayaanimanook found that dunking her bannock in water gave it an even better flavor. For dessert, she and her companions plucked and munched on the plump orange rosehips that presented themselves among the bushes. They were an excellent source of vitamin C. The Baagwaashi Zaa'iganiins region also provided medicinal plants in ample varieties and quantities for those who needed to replenish their supplies. The travellers were then ready to resume their journey up the river. Toward late afternoon each day, they stopped on easily accessible places on the river bank, usually at the same sites every year. Before retiring for the night, Dedibaayaanimanook's father went out for a short trip in order to set two or three traps in a manner he termed niingaani wanii'ige. He accomplished this by canoeing up the river from their camp just before sunset and setting the muskrat traps. Upon resuming their journey the next morning, he retrieved them one by one. He continued with this routine until he had gathered a sizeable collection of muskrat furs even before they reached Namegosibiing. Using the same principle, Dedibaayaanimanook and her niece Bejii Betsy (Gweyesh Annie's daughter) set rabbit snares. They frequently caught spruce grouse along with rabbits.

Gichi Baawitig Big Falls was where the river's current became considerably stronger. Thrusting the weight of his upper body into each stroke, Dedibaayaanimanook's father paddled his heavily loaded canoe against the current. Dedibaayaanimanook and her mother travelled together in another canoe, but they were barely able to keep their craft moving forward, even though they used every ounce of their strength. Nursing her aching muscles, Dedibaayaanimanook admired her father, who was able to ply his way up the river without the adverse effects from which she suffered. Immediately east of Gichi Baawitig, a work camp housed labourers who were building a road from Gojijiing Goldpines to Oojiiwi Zaa'igan[21] around 1939. The Dedibayaashes could hear the muffled sounds of construction echoing through the forest. Throughout different phases of the project, friends and family members were able to find work. "Gii' giishka'aakwewag." Dedibaayaanimanook's brothers Jiins Charlie and Jiibwaat Edward Angeconeb, for example, were hired to cut down trees using a new type of saw. One evening, just as the sun was setting, the Keesicks heard shouts from across the river. Dedibayaash canoed across and brought the two construction workers back for a game of cards.

Whitefish swam in abundance along this part of the river, so Dedibaayaanimanook's mother set a small net near the falls. Her net was just long enough to stretch from one bank to the other. That autumn, when the Uchi road was under construction, Gaamadweyaashiik caught ten jumbo-sized whitefish. She dressed and wrapped the fish, then she and Dedibaayaanimanook took them to the workers' cook, who was so pleased that he gave Gaamadweyaashiik enough groceries to keep the family supplied until well after their arrival in Namegosibiing. From there, the travellers continued up Namegosi Ziibi. It was that brief time of year when leaves dropped from the trees and into the river where they pasted themselves onto the passing canoes and paddles. For a period of about a week, the journeyers were awash in every conceivable shade of autumn. A particular feature that came with this time of year reminded Dedibaayaanimanook of the snow that would soon fall. Before retiring for the night, people were careful to ensure that every tool and piece of equipment was left in an upright position. If a paddle or an axe had been left lying on the ground, the heedless owner was hard pressed to find it the next morning under all the leaves that had fallen during the night.

The river portion of the journey ended when the Keesicks reached the southeastern shore of Namegosibiishishiing Little Trout Lake. From there, they continued to Gojijiwaawangaang, Namegosibiigojijiing, as Dedibaayaanimanook's mother referred to it. In deference to the lives of those who had preceded them, Dedibaayaanimanook's family made a brief stop in order to attend to the upkeep of the cemetery. Twice every year, they undertook the task as a part of their routine for as long as their seasonal journeys continued. They cleared away trees that had fallen during their absence and meticulously pulled out the grasses, weeds and other plant growth that had sprung up. Each grave site received a careful inspection for whatever repairs needed to be done. When the work was finished, people placed coins, jewelry and other similar objects on the graves of their forebears as tokens of respect and affection. A tiny tea kettle—"indakikwaabik," as her grandmother had called it—helped Dedibaayaanimanook to recognize the precise location of her paternal grandmother's resting place.

While their parents were busy with these activities, Dedibaayaani-manook and her cousins spent their time playing beneath the tall ever-greens that grew throughout the peripheral regions of the cemetery. They imagined that the tallest tree was Chief Akiwenz, while the shorter ones were the Chief's wife and various members of the Lac Seul community they had just left behind. Dedibaayaanimanook and her playmates often climbed a tall, straight jack pine at the northern edge of the clearing because its limbs seemed especially designed to accommodate just such an activity.[22]

The Keesicks' stop at Gojijiwaawangaang included a farewell feast before dispersing to their pre-freeze-up camp sites. It was a continua-tion of the old traditional ways. One of Dedibaayaanimanook's uncles described a dream that reminded them of their dependence on the gifts of the earth that made it possible for them to survive. In order to refresh their memory, others of the group specified those numerous benefits, including special places suitably sheltered from adverse weather by the standing forests. Moreover, the self-sacrificing largesse of the timbers provided wood for sleds, toboggans and various other tools. Materials for constructing homes and fuel for keeping them warm, bark for food containers, temporary dwellings, and in the older days, canoes, and even roots for tying and sewing. All of these were derived from the various species of trees. Other types of gifts were mentioned. There were different forms of plant life, for example, that supplied medicine and nutrition, while animals gave up their lives to provide food and material for clothing.

All of Dedibaayaanimanook's uncles, particularly Naadowe Robert, Kiiweyaasin William and Jiiyaan Donald, were blessed with the gift of oratory. They were also endowed with an ability for aadasookewin, that is, the telling of timeless stories. This particular form of story telling was critical to the people in many ways, not least of which was the preservation of the people's historical identity. Although details changed over generations of telling, the main elements of each story were rooted in fact, no matter how far into the distant past they may have occurred. By preserving the people's journey through time, aadasookewin was vital for maintaining the knowledge of who they were as Anishinaabe people. Dedibaayaanimanook's father, uncles and male cousins also exemplified extraordinary powers that came to them as a result of Giizhik Sam Keesick's lifelong achievements. Of all the Keesick brothers, however, Mooniiyaans Thomas possessed the greatest personal power. During their feast at Gojijiwaawangaang one autumn, for example, Mooniiyaans excused himself and stepped outside. He returned a few moments later with a quantity of *white* tobacco, explaining to the group that he had received it from a wemitigoozhi to whom he referred by the name Wemitigoozhi. Making himself known only to Mooniiyaans and only at Gojijiwaawangaang, the personage was of a scruffy appearance. His hair was unkempt and his clothes rumpled, but paradoxically, his home was spotlessly immaculate. As evidence of this being's importance among community members,

Dedibaayaanimanook's cousin Detaginang Frank Keesick was given the ceremonial name Wemitigoozhi. Dedibaayaanimanook was a small child when she watched her uncle Kiiweyaasin William's shaking tent. On another occasion, she witnessed the shaking tent of another of her uncles, Jiimis James. The sacred structure reminded her of a cedar tree being violently shaken in a wind storm, but being young children and not understanding the significance of what was taking place, she and her mates were amused by the phenomenon.

Dedibaayaanimanook's uncle Netawibiitam John and her cousin, Gikinô'amaagewinini (Jiiyaan Donald Keesick's son) had similar spiritual gifts. As evidence of his special power, Gikinô'amaagewinini, who was Oo'oons John Paul Keesick's father, was able to hold fire in his bare hands with no ill effects. Dedibaayaanimanook herself, however, was admonished by both of her parents to refrain from such activities as aadasookewin. Their caution also meant that the name giving role would never be hers, and that she would not be considered to have any special powers in the traditional sense. She did not have these special gifts, in part, because she had not gone on a vision quest. As were all proscriptions, this was taken very seriously. Anyone who attempted to give a ceremonial name without having gone on a vision quest, for example, would cause harm to befall the recipient; the fraud would be exposed and the charlatan denounced before the entire community. In this way, the old system of name-giving ensured that only those who were qualified took on the role, providing assurances to the community that the chosen name was appropriate and honourable. The gift of name-giving was highly regarded because of the special bond it created between the giver and receiver.

As practised in its purest form by Dedibaayaanimanook's forebears, the vision quest journey and the power people attained from such an experience were an integral component of the Anishinaabe experience, practicable only within the context of the Anishinaabe cultural lifestyle. Each successfully completed vision journey imbued the entire community with strength and security. As such, it would have been highly unlikely for non-Anishinaabeg to become practitioners, given the Western mindset about such matters and given the fact that procelytizm was not an Anishinaabe tenet.[23] This degree of traditional spiritualism remained largely extant within the Anishinaabe community of Namegosibiing even during Dedibaayaanimanook's childhood. "Mamaandaawiziwin gii' wanise apii gii' maajiiminikwewaaj Anishinaabeg." However, the generational cohorts of Dedibaayaanimanook's parents and uncles were among the last to follow the practice of acquiring special power as it was applied to benefit others. After the departure of the last generation of Gichi Anishinaabeg (that is, Dedibaayaanimanook's aunts and uncles) that source of empowerment was no longer available due to the destructive effects upon the integrity of the community by residential schooling, the increasing prevalence of the wemitigoozhi's economic/employment system, Christianity and the sickness of alcoholism. Today, in fact, those who wish to become knowledgeable about the old ways have been taught by means of a Western pedagogy with the result that professional eldership is different from the leadership that once prevailed.

Dedibaayaanimanook's father and each of her uncles, elder brothers and male cousins then brought the autumnal feast to a close by sharing their thoughts and plans for the coming winter. Guided by their spiritual power and deeply held respect for all the elements that comprised the natural world, they spoke about what lay ahead for them as the remaining people of Namegosibiing. They discussed the fact that soon after the Treaty adhesion was signed in 1874, people were strongly encouraged by agents of the wemitigoozhi's government, that is, the Indian agents, to give up all their traditional ways and become settlers on the reserves. They observed that their on-reserve brethren received schooling, housing, agricultural implements, livestock and Christian churches as well as gestures of feigned largesse—such as flower seeds—in exchange for their settlement. But they also noted that buying into such an arrangement resulted in greater loss of traditional Anishinaabe ways, and that the more they accepted, the more autonomy they lost and the more difficult it became to make free choices. Other topics were mentioned.

"Zanaginaagwan gaa wii' izhaayeng." Dedibaayaanimanook's brother Jiibwaat Edward Angeconeb had acquired a keen sense about what the future held for them. By being a generation younger than the Keesick brothers (that is, Dedibaayaanimanook's father and paternal uncles) and by working in mines and tree cutting jobs, he had already experienced extensive firsthand contact with wemitigoozhiwag. Jiibwaat was easily able to visualize the difficulties that would quickly, seemingly within the blink of an eye, engulf them both individually and as a people. His insight came from an ability to understand the nature of the wemitigoozhi's value system and way of thinking in terms of their repercussion on everyone and everything.

"Zagaakwaa gaa wii' izhiwinaayeng gii niijaanisinaan." Dedibaaya-animanook's cousin Jôjens George Keesick expressed grave concerns about what lay ahead, and using a metaphor to describe the coming hardships that would threaten their very existence as a people, he likened their future to a dense forest strewn over and tangled with windfalls and thick bushes through which they would have to lead the children. For a few more years, however, the people of Namegosibiing Trout Lake would continue to uphold the old system in ways both large and small. "Minonaagozi indede!" Whenever any one of the Keesick brothers was greeted by a clear morning sky, for example, he would say, "My father looks very well today!" The name "Keesick" is actually the word giizhig, which means day, and by associating a clear and cloudless morning with their departed father, Dedibaayaanimanook's people were preserving their connection with Giizhik Sam Keesick and with what he had given them. Even as the newcomers' encroach-ment into the homelands intensified, they held celebrations and gath-erings and pursued their day to day activities according to what the Gichi Anishinaabeg had taught them.

1. Gichi ogimaakwe is the queen.

2. 1MA34B107/a/32, Hudson's Bay Company Archives, Winnipeg, MB.

3. House of Commons Debates, April 27, 1922, p. 1218.

4. Canon Sanderson also visited Lac Seul during Christmas and Easter.

5. B107/a/33, Hudson's Bay Company Archives, Winnipeg, MB.

6. The approximate translation of the song is as follows:

> Send
>
> Your young girls
>
> Out ...
>
> Spin
>
> Your young girls
>
> Round ...

7. B107/a/32, Hudson's Bay Company Archives, Winnipeg, MB.

8. Coatsworth (1957, p.101) stated that the Quetico Ojibwa used the object as a charm to bring the child wisdom.

9. Mishi Baawitig is the Little Grand Rapids community.

10. Miskwa'oowi Ziibi is Red River.

11. Wiimbaashko Minis was where Dedibaayaanimanook once saw a paddle wheel boat.

12. B107/a/35, p.19, Hudson's Bay Company Archives, Winnipeg, MB.

13. The precise location of Minijing is not known.

14. The Giiwegaabawensag were the Giiwegaabaw (Return Standing) boys, of which there were several.

15. B107/a/35, Hudson's Bay Company Archives, Winnipeg, MB.

16. Ibid.

17. Manidoo Baawitig translates to Spirit Rapids; it was/is a sacred place. Whenever the Keesicks were in its vicinity, they were careful not to make loud noises. They even whispered instead of talking aloud as they portaged around it.

18. Gaaminisiwang, "the Place Where There Is An Island," is a lake that has only one island.

19. Manidoobaawi Zaa'igan was apparently located in the vicinity of Gaaminisiwang.

20. The name Zagadikwaning alludes to a tree that is covered with a thick

growth of branches. In a similar way, the waters of the Zagadikwaning lake was thick with wild rice.

21. Oojiiwi Zaa'igan, Uchi Lake, is east of Confederation Lake; the all-weather road went as far as Uchi Lake and South Bay.

22. Now nearly 100 years old and the tallest in the immediate vicinity, Dedibaayaanimanook's tree continues to stand guard over the burial grounds. It is visible from a great distance on the lake as one approaches from the north, a veritable landmark directing travellers and visitors to Gojijiwaawangaang.

23. There was a parallel teaching in the Sermon on the Mount (Matthew 7:6) in which Jesus admonished his followers not to throw their pearls to the pigs because, not having the capability to understand the value of pearls, the animals would simply trample them underfoot.

CHAPTER 4

Indizhidaaminaaban Namegosibiing

~

When We Lived in Trout Lake

A Cessna 180 airplane flying northeast from Wanamani Zaa'-iganing Red Lake arrives at the place of Dedibaayaanimanook's birth and childhood within twenty minutes. Namegosibiing Trout Lake is approximately thirty air kilometres northeast of Red Lake. Numerous studies have been carried out in recent years about the geophysical features of Dedibaayaanimanook's homeland and a great deal of detailed physical data based on those investigations exists. For example, an Ontario Ministry of Natural Resources (OMNR) management plan identifies the Trout Lake Conservation Reserve that includes Trout, Otter and Little Trout Lakes to have five hundred-fifteen islands. Thirty-four thousand, eight hundred-seven hectares in area, Namegosibiing continues to be a relatively clear lake, reaching a maximum depth of 47.3 metres.[1]

Upon seeing Namegosibiing for the first time, Dedibaayaanima-nook's relative Jiiwe Oojiiwasawaan (Soons's mother) once comment-ed on the extraordinarily rocky nature of its shorelines. But perhaps the most exceptional feature about Namegosibiing was the water, as was evident by the very name that community members gave their lake. Namegosibiing does not refer to a lake, but rather, it alludes directly to the pure, crystal clear waters where the lake trout once thrived. Dedibaayaanimanook's father attributed the origin of this purity to the fact that only streams, rivulets and small creeks—but no rivers—flow into Namegosibiing. In addition, Namegosibiing is a spring-fed lake. This pristine state persisted throughout the eons that

Dedibaayaanimanook's people held stewardship over their traditional use territories, right up until her childhood and a few years thereafter. But beginning in the 1930s, wemitigoozhiwag purloined this steward-ship, and the integrity of the air, land, water, plants and animals—all of the resources—were compromised. The new management regime over the homelands put into place by the OMNR and other parallel state agencies and entities, aimed to destroy the vital relationship and connection with the natural world upon which Dedibaayaanimanook's people based their existence as an Indigenous people. The takeover took place with absolutely no effort whatsoever toward establishing consultation and/or partnership arrangements.[2] Eventually, this alien system would bring in logging activities, followed by commercial fish-ing and the establishment of tourist operations, all of which would concomitantly and effectively result in the physical expulsion of the Namegosbii Anishinaabe people from their homeland. Nevertheless, in their minds, Namegosibiing remained their unequivocal domain, the ancient homelands in which they had been pursuing their many traditional ways of living since a time too long ago to remember.

Dedibaayaanimanook's oral history indicated that each family grouping tended to use specific areas of the lake from early fall to late spring. Dedibaayaanimanook's parents, for example, were the usual occupiers of the northern regions, while her uncle Netawibiitam John and his family remained to the east. Mooniiyaans Thomas and Maajii-giizhigook Mary lived southwest. Being intimately familiar with the characteristics of the entirety of the homelands, but their respective territories in particular, families knew the best places for trapping, hunting and fishing, and in accordance with their obligation to use the natural environment in a responsible manner, they were careful to carry out their practices with the least negative impact.

"Aaniindi giin waa' dazhi biboonshiyan?" Upon arriving in Namego-sibiing, people inquired of one another where they planned to spend the coming winter. The question was necessary because they needed to be careful not to stay at one location for too long a period in order to continue with their diffusive type of land usage. It was a specific strategy, designed to allow the land and the lake to recover after each occupation. As she began to learn about such matters, Dedibaayaani-manook noted the remarkable speed with which the earth was able to cleanse and renew itself under this type of land use management. Between spring and autumn, for example, most traces of the people's tenancy vanished after being absorbed by new growth and cleansed by the rain. Moreover, the people of Namegosibiing acknowledged the rejuvenating ability of the land as another priceless gift, and for that too, they were thankful. Their sense of gratitude nurtured a deeply held respect that guided their every day activities. Making it possible for them to live in a harmonious relationship with the land, the self-reinforcing system of beliefs and values was in fact a sacred covenant. That was the reason why family units needed to tell each other where in their respective regions they planned to spend the first part of the coming winter before they proceeded to those locations while the lake was still navigable. For Dedibaayaanimanook's family, Negiish-kensikaang[3] on Ma'iingani Minis was usually their first stop.

People then needed to consider what type of dwelling they might need for the coming season. There were several styles and combinations from which to choose, depending upon where they were, how long they intended to remain, how often they expected to use the facility and what type of materials were on hand. As an example, Dedibaayaanimanook's sister Gweyesh Annie once put her construction skills to work building a sturdy tepee-shaped structure for her family when they lived at Jiibayi Zaagiing Jackfish Bay. Later, they moved into a more permanent cabin-type building where she glued pages of newspaper and magazines with homemade paste to decorate the interior walls with interesting patterns. Dedibaayaanimanook's uncle Netawibiitam John built a somewhat similar structure at Gaami-nitigwashkiigaag Keesick Bay which he and his family eventually used for storage purposes. This was where Dedibaayaanimanook and her parents spent a few days one spring while en route to Wazhashko Zaa'igan.[4] Adik, who was Zhashagi's father, made a dwelling with logs which he laid horizontally, one upon the other in such a way that the walls gradually curved into the roof. Yet another family lived in a house that had more than four sides and consequently consisted of several walls which came together at obtuse angles. Then there were those who built conventional cabins with horizontal logs, while others built theirs by positioning the logs vertically. Dedibaayaanimanook's father preferred this vertical placement because, in his experience, such a configuration proved most durable. Clay found at various places in Namegosibiing was used to chink these permanent buildings which were, in fact, another example of the wemitigoozhi's influence, since people's homes were always designed and constructed to be entirely temporary during a previous era. In addition, Dedibaayaanimanook's father at various times built a conventional log cabin that extended up to a height of approximately three feet, then he attached a canvas walled tent for the remainder of the walls and for the roof. Particularly during Dedibaayaanimanook's childhood, the Dedibayaash family frequently lived in this latter type of home throughout the entire winter, although Dedibaayaanimanook preferred to live in a tepee style of structure because she was able to lie in her bed and look up through the opening as she fell asleep. Her mother, Gaamadweyaashiik, talked about the same type of homes in which members of her community lived year round when she was a child in Pikangikum. Designed to be entirely temporary, the structures were comprised of walls made of poles covered with large birch bark strips sewn together with tree roots. Gaamadweyaashiik told her about the time she heard wolves sniffing with curiosity at the edges of their home. People used evergreen boughs freshly laid every day for their flooring and mattresses.

Having thus provided for their shelter, the Keesicks were ready for whatever the weather was about to bring. "Nashke igiwe!" At that time of year, Dedibaayaanimanook often caught brief glimpses of black, green and peachy white bobbing up and down in the chilly waters of Namegosibiing as mergansers flashed their autumn plumage. Before too long, frigid weather sweeping down from the north would send all remaining waterfowl fleeing to the south. But with the lake still accessible for canoe travel during this pre-freeze-up period, Dedibaayaanimanook's father took immediate action to ensure that they would have sufficient food to last until the lake was frozen. Big game hunting was foremost on his mind, but he avoided certain animals such as male deer during the mating season. Hunting moose on foot and carrying the carcass home on one's shoulder was referred to by the term giiwose. When people went out for a moose during summer and autumn, they wore moccasins rather than hard soled foot wear in order to move more silently and easily through the woods. Most hunters in Dedibaayaanimanook's family agreed that big game hunting was easier in winter than summer. Another specific hunting term people used was andomoonzwe, which was a reference to moose hunting in a canoe, that is, when the water was still open.

Dedibaayaanimanook's father travelled extensively to hunt, often following streams and rivulets that flowed into Namegosibiing by way of gaining access into the regions most often frequented by moose. Having learned the skills of hunting from his father at an early age, Dedibayaash would remain a successful hunter and trapper despite a childhood incident that left him partially crippled for life. Dedibaayaanimanook once listened to the story about what had happened approximately a year after her father's vision quest. Still a young child at the time, Dedibayaash was struck by a sudden and mysterious affliction so debilitating and painful there were times when he wanted to die. But he overcame the suffering in the same way he had completed the ordeal of his vision quest journey, even though his leg became atrophied. He was no longer able to bend his knee, so he walked with a distinctive limp from that time on. Later, it was learned that the affliction was attributable to the curse of a *Midewin* leader in Lac Seul. Endaso, an elderly man not known to have had any children of his own, was driven by dubious intent. The spiritual leader may have felt threatened when he heard that Dedibayaash had successfully completed his vision quest and now had the special capability to dream dreams. This incident proved to be the first of many lessons to convince Dedibayaash of the necessity to continue in his pursuit of a meritorious life. In his mind, that included the fulfilment of his responsibilities toward the well-being of his family.

One of these responsibilities was to train young male members of the family by bringing them on his hunting excursions. But as vital as it was to pursue moose hunting and train the youth, such trips were especially dangerous during rut season. That was why Dedibayaash was alone one autumn when he set out in search of a moose. Making his way through a dense part of the forest, he suddenly spotted a male moose standing only a few metres away. His appearance seeming to trigger an instant rage in the high-strung animal, it dropped its head and swung a massive rack of antlers that slashed through branches and sent twigs scattering. As an obvious gesture of challenge, its powerful hooves tore at the ground. Dedibayaash gripped his rifle, even though he knew he had no time to use it. With the few seconds he was given to escape, he flung himself into a grove of young birch trees. He heard a loud crack and felt a sharp jolt as one of the antler points grazed his rifle. Heat from the animal's nostrils seared into the back of his hand. The impossibility of avoiding the deadly weapons for much longer was clearly evident when suddenly the animal appeared to realize that Dedibayaash was not a rival. Only after the last echoes of the moose's retreat had faded into the forest did Dedibayaash allow himself to move from his place of refuge. His ability to remain calm in the face of terror—self-discipline was a character trait he had acquired from his childhood journey to Manidoo Minis—had saved Dedibayaash's life that day, allowing him to return home relatively unharmed. Upon hearing the story of her father's harrowing encounter and thinking about what could have happened to him, Dedibaayaanimanook was overcome with angst.

The weeks preceding freeze-up also provided time for the type of activities that allowed children to learn some necessary skills. A prime example was rabbit harvesting, because the animals were a valuable source of both food and fur as winter drew near. Whenever they took up residence in Jiibayi Zaagiing Jackfish Bay, Dedibaayaanimanook's father used a modified version of fur ranching by chopping down several young jack pines a short distance into the woods. Dozens of rabbits gathered to feast on his freshly laid banquet of pine boughs over the next several nights, growing fat so quickly that they were ready to harvest within a matter of only a few days. The method for catching rabbits before snare wire became readily available was to use cotton twine and two long poles. Dedibaayaanimanook's training began when she watched one of her aunts making preparations for the rabbit harvest. First, Gookomens[5] Minogaabawiik assembled thirty pieces of twine, each approximately two feet in length, then she placed a running noose four or so inches in diameter at one end. Next, she placed the pieces of twine on a section of fabric long enough to fit around Netawibiitam's waist and carefully shaped the fabric into a sheath. In the same manner that one draws an arrow from its quiver, Dedibaayaanimanook's uncle was able to pull out a piece of twine as he went from place to place setting up a snare.

A hunter with Gookomens's type of snare used a loose slipknot just above the noose, attaching the twine segment to a long horizontal pole in order to keep the noose positioned in the centre of a carefully prepared passageway on the rabbit trail. A small bent twig on either side of the noose kept the circular shape from collapsing. The other end of the string was attached firmly to the tip of another sturdy pole that was placed over a fallen tree or log to act as a fulcrum. At the far end of the balance pole, a rock was hung to provide the necessary force. A rabbit caught in such a noose was immediately sprung into the air and choked. Once or twice during the night, Dedibaayaanimanook heard a brief, faint cry issuing from the woods as another of the creatures succumbed to its fate.

"Ingii'nitaa ando naadagwe." Dedibaayaanimanook's task was to check the snares, and she always set out as soon as it was light enough to see. The sight of so many rabbits available for their use was amazing! But wherever rabbits congregated in abundance, owls were sure to gather. Dedibayaash set snares for them as well, not only to discourage them from disturbing the rabbits but also because they too were a food source for the family. Dedibaayaanimanook's mother dressed and cleaned the birds, then attached pieces of string to the claw tendons. When the strings were given a tug, the talons closed tightly in a manner that mimicked a live owl's grasp. Their unique toy was not only a source of amusement for Dedibaayaanimanook and her nephew Gichi Jôj, it also gave them a first hand understanding of the mechanism of how an owl catches its prey. As her mother skinned the animals, then prepared the meat for consumption, Dedibaayaan-imanook's training continued. She too would eventually become an expert in these skills.

Although she was born too late to see the use of rabbit skin dresses, she had the opportunity to see how her mother produced a rabbit fur blanket. Gaamadweyaashiik used a moose bone scraper to remove every bit of flesh and fat from the skin until its surface was smooth and clean. Then she cut each of the pelts into one long strip by scoring the skin side of the pelt using a sharp knife and an outward motion. After sewing the strips together end to end, she attached the yarn to a long pole and placed it outdoors where a gentle wind made the fur soft and the skin supple. Rabbit furs were harvested only during the cold season when the pelts were strong and thick. For the blanket itself, Dedibaayaanimanook watched her mother anchor a set of crochet-type loops across the length of a smooth pole with the newly produced rabbit yarn. Gaamadweyaashiik then began to build on the first set of loops, forming rows of stitches back and forth until a blanket of the desired dimensions took shape. On average, a medium sized rabbit fur blanket required at least 70 rabbit pelts. As well made blankets were lightweight and extremely warm, they were not only convenient to carry on trapping journeys that lasted up to ten days, they were also vital for surviving winter nights on the trail.

But there were many other preparations to be made during the wait for freeze-up. Extended travel was restricted for as long as three weeks, so Dedibaayaanimanook's parents were able to spend many hours of each day ensuring that the family's toboggans, sleds, dog har-nesses, trapping related equipment, snowshoes and other implements were in good working order. Even Dedibaayaanimanook's father's homemade mattress received attention. Using the hairs of a moose killed in winter, Dedibayaash re-stuffed his canvas covered mattress. The moose was killed during the cold weather of winter in order to avoid the ticks that were otherwise in the animal's hair. If, however, a mattress needed stuffing during summer, Dedibayaash used grass. Snowshoes were essential for winter travel, and both Dedibaayaanimanook and her brother Jiins watched closely as their mother repaired a pair in which the webs had become loose. Gaamadweyaashiik used a shuttle carved from birch wood, unlike Minogiizhigook who used one fashioned from the leg bone of a moose. The rawhide she prepared was very durable and perfectly suited for snowshoe webbing. Although her brother soon mastered the intricately woven patterns, Dedibaayaanimanook herself did not receive the same level of encouragement to learn. The reason was not because snowshoe repair was an exclusively male task; therefore, it may have been a fear on Gaamadweyaashiik's part that the zigzag patterns would trigger one of Dedibaayaanimanook's migraine attacks.

As the latter part of autumn drew to a close, cold weather settled over Namegosibiing in earnest. Strong winds swept over the lake from the north, and temperatures plunged. Dedibaayaanimanook's parents followed the sequence of events that led to freeze-up. Gradually, Dedibaayaanimanook herself became versed in the terminology that captured the characteristic rhythm of the wind and the writhing water. For example, the lake became a mass of agitated waves that created conditions along regions of northern exposure that was referred to as aasamaa'an. Soon the water began to congeal, but when the newly formed ice attempted to adhere to the shoreline, a fresh series of waves ripped it away and smashed it against the rocks. The term used for the repetition of this pre-freeze-up phenomenon was naakoozigwaa'an. The cold continued to intensify. Sometimes intermittent snow fell, creating soggy, saturated blankets that sank just beneath the surface and helped to lower the lake's temperature even further.

"Geyaabi iinzan baashkinegamaa'an." Standing along the shoreline each morning, Dedibaayaanimanook's father searched for any signs of freeze-up, and when he saw clouds of steam rising from the surface of the lake, he knew they would need to wait for a while longer. In the meantime, Jiins and his mates continued with their hunting and fishing activities, despite the raw weather. Whenever they caught a moose or caribou, they cut the meat into thin strips which they then smoked, along with any fish they had caught, over an open fire. They distributed the food among family members and relatives who were also waiting for freeze-up. Of all the types of food her brother brought back, Dedibaayaanimanook's favourite were the trout backbones that he had smoked. The young men had to eventually haul their canoes from the water and store them away until spring. Thermometer readings finally dropped so low that the ice was able to resist even the strongest waves, and by next morning the upheaval had transformed itself into a picture of white quiescence. However, the ice was too thin to walk on. It would take a few more days of cold, snowless weather before it was thick enough to withstand a person's weight. Four inches was considered safe.

"Ingaagaa—azha miinawaa madweskwadin!" Awakened from her sleep by the sound of the expanding ice, Dedibaayaanimanook sat upright in the darkness one night, but her mother told her not to fear and urged her to go back to sleep. All night long, the brand new ice generated low rumble sounds which people described as madweskwadin. The muffled drum rolls seemed to come from all over the lake. Those who listened carefully were able to hear the subtle changes in timbre as the ice continued to distend. In fact, Dedibaayaanimanook's father knew from the sounds themselves when it was thick enough for safe walking. He taught her the importance of carrying a sturdy pole whenever she ventured onto the ice in early winter because isolated areas of open water sometimes occurred, and the ice did not always freeze at a uniform rate over the entire lake, particularly when a lot of snow had fallen. Unlike today's irregular patterns, the weather in those days produced conditions in which the process of freeze-up occurred in a relatively predictable manner. One stage led to the next in a more or less ordered sequence of events. If the cold weather was accompanied by little or no snow, the ice froze without the formation of slush. Miigwanaangewadin was a term people used to describe the graceful curves produced by large, feather-like crystals that appeared intermittently across the smooth surface of the black ice. Fascinated by the intricacy of their patterns, Dedibaayaanimanook decided to imitate their shapes using glass beads on leather when she began to sew. Later on, when planes arrived into the region, people said that a Cessna-180 required seven to eight inches of solid ice in order to land. A method for informing the pilot about ice thicknesses was to set out a row of small spruce trees on the lake at approximately sixty feet apart. Knowing that each tree represented one inch of ice thickness, the pilot flying overhead simply counted the total number of trees on the lake to know whether it was safe to land.

Once freeze-up finally reached a safe stage, people were once again mobile, free to travel wherever and whenever they pleased. Winter and all of its activities began with enthusiasm, especially with the children. Having been land-bound for so many weeks, Dedibaaya-animanook took the earliest opportunity to venture out. Sometimes she simply remained motionless for several moments, taking in the expansiveness of the lake. Even with her eyes closed, she could feel the limitless spaces of Namegosibiing stretching in every direction, and a sense of freedom filling her with exuberance. Other times, she scampered onto the ice, along the shoreline to where enormous icicles hung from sagging branches, and thick icy blankets draped themselves over the bent cedars. She could have easily sculpted an ice castle, had she thought to bring along her father's chisel. Her father, however, was becoming anxious about their food supply and embarked upon another of his fishing journeys. Using the hooks he had made from an old kettle, he caught and dressed a large number of fish. He sliced them lengthwise, and after scoring them widthwise with several parallel lines, he hung them over a set of wooden racks where they dried evenly and thoroughly in the fresh air. With up to eight horizontal poles holding ten fish each, Dedibayaash was able to process enough dried fish to last for most of the winter. Crows, ravens, gray jays and other creatures never disturbed the drying fish because he placed an old fish net around the structure and covered the fish with several layers of balsam branches. In that manner, Dedibaayaanimanook's father dried trout, jackfish, pickerel and other species. The term people used for fish prepared in this manner was nameteg. "Nametegi'i giskatig!" Dedibaayaanimanook's cousin was once heard to tease his well weathered brother by saying that he resembled nameteg.

A particular species Dedibayaash never caught was sturgeon. He explained that nameg were not found in Namegosibiing because there were no large rivers, such as the Berens River, that flowed into the lake. Other Anishinaabeg from other regions, however, often spoke of catching sturgeon. As a young child in Pikangikum, for example, Dedibaayaanimanook's aunt Omashkiigookwe described how she accompanied her own father on fishing trips. They used a long, fork-like implement to spear sturgeons so large that they had to haul them onto the shore because they were unable to lift them into their boat.

As more and more of the wemitigoozhi's goods became perceived as essential items in the Keesicks' household over the passage of time, Dedibaayaanimanook's father perused their dwindling supplies and decided it was time to visit Wanamani Zaa'igan Red Lake. In a previous time, Dedibayaash would have gone to either Swain Post or the Hudson's Bay Company post toward the east, depending on which one carried what he needed. For many years, Swain's were the better prices with the better quality, but once the town of Red Lake was established, it became the preferred source for supplies, particularly when the independent trader Ken McDougall opened his establishment. As well, the flourishing town had other services to offer, including a bank, general store, cafe, hotel, beer parlour, liquor outlet and, eventually even a movie theatre. Although the discovery of gold triggered the original influx of wemitigoozhiwag into the area, secondary industries sprang up to offer other possible forms of employment. These opportunities drew relatives and friends into the Red Lake area, and the prospect of visiting with them was another incentive to visit the town.

In terms of travel, charter flights from Red Lake, Kenora and elsewhere were available from around the 1930s, so some of Dedibaayaanimanook's relatives were flown to remote sites where they had found jobs. Even Dedibayaash once flew in what was known as a flying boat. "Biniskwe gii' zaagabiwag." When Dedibaayaanimanook's brothers Jiins and Jiibwaat Angeconeb took their first flight in an airplane, they climbed into their seats, one behind the other in the open aircraft. They presented a curious sight to onlookers as the plane carried them rapidly beyond the tree line. Over the course of time, other relatives flew between Hudson and Ikwewi Zaa'igan Woman Lake and various other places in a craft piloted by a man known as Mac. However, Dedibaayaanimanook's father preferred the more traditional modes of travel. One year they were living at Gaaminitigwashkiigaag Keesick Bay, when he and his (step)son Jiins set out across the frozen lake before dawn to purchase a fresh supply of goods from Wanamani Zaa'iganing Red Lake. The two travellers arrived on the northwestern main shore of Namegosibiing just as the sun began its final descent behind Oshedinaa. Known in geological language as a terminal moraine, the Ridge was also referred to as Binesiwajiing. The name alluded to a pair of large indentations, several metres wide, located at the Ridge's center. "Mewinzha Binesiwag gii' dazhewag i'imaa." Dedibaayaanimanook's mother explained that the name was in reference to the Thunderers, who had created the indentations when they nested there during a bygone era.

As daylight succumbed rapidly to darkness, Dedibayaash and Jiins prepared for the night by collecting firewood, then they dug out a small space in the snow bank at the foot of the tall balsam firs where they built a fire. During Dedibaayaanimanook's early childhood, matches were not in common use. Instead, people carried sufficient flint and tinder as well as a piece of special metal in order to start a fire and keep it burning. In those days, both men and women smoked a pipe. Dedibaayaanimanook once watched as her paternal grandmother filled her store bought pipe with a mixture of tobacco which she interspersed with tiny pinches of tinder. She then struck the flint against a piece of special metal she called apis to create a little shower of sparks that tumbled into her pipe. When not in use, Nookom's smoking paraphernalia remained in her gashkibidaagan. This was a little bag, customarily made from the skin of a flying squirrel and lined with fabric, that was presented to the family matriarch by one of the young women who had married into the family. In a manner similar to that of Dedibaayaanimanook's grandmother, travellers often used a small quantity of tinder to keep their campfires aglow until dawn.

Dedibayaash and Jiins, however, allowed their fire to die after their meal, then they covered the warm earth beneath with several balsam boughs and prepared their bedding on top. The two fell asleep without difficulty, sedated by the exertion of their day-long journey. As night progressed, twigs and branches crackled and snapped in the sub-zero temperatures. These sounds were described by the phrase gii'madweyaakodadin. A deep rumble rolled across the icy stretch they had just crossed, announcing the birth of yet another pressure ridge. Each fissure etched a jagged line into the frozen surface of supine Namegosibiing. During the most frigid period of the post freeze-up season, ice could expand to thicknesses of several feet within a matter of a few days, but the reverberation of these developments failed to disturb either of them, reposed as they were in the warmth of their rabbit fur blankets.

Regardless of the time of year, people were in the habit of getting up once or twice during the night. The custom allowed them to track the course of the constellations across the night sky and develop familiarity with the stars' positioning throughout the seasons. Dedibaayaanimanook, too, was well familiar with the Big Dipper as well as the Antler and other celestial bodies. Her mother explained that the various alignments of another constellation, known as Odaadawaa'amoog—the Orion's Belt—informed people about how much snow was expected to fall. One winter evening during the latter part of February in 1939, a very bright "meteor" was seen to pass overhead at Lac Seul. Travelling from east to west, the heavenly body appeared to burst into a brilliant shower around 8:00 in the evening.[6] The winter that Dedibaayaanimanook and her family were at Kejick Bay Lac Seul, one of her cousins witnessed a similar phenomenon while out on the lake on a moonless night. Maashkizhiigan saw the sky light up when a body they referred to as a gwiingwan flashed across the sky, trailing a spectacular shower of sparks. If a loud sound was heard when a gwiingwan disintegrated, it was described as babiidikwe. It was a sign that the snow was going to be deep.

On cold, clear, moon lit nights, one often noticed fine, powdery ice particles floating down, seemingly from nowhere. This phenomenon was referred to as ningôwanise. "Aazha miinawaa wanangoshag binanjigewag!" As he came in from the frigid outdoors, Dedibaayaanimanook's father once explained to her that this occurrence happened because the stars were once again dropping their food crumbs onto the earth. The habit of getting up at night also allowed people to monitor the comings and goings of the moon. People observed that each new moon of the year had a distinctive orientation and positioning in the sky, therefore they were able to use the phenomenon to mark the beginning of a new month. Similarly, the last quarter of each moon signaled the end of its month. Seasoned practitioners such as Dedibaayaanimanook's parents were familiar with the precise set of lunar characteristics specific to each moon of the year. They also knew about the phases and name of each moon, plus the number of days between each. With the sun, moon and stars providing information about time and direction, people did not have a need for calendars, watches or maps. But the people's systems of reckoning were soon superseded by these devices when the wemitigoozhiwag arrived. Younger generations became confused because the two methods did not produce perfectly coinciding months, but Dedibaayaanimanook and Gichi Jôj were among the few who were versed in the traditional convention. Both her parents had determined the two children would have the correct information because it had always served them well. It was with this kind of heavenly knowledge that Dedibayaash and Jiins were able to fix their direction as they set out on the second day of their journey several hours before even the first faint signs of daybreak were visible to the east. They went as far as East Bay, where they stopped for their second night on the trail. When Dedibaayaanimanook and her parents, along with her uncle Jiiyaan and his family, once travelled the same route, this was where they too had rested for the night. Waabashgosiwagaang Post Narrows lay just a few miles ahead. At the time, the tiny village included a Hudson's Bay Company trading post, but only a traditional cemetery remains there today.

Another day's journey brought Dediabaaynimanook's father and her brother to the town of Wanamani Zaa'igan Red Lake. Before the arrival of wemitigoozhiwag, the name Wanamani Zaa'igan referred to the lake and the community of Anishinaabe people who resided within the surrounding region. But the name began to refer to the municipality after it was established as a mining town. From that time on, Dedibaayaanimanook's people used the word Oodenaang to refer specifically to the town of Red Lake because it was the closest commercial center to Namegosibiing.

Dedibayaash and Jiins arrived at the outskirts of Red Lake and immediately called upon relatives whom they had not seen for several months, in some cases. The relatives were eager for news from Namegosibiing, but the travellers had little time to spare. Bypassing the Hudson's Bay Company store, they sold their bundles of fur to McDougall because he showed an interest in continuing to do business with them. The Hudson's Bay Company, on the other hand, had became entrenched in retail, having transformed itself from a string of trading posts to a chain of department stores across the country, and remote retail outlets became Northern stores. Since there was a bank in Red Lake, Dedibayaash made deposits, then purchased groceries for the family. He also bought gifts for Dedibaayaanimanook and her mother. After giving the assortment of fabric, hair pins and brooches a close inspection, he chose ribbons in several colours for Dedibaayaanimanook and a quantity of fabric for Gaamadweyaashiik. He knew that some of the thick, canvas-like material along with flannel were a wise choice for the winter, having heard Gaamadweyaashiik mention that she would not need the cool, smooth textured waasikwegin until summer. He also decided to leave needles, threads and other notions for a future visit. Thus, their brief shopping experience came to an end. They secured their supplies to the sled, then retraced their steps northeastward, back to Namegosibiing, where Dedibaayaanimanook and her mother were anxiously awaiting their return.

Until she was around nine years old, Dedibaayaanimanook enjoyed a relatively carefree childhood. This was true mainly because her parents' intent was to protect her from undue stress in order to avoid the headaches from which she had been suffering. But in addition to her participation in the harvesting of rabbits, she took on more work as she grew older. The errand she found most enjoyable was gathering fire wood for her mother. One need only to imagine what life would be like without any means for heating one's home or cooking one's food to realize how crucial this responsibility was for the family's well-being. As a special dream gift from one of her paternal aunts, Dedibaayaanimanook became knowledgeable and skilled in the various aspects of wood gathering. For example, she learned that dry wood was best because it produced more heat and less smoke and it was easier to cut and lighter to carry than green wood. Due to its moisture content, wood lying on the ground was to be avoided unless meat or fish was being smoked. Instead, she searched for dead trees that were still standing. Dedibaayaanimanook knew that gathering firewood was physically exhausting, so one of her methods for making a load easier to carry was to gather the wood into a pile, then tie it all together in a bundle that she carried home on her back. Whenever she had the use of her parents' wood saw, her mother cautioned her to use it with care. It meant having to use either an axe or half a saw blade—which was impossible to do!—if it broke. Unfortunately, that very thing once happened during a moment of childish carelessness. With her work suddenly twice as difficult, Dedibaayaanimanook soon understood the reason for her mother's admonition. This rueful experience was one of many lessons on circumspection that she would not soon forget, even though her father was able to replace the broken blade soon after the incident and she once again enjoyed her outings.

None of this is to say that Dedibaayaanimanook's life was without some avenues for amusement, particularly during the early days when she first began her wood gatherer occupation. As with most other children, she was quite capable of finding ways to turn work into fun. One of her favourites was made possible after a fresh blanket of snow had just fallen. It was a game of daring and a test of adroitness that began by taking hold of an evergreen branch and giving it two or three vigorous tugs to see how long she could remain stationary while looking upward as the snow started falling from the highest branches of the tree before she ducked. On occasion, Dedibaayaanimanook misjudged her timing and the powdery snow landed on top of her face. *"Ishe'hay!"* But her shrieks were loudest when small amounts tumbled down the back of her neck. At other times, she was accompanied by her young nephew Gichi Jôj George Trout. Ostensibly, he came along to lend a helping hand with the wood, but the two usually expended their energies shaking snow on top of one another. When they returned home with only a meagre supply of wood—but covered over with snow—Dedibaayaanimanook's mother knew how they had been spending their time.

"Niwii'andawagoodoo, nimaamaa." Dedibaayaanimanook received her own set of rabbit snares when snare wire became more readily available, and she was eager to prove that she was capable of fulfilling her new responsibility. Setting them was a task even more to her liking than collecting wood. For one thing, it was less strenuous. All she needed to do was locate well used rabbit trails close to the evergreens where she positioned each snare directly in the middle of the path, one or two inches above the ground. Several young deciduous twigs and pine boughs placed upright in the snow on either side concealed the wire from the rabbits and encouraged their approach. Unlike trapping, no other bait was necessary. Typically, Dedibaayaanimanook was on the trail at the first sign of dawn, hurrying into the woods to check the snares. Once or twice, every snare presented her with a fluffy white gift which she contributed toward the family's food supply—and a new rabbit skin blanket. The same snaring method was effective for catching the ground-dwelling grouse with a rusty colored band across the tip of its tail. Spruce grouse were delicious when her mother used it for making a type of stew. According to the teachings of Gaamadweyaashiik, the use of a gun or a sling shot was not appropriate for a girl. Catching larger types of animals was therefore not likely for Dedibaayaanimanook. However, as a child, she was content with snaring rabbits and grouse, and leaving the game animals for her male relatives.

Throughout the winter season, both planned and unexpected events interposed in the family routine. The winter Dedibaayaanimanook's cousin Detaginang Frank Keesick and Gichijen were married, Gweyesh Annie and her husband Jiibwaat Edward Angeconeb decided to hold a feast. The Dedibayaashes were living at Gaaminitigwashkiigaag, so they did not have to travel as far to attend the gathering as those who came from Pikangikum, Ikwewi Zaa'igan Woman Lake and Aanziko Zaa'igan Otter Lake. Included among the guests was Jaaniiye Alex King, a cousin of Dedibaayaanimanook's mother and the father of Bezhigoobines Frank King, the one who would later become Gweyesh's son-in-law when he married her daughter Bejii Betsy. Gweyesh's large drum turned out to be the main attraction of the dance that took place during the gathering because it was the only time such an instrument was ever in Namegosibiing, as far as people could remember. One of Giizhik Sam Keesick's admonitions for his children and grandchildren had been that they refrain from any spiritual ceremonials that specifically incorporated the use of a large drum, and until very recently, his descendants have upheld his wishes in that regard.[7] However, a hand held drum existed in Namegosibiing during Dedibaayaanimanook's lifetime. It was constructed by her father.

Using two pieces of cedar approximately 3 1/4 inches wide and 1/4 inch thick, Dedibaayaanimanook's father began by bending the strips into a circular shape 15 inches across. Pliability was attainable by carefully ladling hot water over the wood. After stabilizing the circular shell with a length of cotton twine, he anchored strips of rawhide on opposite sides of the drum to form the handles. Then he stretched a piece of rawhide leather over both faces and whip stitched it into place using double stranded white thread. It was very important that both faces be completely covered. Next, he applied charcoal black to the rawhide, overlapping the design onto the drumhead by up to half an inch. To ensure a degree of adsorption and to prevent the charcoal from wearing off with use, he mixed it with a fine powder that he made by crushing the bones of moose ribs. Finally, Dedibayaash took a long piece of white thread and proceeded to string together several eagle quills, each measuring a quarter of an inch in diameter and cut into a length of 3 3/4 inches.[8] He pulled the thread across the drumhead, securing its ends to the sides of the drum with small nails. During informal family gatherings, Dedibayaash often sang as he accompanied himself on the drum. The songs that an individual sang belonged only to that person; the lyrics were considered very personal and were not normally shared with anyone. For that reason, people who wished to sing had to develop songs of their own. Dedibayaash's drum became separated from the family after he passed on, even though it continued to remain in Namegosibiing. For many years, it hung as a decorative object on the dining room wall of Sarah Yates's Trout Lake Lodge. Today, however, Dedibayaash's drum is back in the family's safekeeping even though it is no longer in Namegosibiing. One of his granddaughters now keeps it in her home.

Another feast that Dedibaayaanimanook remembered was a special feast her parents held for their Namegosibii Anishinaabe brethren. She remembered because it was the last gathering her parents ever had. By that time, Gwiiwije'oons Johnson, the eldest child of her cousin Detaginang Frank Keesick, was a few months old. As was their custom, the Dedibayaash family waited for the fish to spawn before proceeding from Negiishkensikaang on Ma'iingani Minis to their winter site. They began to make preparations for a feast to celebrate the Christmas season as soon as they arrived. Dedibaayaanimanook's father, who still hunted moose at the time, set out on a special hunt and before too long, he shot a large moose. Working entirely outdoors over an open fire, he prepared the fresh meat in several different ways, and when he returned home, his toboggan was piled high with fresh meat. Dedibay-aash also included fish on his portion of the festival menu. Meanwhile, Dedibaayaanimanook's mother set to work preparing rabbit, ruffed grouse, muskrat and other types of meat. She painstakingly pounded moose bones into a fatty substance that produced an unusually delicious flavor. By that time, however, not many were continuing to use moose bones in this manner. Few people, aside from Dedibaayaanimanook and her parents, had ever heard about the particular dish, much less experienced its wonderful taste. Soon the day of the feast approached, and Dedibaayaanimanook's parents were nearly finished with their preparations. Dedibaayaanimanook herself could hardly wait for the guests to arrive.

Not that many opportunities presented themselves for Dedibaaya-animanook to wear her finest clothes, but this was certainly one of them. When the much anticipated day finally arrived, she put on an outfit that her mother had made from fabric purchased by her father, then she pinned on the Husdson's Bay Company coat-of-arms brooch that her father had brought back from the trading post. She had several, but on more than one occasion, her brother Jiins approached her about taking one of them along with him on his trips to visit with friends. Each time, he promised to replace it at his earliest convenience, but that never seemed to happen, and Dedibaayaanimanook soon found herself down to her last few pins. Just as she had surmised, Dedibaaya-animanook later learned that her brother was using her jewelry as gifts to impress his female friends.

Dedibaayaanimanook had thick, luxurious hair that cascaded to the floor around her as she sat down. From time to time when she was a little girl, her mother extracted otter's tail oil which she used to infuse a silky, lustrous texture to her raven black hair. Dedibaayaanimanook fastened a barrette to anchor her hairstyle firmly in place, and then she was ready for the arrival of aunts, uncles and cousins, all of whom would be similarly befittingly attired. The feast lasted for as long as the food did, over the course of several days. "Majote'amawaadaa sa miijim!" The Gichi Anishinaabeg who were present made certain that a small portion of food went into the fire for those who had come and gone before them. It was the manner by which people paid their respects to the ancestors. "Hoo' miigwech!" When the feast was finished, each of Dedibaayaanimanook's uncles expressed his gratitude for having been given the opportunity to partake of the special celebration and for all the effort that had made it possible, and the event that Dedibaayaanimanook would remember for the rest of her life came to an end. On a different occasion, Dedibaayaanimanook and her family were living at their camp in the northwestern part of Namegosibiing just before Christmas one winter when her cousins Maashkizhiigan and Oshkaandagaa Charlie Ashen, her uncle Jiiyaan Donald and their families, all journeyed across the lake for a visit. Her father immediately went out and killed a moose at a nearby beach for the visitors. Although his reasons were known only to himself, it was the last time that Dedibayaash ever killed a moose.[9] Thereafter, Dedibaayaanimanook's brother Jiins Charlie took on the role of the family's moose hunter. Dedibaayaanimanook was around ten years old at the time.

Special feasts and celebrations were happy occasions for everyone, but Dedibaayaanimanook's people were not immune to tragic events. Even though they lived in Namegosibiing, where they were removed from the fullest force and most immediate impact of the larger, non-Anishinaabe communities springing up everywhere, the people were increasingly affected. For example, incidents of alcohol abuse, along with its negative and highly disruptive effects on the community, were becoming more frequent. These ocurrences had unimaginable consequences upon the psyche of individual members. The Keesicks were once living at Gaaminitigwashkiigaag when they heard a sharp crack as a rifle discharged. But it was not the ordinary shot of a hunter. Although the event took place within a matter of a few brief seconds, it seemed to Dedibaayaanimanook's mother that she had been staring forever at the hanging laundry and the snow beneath it, all spattered in crimson. The victim suffered a massive wound to his forehead, and even though he continued to breathe for several hours into the night, Dedibaayaanimanook's mother knew there was no possible way that he would survive. He had lost too much blood. As he expelled his final breath, Gaamadweyaashiik knew she would never forget what she had just witnessed. No one, not even Gaamadweyaashiik, anticipated that Dedibaayaanimanook's cousin was so filled with despair that he would take his own life.

Four families were living together on the south facing peninsula that forms the northernmost region of Gaaminitigwashkiigaag when another incident occurred. A child was accidentally shot. *"Aazha ninisigoo!"* Dedibaayaanimanook's close friend and sibling, Niingaana-ashiik Mary came staggering from the woods, her piercing screams preceding her. Crying out that she was being killed, she collapsed by the family's cabin. It was learned that a bullet accidently discharged from Dadens's rifle had ricocheted off a nearby jack pine, leaving a superficial wound in his young sister's side. Although the bullet had lost much of its velocity, the force of its momentum was terrifying and painful. All four families relocated immediately after the accident. The move was a gesture of compassion for Baswewe and for the little girl they had nearly lost.

Particularly during the winter season, when survival placed great demands on their skills and tested the limits of their endurance, maintaining a close relationship with one another was crucial. As a result, Dedibaayaanimanook was strongly attached to her Gaaminitigwaash-kiigaag siblings—that is, her first degree cousins—Meniiyaan Mary Ann and Mazinigiizhik James. Since cousins were in fact siblings according to the Anishinaabe custom, Dedibaayaanimanook always referred to her cousin Meniiyaan as her older sister. Even though Dedibaayaanimanook was at least three years younger, her sister/cousin never failed to treat her as an equal, and even when Meniiyaan became a teenager, the two continued to remain close. The last time Dedibaayaanimanook saw her sister in good health was on Namegosi

Ziibi Trout Lake River, at Adikamegwaaminikaaning Where the Whitefish Spawn. When Meniyaan died, Dedibaayaanimanook lost both a sibling and one of her closest and dearest friends. She knew that her sister had died of alcoholism. More than once, Meniiyaan had expressed a wish to be buried in her Namegosibiing homeland, but circumstances dictated that she be laid to rest at the traditional cemetery in Gojijiing Goldpines.[10]

Dedibaayaanimanook had close relationships with other relatives as well. Until he married, her half brother Jiins remained a member of the Dedibayaash household. Jiins, who had a knack for seeing humour where others did not, showed a special, invaluable skill in wood carving that emerged in his early teens. He also learned to enjoy cooking. Dedibaayaanimanook once watched as he stood stirring what he referred to as his French cuisine. It was a special recipe that included dried apples and raisins. Even though she did not spend a great deal of time with Jiins because he was a full time trapper/hunter who was out on expeditions most of the time and because he was considerably older than she, Dedibaayaanimanook valued what they did share together. He told her stories about his adventures and those of others in the family. For example, there was the description of the incident when his sisters Gweyesh Annie and Gichi Jôj's mother were sent out on a family errand. It happened several years before Dedibaayaanimanook was born. Setting out from their home at Gaaminitigwaashkiigaag one early morning about a month after freeze-up, the two young girls headed off toward Negiishkensikaang on Ma iingani Minis in order to bring back a supply of dried fish for the family. They were not expected to return until late afternoon. But as dusk began to settle over the lake and the two girls still had not returned, family members became concerned. Finally, around mid-evening, Minzhinawebines Sam and his cousin Baabiijinigaabaw set out for a search. Being a cloudless night with the Big Dipper clearly visible toward the northern sky, they had no difficulty finding their way across the ice. Approximately halfway to Negiishkensikaang, they noticed two small figures about to disappear behind an island about a mile off course. The brothers knew they were the two girls, so they waved their arms and shouted as they ran toward them.

"E'zhôshkonibiikaag osha." The girls were perplexed by the agitation with which they were greeted, explaining that their delay was due to the slushy conditions around them. By reason of their relative inexperience, they had been unaware of the dangers of straying off course on a cold winter's night, despite the fact that their intent for having detoured meticulously around even the smallest amount of slush was to prevent the dogs' paws from freezing. Minzhinawebines took the opportunity to enlighten the girls about their folly by gesturing to a momentarily brilliant segment of the auroras undulating across the skies above them. When he likened the degree of their folly to someone relying on the northern lights for travel directions, the youngsters understood his point and were chastened by his lesson on common sense.

Maintaining close relationships with one another was a necessity with community members, whether they were adults or children, and no matter the distances that separated them, they visited frequently in order to socialize, exchange small gifts, and otherwise make sure that all was well. When Dedibaayaanimanook's nephews Gichi Jôj George Trout and Niksaandan George Sam Keesick were attending school at Zhashagiwi Baawitig,[11] for example, Dedibaayaanimanook's brothers went to visit the two children on the family's behalf. Many of Dedibaayaanimanook's kin were schooled at Zhashagiwi Baawitig. "Gaa gii izhi awakaanaawaaj abinoonjiizhag," meaning that this was the place where Anishinaabe children were routinely treated as though they were slaves with no rights as humans whatsoever, was a phrase frequently used to describe the institution. During his boarding school confinement, Niksaandan once declined an invitation to join a group of classmates who were planning to escape. The young boys succeeded in getting away, but not sure which way was home, they took an equally dangerous chance by jumping a passing freight train. One of the escapees, a lad they referred to as Waabigozhiish, fell from the train and broke his neck. Despite his serious injuries, he actually survived the fall. Walking from Jiibaayi Zaagiing to Pelican residential school and back to visit the children took Jiins and Jiibwaat a little more than two weeks.

Since the Dedibayaash Keesicks spent their winters with the Jiiyaan Donald Keesick family, Dedibaayaanimanook enjoyed a loving, if not always perfectly happy, relationship with her sister Moshish Mary. This was due in part to a habit that Moshish Mary had of belittling her. "Indogonaa giin Jesus ozidan!" Deciding it was time to take the offensive, Dedibaayaanimanook once came up with what her sister apparently took to be a good response. But just what the Lord's feet had to do with their quarrel was unclear! It was far more typical for Dedibaayaanimanook to try to hide the hurt she felt and to stay away from her sister whenever she was in a less than amiable mood. Invariably, a remorseful Moshish came calling within a day or two, having grown weary of her own company.

The two Keesick families were living together at Jiibaayi Zaagiing one winter when Dedibaayaanimanook's and Moshish Mary's parents instructed them to prepare for a trip. They were to go to Gaaminitigwashkiigaag, the large irregular bay that faces northwest approximately halfway along the eastern shoreline of Namegosibiing. It was the place of Dedibaayaanimanook's birth. A peninsula called Getewaakaa'iganiing lay just to the southwest. At various times, the Dedibayaashes also lived in the Gaaminitigwashkiigaag region of Namegosibiing, but Dedibaayaanimanook's uncle Netawibiitam John Keesick, his wife Minogaabawiik and their children usually spent the entire winter at that location. Later, Netawibiitam's son Detaginang Frank Keesick and his family would also make Gaaminitigwashkiigaag their winter home. In fact, it was for those reasons that the location came to be called Keesick Bay by the wemitigoozhiwag who eventually arrived and settled in Namegosibiing. Dedibaayaanimanook's parents had learned of Netawibiitam John's failing health, and that he was now unable to walk. As he lay in bed, the ache in his lower legs became so intense that only when his knees were bent and bound tightly with ropes nailed to the floor was the pain lessened. In response to the news that his condition had rapidly worsened, the two young cousins hurriedly prepared to go to Gaaminitigwashkiigaag and offer a helping hand to their aging aunt, Gookomens Minogaabawiik. They were to help her with fire wood and any other chores that needed doing. They were told to stay for as long as Gookomens needed them.

During the early hours of dawn, Dedibaayaanimanook and Moshish left Jiibayi Zaagiing. They were able to make good progress by not stopping for the side trips that were usually part of their adventures together. With late winter having advanced to where the snow was now of a crystalline texture, Dedibaayaanimanook was reminded about how people used the zeseganaagoon specifically for making tea. Whenever they were out on the ice and wanted to stop for a break, they collected clean slush if it was available rather than chop a hole to get water. But the girls did not make such a stop this time. They did, however, pay close attention to the ice conditions, pausing periodically throughout their journey only to ensure that the dogs' paws were free from cuts and other injuries. Just before dusk, they were finally within sight of their destination. Approaching their uncle's cabin, they noticed that the window curtains were all drawn, and without exchanging a word, they both knew that their uncle had already died. The cousins' extended stay at Gaaminitigwashkiigaag became a source of comfort for their elderly aunt Gookomens, as the community fondly referred to her. After Netawibiitam John's burial, the people of Namegosibiing held a special feast to honour the life of their beloved brother.

1. The original version of the <u>Trout Lake Conservation Reserve Resource Management Plan, C2334, November, 2005</u>, a document the Ontario Ministry of Natural Resources (OMNR) produced, contains several inaccuracies in one of the appendicies in which there is a discussion about how the traditional Anishinaabe people of Namegosibiing did or did not use fire as a forest management tool.

2. OMNR's lack of consultation has continued to this day. For example, OMNR's regional officials ignored the advice of Namegosibii Anishinaabeg about publishing an article that had no references or sources for what was being claimed in a part of their 2005 document (see Note 1 above).

3. Negiishikensikaang is literally, "Where the (Small) Cedars Grow Along the Shore."

4. Wazhashko Zaa'igan translates to Muskrat Lake; it is now known as Joyce Lake.

5. Dedibaayaanimanook referred to her aunt Minogaabawiik as Gookomens, which means "your little grandmother" because Minogaabawiik was petite and slender.

6. B/107/a/35, Hudson's Bay Company Archives, Winnipeg, MB

7. As alluded to previously, Giizhik.Sam Keesick's teachings included Christian elements. There are some who think those elements weakened the old system of beliefs. Others viewed them as supplemental and even complemental. Given the integrity of his character and the extent of his understanding about such matters, Giizhik may have intended to draw out the commonalities that existed between the two systems in their purest form. For example, Giizhik often made reference to the virtue of self-denial and spoke of the altruistic spirit of Gizhe Manidoo, the one whom Christians call Jesus Christ. He talked about the meaning of suffering in the hands of unjust persecution, and that there would be another time in which wrongs would be set right. Being well aware of political realities (he was a Band councillor for several years), Giizhik took on a more pacifist position, particularly in his latter years. It is not to say that he was passive, even though Anishinaabe peoples were historically described as passive by the dominant culture in Canada. (Dominant in this context is always used to mean "exerting control or power" rather than "qualitatively superior" – domineering, not paramount.) Respect, toward nature and fellow humans, was one of the pillars on which Anishinaabe culture was built. Therefore, living in a manner that gave respect was clearly evident in behavioural patterns of the traditional people. That demeanor, of course, was perceived and interpreted as passivity,

hence weakness, when viewed from the eyes of a dominant culture. Historically (and even to this day), there has been no place or patience for anything interpreted as weak.

8. The quills imparted a particular resonance when Dedibayaash struck the drum.

9. The Keesicks usually ate deer meat beginning in late spring after it replaced its thick winter covering with the more characteristic reddish brown summer coat. Venison was in fact the family's main source of meat protein (miijim) throughout summer and early autumn, although males were avoided during rutting season due to the strong bitter flavour of the meat. Moose was most often a winter food source.

10. The traditional cemetery at Gojijiing Goldpines has since begun to fall into disarray.

11. When people mentioned Zhashagiwi Baawitig, located fairly close to the Lac Seul community, they were referring to the residential school that was located at Pelican Falls. Dedibaayaanimanook's nephews, Niksaandan and Gichi Jôj, were approximately her age because she was born when her parents, both previously married with children, were in their mid-forties. Hence, her (half) siblings and many of her first degree cousins were already young adults by the time of her birth. It was Niksaandan George who, as a toddler, elicited chuckles from the adults when he referred to one of his elderly aunts as "ingiishki joozhish" (literally, my *cut-in- half* aunt) in his attempt to say "ingichi doozis" (my great-aunt).

CHAPTER 5

Ingii'ondaadiziminaaban

~

We Used To Make A Living

"Indizhichigemin e'Anishinaabewiyaang," was how it was explained that Dedibaayaanimanook's people pursued their livelihood in ways that were wholistic and self-reinforcing. This was another way of saying that their social and economic systems and structures allowed them to derive their sense of self as Anishinaabe people from all the activities they carried out on a day to day basis and from the methods by which they did so. Trapping and hunting were examples of principal activities that dated as far back as collective memory stretched and beyond. Catching fur bearers was essential for carrying out trade with other nations, and hunting was necessary for personal consumption. The activities were practised in ways that maintained the old customs. In fact, they were all part of the old customs handed down from the ancestors, representing the many elements that comprised what it meant to be Anishinaabe.

Living off the land was not for the faint of heart or those un-accustomed to being out of doors. But it was well suited to the people of Namegosibiing because they were neither faint hearted nor housebound. The activities that kept Dedibaayaanimanook's father and other members of the family occupied typified their traditional Anishinaabe lifestyle. Spending so much of his time on the hunting and trapping trails, her father was intimately acquainted with the regions that encompassed the family's traditional use territories. He routinely embarked on trips that lasted up to five days or longer, and although he used sled dogs, he always travelled the distances of his traplines entirely on foot. The trips he took over the vast expanses of the traditional land use territories northeast of Namegosibiing—as far away as Memegweshi Zaa'igan,[1] Niki Zaa'igan[2] and Gaamanga-dikamegokaang[3]—were evidence of his physical endurance and his dedication to providing for his family by maintaining this traditional way of life. Each one of his outings was a potential encounter with a moose, deer or other animal, and for that reason Dedibayaash never ventured anywhere without his rifle, which he had purchased for an undisclosed amount. Back when the fur trade with the wemitigoozhi-wag first began, gun technology was far from perfected.[4] Accidents involving firearms continued to happen since that time. For example, Dedibaayaanimanook's cousin Omooday Paul lost the middle finger of his right hand when he inadvertently shot himself while loading his rifle. But the fact that Omooday's wound healed without infection or other complications was indicative of the people's medical know-how, their knowledge of how to utilize the natural materials that existed around them without negative side effects. Moreover, the makeup of the community itself was such that there were members versed in several different applications of traditional medicine. For example, one individual among the Keesicks treated tuberculosis, the sickness that historically took so many lives. The group as a whole was thus able to maintain enough knowledge to treat a wide range of medical problems at any given time, exemplifying the customs of self-sufficiency handed down from the ancestors.

As another form of inheritance, Dedibaayaanimanook's father and uncles came from a long hunting tradition. "Gii'onashkinachigebani'o-wag" was Dedibayaash's precise description that alluded to the legendary hunters of old, who were so adept that they were able to load their rifles, take aim and fire in one continuously flowing motion sufficiently silent not to scare off the animal. Even though cow horns were once readily available at the Hudson's Bay trading post, they had become obsolete by the time of Dedibaayaanimanook's birth, but her father's one sentence description was a reference to how expertly these objects were used in bygone days to fill a rifle with gunpowder. Dedibayaash's depiction was also an indication of the type of hunting skills he and his brothers had inherited.

Another long-standing custom given to the people related to the simple and highly efficient strategy of using dogs. The animals were kept for work rather than pets, but that was not to say that people did not have a high regard for their dogs. Indeed, they had a special relationship with them because they served several vital functions. For instance, dogs were necessary for pulling toboggans and sleds in winter. They also helped in the hunt. When Dedibaayaanimanook's mother was a young girl, she had a dog that her father took on hunting trips in order to help with the chase. By running ahead and distracting the moose, it kept the quarry at bay long enough to allow the hunter to approach to within firing range. The dog's work usually took place during spring when the snow began to melt and was no longer so deep as to impede its ability to run. But Dedibaayaanimanook also heard about the last time her maternal grandfather ever took the dog on a trip. Having apparently misjudged its distance from the moose, the unfortunate creature was injured by a powerful kick that shattered its hind leg. Another potential danger for the dogs were porcupines. Since they were not allowed to ride in canoes and boats during river travels, dogs needed to follow along on land. At least one, usually the youngest, was sure to arrive at the campsite with its muzzle covered in porcupine quills. Whenever that happened, Dedibaayaanimanook's mother bundled the dog tightly in a blanket before attempting to remove the quills. Any quills inadvertently left embedded led to infection and pain. Porcupines were equally a potential danger in winter. But dogs also provided companionship when travellers were away from their families, and if a hunter was in dire circumstances, they were a potential source of warmth and even protection. While people were mindful of the health and well-being of their dogs, there were those, such as Dedibaayaanimanook's cousin Oshkaandagaa, for whom their teams were a source of much pride. This was clearly evident in the time and effort it took to make them colourful, elaborate harnesses.

People also had a bond with their dogs which was apparent in such ways as the colourful names they often gave them. Dedibaayaanimanook's father, for example, once had a special dog to whom he gave the name Gijigaa'ajoosh, while her uncle Netawibiitam John named his Baash-kine. Her brother Jiins's dog was Ma'iinganens,[5] who, unlike another he named Gagiibaadiz, was known for his intelligence and obedience. Dedibaayaanimanook's Asemaa proved to be a loyal, hard working sled dog. Then there was the elderly woman who referred to her dog's puppies as her grandchildren.

The process of handing down knowledge about the various aspects of the old ways came in the form of experiential instruction that began at an early age for the children of the community. Because most of her half siblings were into adulthood when she was born, Dedibaay-aanimanook's circumstance was such that her parents were able to provide her with more time and attention than would otherwise have been possible. In fact, their parenting style was quite similar to that of grandparenting. Dedibaayaanimanook, for example, was sometimes allowed to accompany her father on some of his shorter traplines. Each was a form of learning. When they were living at Gaaminitigwashki-igaag Keesick Bay, she and her father embarked on a short jaunt that took them into an area replete with muskrats. The animals, living in dwellings made from mud mixed with the roots and stems of various aquatic plants, organized their living space into a type of "kitchen" in which they ate and another area for resting and sleeping. Dedibaay-aanimanook's father began by forming an opening at the top of the mound. Then he reached down and placed a trap inside each of the eat-ing areas. Whenever she was invited along, Dedibaayaanimanook ran ahead, down the trail to each of the mounds and eagerly flipped open the top with her mitten. There she usually found a heap of luxurious brown fur atop the sprung trap. Once or twice, however, her only find was a forlorn little forepaw. The trail Dedibayaash followed was described as gakiiwemog, meaning that there were places where it cut through the woods rather than keep to the winding little creek that flowed into Namegosibiing from Manoomini Zaa'igan Rice Lake.

While on one of these outings, Dedibaayaanimanook's father left her to rest for ten minutes or so while he went on ahead. Dedibaaya-animanook stood and watched her father disappear into the woods, but being a small child with an active imagination, she soon convinced herself that she was never going to see him again. There was little else to do but sit down in the snow. As she envisioned her fate, an overwhelming sense of loneliness came over her. She began to cry. Before too many moments had passed, however, Dedibaayaanimanook's thoughts were interrupted by the sound of approaching footsteps. "Ind-ede!" The sight of her father emerging from the woods dispelled her gloomy thoughts, and with a rush of sudden joy, she scrambled to her feet and hurried toward him. Later on, when she was old enough to think about such matters, she would realize that family members took care of one another.

During their lifetime of travel throughout their traditional use ter-ritories, Dedibaayaanimanook's people acquired a vast body of know-ledge that reinforced what had been given them by their predeces-sors. Much of that information related to the animals that co-existed with them. There was one particular animal about which her father spoke, a rare creature the tracks of which he came across only twice. They were those of a feline, but much larger than a lynx's. The secret-ive interloper appeared to have a definite preference for travelling above ground by moving from tree to tree in the woods along a southeast-northwest corridor. Before Dedibaayaanimanook's birth, when wooden traps were still in wide use, her father saw a set of the animal's tracks at Goshkwegaawinigam Swain Lake. He decided to set out one of his traps to catch the animal, but when he returned the next day, he discovered that a wolverine had torn the trap into pieces and consumed the bait. Although he respected all creatures, Dedibayaash identified only two animals he feared—the wolverine, for its extraordinary strength, intelligence and courage, and the sphinx-like cougar for its incredible stealth.

All the men of Namegosibiing were skilled in the outdoors. Dedibaayaanimanook's brother Jiins, for example, spent the vast majority of his time on the trapline before he married. As other trappers were in the habit of doing whenever they unexpectedly came across the tracks of a fisher, Jiins once decided he would follow a set of the footprints until he caught the animal, no matter how long it took. The venture continued on for three days as he trailed the fisher to its burrow. Not having intended to go so far that day, he had not brought along either food or overnight gear. "Indoonji ganawenimaa osha." Sometimes Dedibaayaanimanook could hear her mother weeping quietly in the night as she worried for Jiins's safety, even though Dedibayáash attempted to reassure her. Jiins, on the other hand, was never aware that his extemporaneous journeys caused his mother so much anxiety. Hunters embarked on such a trek because that particular type of fur pelt was greatly valued, yielding among the highest of prices. The fact that Anishinaabe people took such trips as Jiins's impromptu trek attested to their stamina. People had the knowledge and skills necessary to survive tremendously adverse conditions. Moreover, Jiins's preference was for clear, cold weather whenever he travelled. He found that cold temperatures made walking a distinct pleasure, even after a fresh blanket of snow had fallen because the powdery granules slid effortlessly off his snowshoes. On that kind of winter's morning, he was typically already several miles into the trapline when the first rays of light appeared over the eastern skies. Journeys to the trading post, on the other hand, began either in early morning or late evening, depending on where the family was living, where Jiins intended to purchase the groceries and other supplies and where along the trail he planned to spend the night. Once the warm weather of spring arrived, the snow needed a different strategy because it was sticky and heavy with moisture. Dedibaayaanimanook's father advised her to carry a walking stick in order to tap the snow off with each footstep.

Although this procedure reduced her rate of travel, it was preferable to the undue stress on her snowshoes when the clammy snow attached itself in increasingly voluminous clumps.

Successful Anishinaabe hunters, including Dedibaayaanimanook's father, uncles and brothers, traditionally had a special connection with the animals on whom their survival depended. Standing behind a birch tree, Jiins once watched with wonderment as a moose feasted on a grove of saplings. He was suddenly struck by the ease with which the animal was able simply to reach out for the food it needed, in contrast to the effort humans needed to expend in order to eat. By way of expressing his esteem and admiration for the animal, Jiins dedicated a special song to it. Later, he told Dedibaayaanimanook about his epiphany, and even though he had shared the words to his song with her, she was duty bound not to reveal them. The song was an expression of his relationship with the animal, and because the words were his, the right to divulge them was his alone.

Another example that illustrates the type of association that existed between the people and the animal beings happened one night on the trail when Jiins experienced a remarkable encounter with wolves. Nightfall was closing in, but a fair distance across the frozen lake still lay between him and land. The wind began to whistle. It blew with increasing intensity, picking up the snow and strewing it forcefully around him. As he pressed on, Jiins noticed the indistinct form of what appeared to be a wolf in the stretch ahead. He decided it was best to continue his pace, and to his great relief, the creature moved aside when he drew close. Jiins soon noticed, however, two other large timber wolves. They were keeping pace with him on either side. It seemed as though time itself had somehow frozen, and Jiins was locked in a swirling universe of snow and wolves when suddenly the animals began to merge into the night's darkness. Once again, Jiins found himself alone on the trail. Although the wolves' intent may never be proven as a scientific fact, they had clearly served to prevent the solitary Anishinaabe from straying off course that frigid night in Namegosibiing. In effect, they had saved his life. Dedibaayaanimanook herself knew of no tradition indicating that people needed to have an inordinate fear of wolves. The animals did not have a reputation for harassing, hunting or otherwise harming anyone. Instead, people recognized that they too had just as much a rightful claim to inhabit the earth as humans, to maintain their space and fulfill their need to survive. As co-inhabitants of the earth, therefore, wolves were accorded proper deference.

The Dedibayaashes knew of an Anishinaabe woman named Mrs. Sapay (Njôy Anderson's mother) who owned a dog that was in fact a wolf. Known to be faithful and obedient, the creature was so gentle that Mrs. Sapay's small children played fearlessly with it. Later, Mrs. Sapay herself was rarely without it. When she journeyed from Gojijiing Goldpines to Swain Lake to visit her daughter, for example, she was companioned by her devoted wolf dog. Remarkably, the two actually ran—rather than walked—the entire distance. Those acquainted with Mrs. Sapay knew that it was entirely within character for her to have run that distance. A unique woman, she performed all work related activities and tasks normally carried out by the men of the community with such skill and competence that people spoke of her with certain admiration. On another occasion, Mrs. Sapay and her husband stopped at the Dedibayaash Keesicks' camp along the way, but this time she was without the wolf. She informed her inquisitive hosts that her faithful companion had simply felt too lazy to make the journey. Later, Dedibaayaanimanook's mother explained that a powerful dream made it possible for Mrs. Sapay to receive the gift of a tame wolf.

None of this, however, was to say that people were oblivious to the fact that wolves could be very dangerous under certain circumstances. The time Dedibaayaanimanook was an infant and she and her parents were at Memegweshi Zaa'igan, for instance, a group of relatives out on a journey unwittingly found themselves between a pack of wolves and a moose the animals were tracking. The travellers realized that they had inserted themselves into a group of carnivorous animals on the verge of a kill. By exercising great care, however, they were able to withdraw from the situation without harm. Anishinaabe wisdom was unlike that of the wemitigoozhiwag's tradition, in that no attributions of inherent malevolence existed against wolves. On the other hand, a fox could be quite a different matter. Under certain conditions and on a non-physical plane, owls, fox and two or three other creatures were sometimes prepared to implicate themselves in the use of what is referred to as evil medicine. The fox being, for instance, was able to terrorize the intended victim by uttering loud, unearthly cries or by appearing in strange and grotesque forms. A disturbing episode with one of the creatures happened to Dedibaayaanimanook's cousin Detaginang Frank Keesick and his wife not long after they were married. While he was away on an overnight journey into the family's hunting territory, Detaginang left his wife Gichijen at home. Their relatives had already departed for their winter camp sites, so Gichijen was completely alone with her small dog. As evening shrouded the landscape in darkness, she sat close to the tiny stove, enjoying its warmth. Her dog was still somewhere outdoors. Suddenly she became aware that it was barking from off in the distance. As she listened, she realized that the dog sounded agitated and was running swiftly.

"Indogo e'gagwe dabaziij." When her dog reached the tent, Gichijen could see the outline of its form while it crouched backwards against the canvas. Gichijen was paralyzed with fear, unable to imagine what could possibly have caused her dog to retreat with such obvious terror. Dawn began to break when she awakened. At some point in the night, she had fallen asleep. Even though she wished that the events of the night before had simply been a terrible nightmare, she knew they were very real. After several moments, she forced herself to go outdoors for a fresh supply of firewood, and as she made her way toward the pile of wood, a slight movement caused her to glance toward a tall spruce tree. Standing half hidden behind the evergreen was a misshapen, pole-like personage. It watched her with piercing eyes. Later that day, Detaginang returned from his trapline. He and Gichijen immediately packed and began the long journey back toward the south where his uncle Mooniiyaans Thomas Keesick used Anishinaabe medicine to treat her trauma. While they were there, they learned that several months previously, a young man from Gichijen's community at Bizhiwi Zaa'igan Cat Lake[6] had wanted to marry her. However, she unintentionally insulted his entire family by rejecting the young man's offer when she chose to marry Detaginang Frank Keesick instead. Amassing his powers, the man's father had invoked the animal's apparition to avenge Detaginang and Gichijen's perceived offense.

A further example involved an even more dangerous animal. It was an incident that began just as the Keesicks were embarking on their river journey home one autumn when an Anishinaabe from another community approached Dedibaayaanimanook's uncle Jiiyaan for money. With barely enough for his own needs, Jiiyaan turned down the request. He and the rest of the family thereupon resumed their journey up the Namegosi Ziibi toward Namegosibiing. When they reached Waaboozo Baawitig Rabbit Rapids, Jiiyaan and his entourage made one of their stops for a night's rest. Maagii had already gathered wood and built a fire, so she was tending to their infant while a fellow traveller lay resting on his sickbed close by. As he sat next to the fire enjoying its generous warmth, Jiiyaan became aware of someone approaching from the underbrush. He rose to greet the stranger, but without warning, he found himself facing a gigantic bear. Before he could react, a set of powerful claws began raking fiercely over him. Maagii instinctively shifted her infant and seized her axe. But she did not have to use it because the attack ceased as abruptly as it had begun. Gweyesh Annie and others who were camped further along the riverbank heard the commotion and, grabbing their rifles, came running to help. However, the creature had already disappeared into the river's darkness, leaving Jiiyaan bleeding from massive wounds. The family had just felt the wrath of the offended Anishinaabe who had approached them for money. Certain members of the Keesick family, however, had the power to countervail such forces. In that particular case, it was Dedibaayaanimanook's father who intervened to save his brother's life. Jiiyaan and his family eventually reached Namegosibiing where he made a slow recovery.

Understanding this type of curse that directly incorporated certain animals in a struggle between opposing forces was vital for the security of the community. To overcome such a threat, the community needed members who were gifted with the kind of spiritual and moral integrity that imbued them with personal power. Dedibaayaanimanook's father and her uncle Mooniiyaans Thomas were these types of individuals among the Namegosibii Anishinaabeg. Dedibaayaanimanook's father once explained that the effectiveness of what is known as evil medicine depended on its user's ability to conceal his or her identity. In Gichijen Keesick's case, Mooniiyaans Thomas was able to treat her state of terrorization by using his power to identify the perpetrator of the act.

"Misawaa ganabaj daagii' mamaanzhiiwag Anishinaabeg." The use of one's power for carrying out acts of revenge and intimidation against others was by no means a novelty, but with the negative impact of wemitigoozhiwag on the people's lives, fewer individuals had the ability to counter evil medicine. In fact, some wondered whether Anishinaabeg would eventually lose their ways of integrity and honour, because the arrival of the wemitigoozhi's disparate systems into the homelands tended to erode the old ways very rapidly. Among Dedibaayaanimanook's people, for example, the notion of registration that legally specified trapline boundaries for each trapper was at one time unheard of. Instead, people recognized that a trapline was where each family group customarily travelled and lived, in order to pursue a livelihood. It was part of the larger traditional use territory to which human families were just as connected and upon which they were just as dependent as the many non-human ones. Originally, people respected one another's traditional lands, but once the wemitigoozhiwag began to trap within the homelands, licenses indeed became necessary. Despite these developments, trapping continued to be meaningful for the people for as long as their values remained rooted in the land.

The nature of the tradition of trapping was such that trappers needed a good understanding about how a pelt was evaluated if their intent was to engage in trade. They needed to know, for example, that a grader examined the condition of each pelt, looking at colour, amount (length and density) of fur, straightness of hair and signs of damage. Depending upon the current fashion in the case of trade with wemiti-goozhiwag, fur density could be more important than size for some animals. The darker color of a muskrat might be in high demand one year, then of little worth the next. Overall, the best furs fetched the highest prices, and were destined either to adorn or become the end user's most expensive garment or accessory. These types of character-istics were used to categorize the quality of various furs, and for the best possible return for their efforts, trappers referred to those criter-ia when deciding what to harvest and when. Dedibaayaanimanook sometimes heard her father express concern when uncontrollable factors such as adverse weather conditions affected the fur harvest or when the quality of a fur was damaged when animals fought one another or struggled to escape from a trap or a predator. There were times when Dedibayaash needed to travel unusually long distances to obtain what was most in demand at the trading post. At other times, severe weather made trapping either difficult or untenable. In the early 1930s, for example, when Dedibayaanimanook was around ten years old and her nephew Niiyoo Leo Angeconeb was still in a cradleboard, Namegosibii Anishinaabeg experienced an exception-ally heavy snow fall that made for an anomalous, difficult winter.

"E'niibawij moonz ogii'daangishkawaan goon omisadaang." The snow came right up to the underbelly of a fully grown, standing moose. As a result, moose, deer and caribou were largely immobil-ized, confined to a severely restricted feeding range. They were unable to outrun the predators and became easy prey. Hunters were able easily to track them, but the animals were lean and stressed. Other types of animals were also adversely affected. People noticed the sudden disappearance of rabbits, spruce grouse and other small, non-hibernating ground dwellers. Their tracks, usually so plentiful and always so familiar, all vanished from the landscape that winter. Snow covering the entrance into the animals' dwellings became hard as rock, locking them in icy coffins. They suffocated, starved or froze to death. People had to wait for animals from surrounding areas to come in and re-populate the land, but in the meantime, harvesting activities yielded little. No matter what the weather conditions were, however, trappers had also to contend with the Hudson's Bay Company's fur pricing practices which ostensibly reflected "what the market can bear." This underlying philosophy, that remained central to the European value system, was contradictory to how Dedibaayaanimanook's people thought about the usage of animals, furs and anything else. To continue with their partnership with the land and live up to their obligation to live in harmony with the natural environment, people understood their part of the bargain was to take only what they required to survive. Therefore, acquisition and accumulation beyond those requirements for survival were contrary to their agreement, and that was the reason why people were highly skeptical when they saw the wemitigoozhi's typical behaviour of over-consumption and over-harvesting. Furthermore, the wemitigoozhi's system of endless pursuit of greater accumulation and profit was illogical because it failed to take into account the fact that the earth's resources were finite, requiring careful handling and management. Otherwise, the people saw the day would come when there would be nothing left to harvest. What was most unsettling of all, however, was that the people of Namegosibiing themselves were becoming increasingly drawn into the newcomers' system, even despite their best efforts.

As another corollary to how they saw their relationships, Dedibaayaanimanook's people were not inclined toward political activity such as the formation of trappers' associations as a means for influencing prices, at least not initially. Instead, their efforts were focused on producing a quality product by taking every precaution to minimize the negative effects of adverse conditions. Given the general acknowledgement that their way of life—their very existence—depended on a healthy homeland, Dedibaayaanimanook's mother was an example of a practitioner of the traditional Anishinaabe ways. Gaamadweyaashiik was mindful of how she carried out her daily activities, and conservation, re-use and re-cycling were the terms that accurately captured her way of doing things. As the family member who processed what the family trappers brought home, she cleaned the skins and repaired the tears and holes. Whenever Dedibaayash or Jiins brought back a pelt so badly damaged by ravens or other means that it had no commercial value, she salvaged it for decorating moccasins, parkas and mittens in place of fabric or ribbon. Most furbearers and other types of animals were a source of food for the family because, as Dedibaayaanimanook heard her mother explain so many times, animals obtained their nourishment from medicinal plants, whether the plants were aquatic or terrestrial. That was why rabbits, beavers, muskrats and even bears were all healthy sources of nourishment for humans at that time. Dedibaayaanimanook recalled that a porcupine produced especially delicious meat. Whenever individuals avoided eating certain types of animals, their reasons were based on a dream. Gaamadweyaashiik, for instance, prepared the meat of a bald or golden eagle that Dedibayaash occasionally brought home, even though she herself did not partake of it. Similarly, Dedibayaash did not eat beaver. Gaamadweyaashiik used all parts of an animal even though not everything was suitable for human consumption. As an example, the brain matter of an animal was not eaten. Instead, it was put to other uses such as the production of leather.

During the latter part of spring when they were still in Namegosi-biing, Dedibaayaanimanook enjoyed special outings with her mother to search for various types of food plants. She received instruction on how to recognize the shoots of an aquatic plant with rootstocks that were edible only during that time of year. Another excellent source of nutrition highly recommended by Gaamadweyaashiik was a car-rot-like plant that grows in the water along the shoreline. While many plants were safe for human consumption, there were those about which Dedibaayaanimanook was cautioned by her mother. This included two specific types of plants. Most of what Gaamadweyaas-hiik harvested was eaten freshly picked, because, as she explained to Dedibaayaanimanook, they provided maximum nutritional benefit when eaten raw. Dedibaayaanimanook's mother had also acquired knowledge about the healing properties of various plants and other materials and the techniques for their usage. For instance, she knew how to make incisions painlessly in order to treat certain ailments. When Dedibaayaanimanook was suffering from a severe headache, Gaamadweyaashiik once made a small incision in her scalp, then applied a piece of special stone to the cut. Other individuals used the same method. Joe Paishk's grandfather, Moozhonii, once incised his daughter-in-law Jii and healed her of a severe headache. Dedibaaya-animanook's father actually applied the treatment to himself by cutting a set of short parallel lines on one side of his head, then using a piece of the stone. Some who were trained in medicine made use of a specific type of flower, while others used a special remedy known as azhaason mashkiki for treating headaches. These therapies, which included use of natural anesthetics and disinfectants, were evidence of the body of knowledge possessed by Namegosibiing's practioners. Both of Dedibaayaanimanook's parents were of this fraternity.

Just as her father had undergone many hardships, Dedibaayaani-manook's mother, Gaamadweyaashiik, survived numerous adversities during childhood which influenced her beliefs and practices. One tragic experience was the loss of her eldest sister in a drowning accident at Gull Rock Lake. Another incident that indicated the degree of trauma through which Gaamadweyaashiik and her siblings lived began on a bitterly cold morning when she and her younger brother were sent out to visit relatives who resided several miles away. With a strong wind already blowing, the snow turned visibility into a whiteout. But the children were driven to obey their mother, and they continued onward. At that moment, Gaamadweyaashiik thought she could hear the baying of wolves above the howling wind and instinctively, the two began to flee. Although the wolves ceased their chase upon perceiving the human children, Gaamadweyaashiik's brother was seized with such fear that he continued to run until he was completely exhausted. He began to cough uncontrollably, barely able to breathe. The two young siblings survived their journey, but Gaamadweyaashiik's brother developed breathing problems that progressively worsened. He died shortly thereafter. In another incident, Gaamadweyaashiik was busily mending when she asked her mother to pass the scissors. Her mother, with no forewarning, simply flung the scissors toward her, hitting her beneath the eye. "E'indaanisens—ganabaj isa ginisin!" As blood gushed from Gaamaadweyaashiik's wound, her mother cried out in panic, fearing that she had surely killed her. As a young adult, Gaamadweyaashiik resolved that she would never treat others, much less her own children and family members, in such a manner. Rather, she acted with patience, kindness and a forgiving attitude toward her fellow humans because she saw the survival of her childhood to have been a gift. It was a gift that helped her to show Dedibaayaanimanook about living a full, productive life.

Other blessings Dedibaayaanimanook received from her mother were all of the abilities and traits necessary to provide for the family's clothing. For example, Gaamadweyaashiik once knitted Jiins a pair of woolen socks which she decorated with a border of reverse k's in brightly contrasting colors. When Jiins put them on with his jodpurs one day, family members knew that he intended to visit a special friend living in another community. He presented a strikingly handsome figure, the pair of tassels his mother had attached to the outside edges of his socks bobbing up and down with an air of festivity as he strode facilely down the trail. In a similar manner, Dedibaayaanimanook would one day provide for her own family.

As she watched her mother working with furs, beads, leather, fabric and ribbons, Dedibaayaanimanook learned various techniques such as those necessary for making the solidly beaded belt that she sold to a relative in Lac Seul for three dollars. She also gained knowledge about how to catch squirrels and weasels and sell their furs. One year she received 25 cents for each squirrel pelt and 50 cents per weasel fur. The Dedibayaashes were living at their winter camp on the western main shore of Namegosibiing when Dedibaayaanimanook even caught and skinned a skunk. But generally speaking, the role of trapping belonged to the male members of the family, not Dedibaayaanimanook. That did not, however, preclude her becoming knowledgeable about the oral traditions associated with the profession.

Although the family's trappers accumulated large quantities of fur pelts, they had abandoned the old practise of going to the Hudson's Bay Company by the time of Dedibaayaanimanook's childhood. Instead, they hauled their bundles to the independent traders at Swain Lake, Red Lake and other posts further afield. In addition, traders had once hired runners to pick up furs from the various communities in former times, but the practice that was characterized by having someone go from community to community in order to trade goods for furs was largely a relic of the past. The only notable exception was a wemitigoozi who collected the Keesicks' furs and took them to Swain Lake when Dedibaayaanimanook was a toddler. The man, a Mr. Brown from Gojijiing Goldpines, had adopted the Anishinaabe name Waabinini for himself. He and his travelling companion, Charlie Bannatyne (Gichi Jii's father), always brought along a quantity of basic staples such as tea, flour and lard for the families whose furs they were out to collect. The Dedibayaash family lived at Gaaminitigwashkiigaag Keesick Bay during the early part of winter, and their camp lay directly along the route that took the fur collectors to Swain Lake. Waabinini, whom Dedibayaash knew from his work during the summer, and Charlie, spent the night with the Keesick family on more than one occasion. Dedibayaash's brother Jiiyaan once dropped by and as the four spent the evening playing cards, Waabinini bounced little Dedibaayaanimanook on his knee. He too had a daughter approximately the same age. Dedibaayaanimanook was too small to remember Waabinini, but her father told her these stories about him.

During the mid-winter season, Dedibaayaanimanook's father trapped mainly for muskrat and otter. He rarely caught martens and did not hunt wolves, although he occasionally found one in one of his larger traps. Ever aware that their food, clothing and income derived from the fur bearers that included muskrats, rabbits, bears and beavers, Dedibayaash was careful to avoid killing more than they needed.

People held all creatures in high regard, but the beaver, "Ogimaawi-nini,"[7] as Dedibaayaanimanook's father referred to it, was particularly esteemed for its unique attributes. "Indogo wemitigoozhiwag endaawaaj!" Dedibayaash once made the observation that the animals set up their living quarters in much the same way as wemitogoozhiwag. "Gii'on-zaawaabikowimiishidoone gaagii' waabamag." By way of explaining why he likened beavers to wemitigoozhiwag, Dedibaaya-animanook's grandfather Giizhik once told his children about a dream he had just prior to leaving for a hunting trip. He dreamed that he met up with a wemitigoozhi whose golden beard gleamed brilliantly in the sunlight. Early into his hunt the next day, Giizhik was taken aback when he came upon a large beaver with long golden whiskers.

Another experience about which Dedibaayaanimanook heard from her father involved an incident in which a relative was bitten by a beaver. As Gôkwad attempted to remove a live beaver from his trap, it locked its incisors firmly onto his gloved hand. Gôkwad realized the impossibility of simply shaking it off. Even if his partner had grasped the creature from behind and pulled, their combined efforts would have served only to exhaust them. For that reason, he decided to relax. After a long wait, the determined animal finally released its hold on his hand. At this point, one may wonder why it was that the hunters did not do what would appear to have been expedient for the moment by simply killing the animal. The reason why Gôkwad did not destroy it was due to the unusual nature of the circumstances. It was a rare opportunity to witness firsthand and at a close range the animal's courage and strength of will in defending itself.[8] Furthermore, the event was a reminder for Gôkwad and his companion about the Anishinaabe tenet that places value in the life of even one animal and the role it plays in and for the world in which it lives. The incident compelled them to recognize the beaver's strength of character and preserve its life. Finally, it was a valuable form of learning for all who heard about it because it underscored the human's responsibility to honour the earth and its non-human creatures.

Dedibaayaanimanook knew that her father rarely brought home a beaver because he rarely caught an animal for which he had not set a trap. The entire Dedibayaash family was not in the habit of eating beaver meat. Most often it was a muskrat that Dedibaayaanimanook's father caught for food and for fur. As noted previously, one's personal vision dream provided guidance as to whether certain animals were to be avoided as food. Dedibaayaanimanook's father, for instance, did not eat the meat of a male caribou as a result of an instruction that came to him in a dream. For the same reason, her uncle Mooniyaans Thomas shunned porcupine meat, and her paternal grandmother Nookom did not consume pork. So powerful were these dreams that anyone who ate proscribed foods risked illness, insanity and even death. In fact, it was the accidental consumption of a proscribed substance that caused the death of Dedibaayaanimanook's aunt Maajiigiizhigook Mary. But aside from that type of restriction, all wild animals were a potential source of food during Dedibaayaanimanook's early childhood in Namegosibiing. People did not need to be concerned that the meat was in any way contaminated by what the animals ate because people's activities did not result in harm to the health of the air, land or water, and the animals flourished freely and healthily within the natural system of their respective habitats.

Since the era of Dedibaayaanimanook's people, however, another system of stewardship took over the homeland, and the situation changed drastically. For example, rabbits and hares have learned to live in urban-like settings such as Red Lake. But Anishinaabe knowledge would advise that such creatures are unfit for human consumption due to the contamination of their food sources by the various chemical poisons applied to plants. Even wild animals of what remains of the former boreal forests of Dedibaayaanimanook's homelands are no longer healthy as they were when her people were the sole managers. The Ontario Ministry of Natural Resources (OMNR) formed partnerships with private corporations to spray herbicides and other forms of chemicals on vast tracts of forest in order to control or eliminate vegetation deemed to compete with species harvested by the logging companies.[9] During those early pre-OMNR days, Namegosibiing supplied the people's needs, both spiritual and physical, and being the place of their home, it supported their customs, culture and world view. For their part, Namegosibii Anishinaabe harvesters and hunters together with their families pursued their vocational activities with a degree of care and deference that contrasted noticeably with the methods that were introduced into their homelands by the wemiti-goozhiwag.

1. Memegweshi Zaa'igan, Mamakwash Lake, is northeast of Namegosibiing.

2. Niki Zaa'igan, accurately translated as Goose Lake, is north of Memegweshi Zaa'igan; both lakes are part of the Berens River system.

3. Gaamangadikamegokaang (Where the Large Whitefish Live) is somewhere northeast of Namegosibiing.

4. Problems with merchandise in general could be traceable to such factors as the quality of material used in manufactured goods, quality of workmanship and cost reduction efforts. In the early 1600s, the iron used in a pair of falconets (small cannons) became so brittle in the cold weather that they malfunctioned. At one time guns, gunpowder and flints provided by the Hudson's Bay Company were not of the same standard as those of the French. See Elizabeth Mancke's monograph titled "A Company of Businessmen: The Hudson's Bay Company and Long-Distance Trade, 1670-1730," p. 55.

5. The meaning of "Gijigaa'ajoosh" is unknown; a ma'iinganens is a coyote. The term can also refer to a small wolf.

6. Bizhiwi Zaa'igan is now referred to as Cat Lake; however, the correct translation is Lynx Lake.

7. Ogimaawinini is literally, the leader or "boss man."

8. As a recent example of the beaver's ability to survive, a family of the animals continues to live in the Seine River within the city limits of Winnipeg in South St. Vital where old growth forests along the river banks are protected in their natural state. Anishinaabe wisdom cautions anyone who may suddenly happen upon a beaver along the trail. The best thing would be to back away and allow the animal sufficient space and time to escape into the water.

9. Ontario's policies have resulted in the transformation of boreal forests into gigantic tree farms that benefit logging companies. OMNR officials have largely disregarded concerns for bio-diversity.

CHAPTER 6

Gaagii'ikidoj Nimishoomis

~

As My Grandfather Predicted

One cold day in January of 1939, a small aircraft proceeded northeast, purposefully toward Namegosibiing. It flew over Bizhiwi Minis Cat Island,[1] then traced a wide circle above Ma'iingani Minis Wolf Island before making a gradual descent. After a bumpy touchdown, the craft taxied to a stop just off the western shore of the island. A passenger jerked the handle downward and the door of the plane opened. As he alighted, the compacted snow crunched stridently beneath his boots. He glanced briefly at the large island in front of him, then directed his gaze toward the lake's northern regions. A sudden gust of wind struck forcefully against his naked face, and blinking the freezing tears from his pale gray eyes, he tried to distinguish island from main shore. The wemitigoozhi could see no signs of life other than the trees. From where he stood, the entire landscape appeared uniformly untouched.

At that moment, but many miles to the north, an Anishinaabe man stopped from his work. Dedibaayaanimanook's father searched the southern horizon from his vantage point at Jiibaayi Zaagiing Jackfish Bay. Dedibayaash wondered whether it was indeed the sound of an airplane he had just heard from off in the distance. But others later concurred that they too heard a faint drone from the general direction of Negiishkensikaang on Ma'iingani Minis. After Dedibayaash and the others ended their brief discussion, a contingency set out across the lake to see what could possibly have been the reason for a plane to land at Ma'iingani Minis. Dedibaayaanimanook too was rather curious about the matter. She was just three months short of her seventeenth birthday. Hours later, the investigators returned with their findings.

"Amii'i wii' giigooyikaadeg gi Namegosibiiminaan!" was their stunning announcement. It sent shock waves throughout the community as people immediately absorbed its meaning. Years earlier, Dedibaaya-animanook's grandfather Giizhik Sam Keesick had talked about a time when wemitigoozhiwag, the white men, would arrive within their midst. The plane's landing at Ma'iingani Minis that January day in 1939, signalled the beginning of his prediction's fulfillment. Having procured a license to begin harvesting Namegosibiing's fish, these wemitigoozhiwag were in fact fishers who had just unloaded a plane full of gear at the island. The people's home was about to be commercially fished.

Not long after the arrival of the foreigners, people decided to move away from Ma'iingani Minis. They had chosen to set up a winter camp on a tiny island toward a more westerly part of the lake, close to Oshedinaang Trout Lake Ridge. But the wemitigoozhiwag were not destined to remain there for long either. Due to an unfortunate turn of events, their little cabin, along with all of its contents, burned to the ground. Although no one was injured, it was a setback for the partners, and they were once again in search of a new camp site. They had already seen an island in the north central region of the lake, but not lying directly in the path of the Namegosibii Anishinaabegs' usual comings and goings, it had no name. Not all the islands of Namegosibiing had names. In fact, there were only a few that did. For their purposes, however, the arrivals' final choice was ideal in terms of shape, size, prevailing winds and directional orientation. The bay was a perfect size for planes to land and take off. Although their camp faced northeast, a closely situated chain of islands formed a protective barrier that broke the immediate impact of the northerly winds. In addition, the island was not too far from the travel routes that the

Namegosibii Anishinaabe people most often used. Before long, the wemitigoozhiwag began referring to the island on which they now lived as Camp Island and it soon became "theirs."

Over the next several weeks, the people of Namegosibiing ventured across the lake to have a look at the fishers. Dedibaayaanimanook's two brothers Jiins Charlie Angeconeb and Jiibwaat Edward Angeconeb, as well others, visited Giigooyikewinini[2] and made their acquaintance. With the exception of Naadowe Robert, who was now residing in Osh-kaandagaawi Zaa'igan Nungesser Lake, all of Dedibaayaanimanook's uncles eventually met the man on at least one occasion. Later that same winter, Naadowe Robert expressed a desire to see Namegosibiing one last time while he was still able to make such a journey. Upon hearing that his elder brother was planning to visit, Dedibaayaanimanook's father began immediately to make preparations for a shaking tent ceremony. Dedibayaash wanted to be sure that Naadow's final visit would be celebrated and remembered. Jôjens and Jiimis, two of Dedibaayaanimanook's cousins, went to Oshkaandagaawi Zaa'igan to bring their father to Namegosibiing. Since the arrival of Giigooyikewinini was the topic of everyone's conversation, Naadowe heard a great deal about the newcomer, but he would not personally meet the wemitigoozhi who now claimed Namegosibiing to be his home.

Jiiyaan Donald Keesick was one of the first of Dedibaayaanimanook's uncles to cross the frozen lake to Camp Island. "Ezhi niiskiingwej e'waabamishij!" was how Jiiyaan described his first encounter with Giigooyikewinini, the one evidently in charge of the operation. The wemitigoozhi had paused from his work when Jiiyaan approached, and as they stood facing each other, Jiiyaan could not help being taken aback by the paleness of the stranger's blue-gray eyes. He also noticed that the newcomer looked him over quite thoroughly, then made a slight face and shook his head. It seemed an odd way to greet a visitor, but as Jiiyaan surmised with a chuckle, something about his appearance apparently did not sit too well with the man. Perhaps it was a reaction to the fact that Jiiyaan was in the habit of wearing his garments until they were beyond well worn so that, at any given time, his clothes were liable to be in a tattered and threadbare condition. The entire Jiiyaan family usually managed without a whole lot of material possessions. Although he and his wife Maagii Maggie always wore some type of footwear, there were times when their children had no shoes whatsoever. Dedibaayaanimanook remembered that her young cousins made a habit of darting across the snow in their bare feet for a visit, usually arriving during mealtime. They stood by the door and huddled together for warmth, watching in silence while Dedibaayaanimanook and her family ate until Dedibayaash handed them each a sandwich. The youngsters then returned home as quickly as they had come. The Jiiyaan family's lack was evidence of times when their shortages were particularly acute.

"Gigozimin iidog!" Dedibaayaanimanook recalled the time that her uncle and his family were preparing for a long journey, but this time, the Jiiyaan children were all seen with shoes. Upon hearing someone making a comment about their footwear, one of youngsters exclaimed that they were, after all, moving. It was quite possibly the child's way of inferring that it should have been obvious to anyone that they would wear shoes for such special events as a journey. Perhaps, too, there was an element of similarity in the way people reacted to the children and how Giigooyikewinini demonstrated his understanding of Jiiyaan's state of well-being.

A few days after Jiiyaan's return from Camp Island, others ventured forth to make an acquaintance. Depending on the time of day, Giigooyikewinini could be out on the lake lifting nets with his fishing partners or at home repairing dog harnesses, cleaning and filling naphtha lanterns, de-icing sleigh runners or sharpening ice bars, fish hooks and various other implements. At other times, visitors were liable to find him hammering fish boxes together, mending nets or preoccupied with other similar types of maintenance work. Then one day, people learned that the operation, which had originally been set up as a partnership, was dissolved and Giigooyikewinini's partners were gone. He was left on his own and in need of help, and for that reason, Dedibaayaanimanook's two brothers decided to work for him. Thus began a close association with the wemitigoozhi. One of their first observations was that he seemed to be settling well enough into his new environment that he would probably make a success of his fishing venture. It seemed very likely to them that he would be staying. Another interesting bit of observation was that Giigooyikewinini kept endless records about practically everything. He not only wrote down the fish that were caught, who worked for him, when planes came in, what supplies arrived and much more, he also entered a brief summary of each day's events into a journal. Tiny notations about weather conditions and other miscellany were written every day on a calendar that hung from a nail in the wall next to the kitchen table. It was evident that Giigooyikewinini was meticulous and well organized.

Just as they did every year at that time, Dedibaayaanimanook's parents and relatives sorted their gear, setting aside everything they would not need until their return in autumn. Dedibayaash bundled all the family's winter equipment in canvas and cached it away. Earlier that spring, he had purchased a small outboard motor, and they needed gasoline before leaving for Lac Seul. Jiins had just shot a moose, and with plenty of food to share, he decided to visit Camp Island and barter fresh meat for a supply of gasoline. "Wiijiiwishinaan isa, Ikwezens!"[3] When Jiins and Jiibwaat invited her, Dedibaayaanimanook decided to accept their invitation and accompany them to Camp Island. It was the first time she ever saw the one who was now making a substantial impact on the affairs of the community. The three returned, and the family was ready to set out. Keeping to the most direct route took them to the western shores of Ma'iingani Minis where they stopped to rest. Surveying the logs, tree stumps, clearings and other signs of occupation where Giigooyikewinini and his mates had first lived, they were reminded that wemtigoozhiwag were now living in Namegosibiing. They thought about all the changes that had been set in motion that winter, and they continued their journey, following the familiar old landmarks that took them through a maze of islands and reefs toward Gojijiwaawangaang. As Namegosibiing disappeared from view, Dedibaayaanimanook tried to ignore her longing to stay.

The Keesicks pitched camp where they had always done before, across the channel from the traditional cemetery at Gojijiwaawangaang. They resolved to carry on with the ancient ways they had learned from those at whose final resting place they briefly paused. Although there was no way they would have known at the time, the location would become a special place of burial some 50 years later. Then Dedibaayaanimanook's father planted several rows of potatoes in the sandy soil at the top of the hill that sloped toward the rising sun. After that, they resumed their journey south.

The people of Namegosibiing did not know of anyone inhabiting their homeland during the summer months. Had others been using the lake in their absence, they would have certainly known. From now on, however, that would all change because the unthinkable had finally happened. Wemitigoozhiwag were occupying Namegosibiing, year round. They continued on, across the shallow waters of Aanziko Zaa'igan Otter Lake, through the passageway that took them south, then northeast into Namegosibiishishiing Little Trout Lake. They crossed the lake, stopping for lunch on the northern shoreline before proceeding toward the headwaters of Namegosi Ziibi Trout (Lake) River. Once again, they embarked on their down river journey to spend a busy summer in Obizhigokaang Lac Seul. However, Namegosibiing was never far from Dedibaayaanimanook's thoughts.

When the nights began to feel cool again and autumn's colors took on a subtle appearance, Dedibaayaanimanook and her parents did not prepare for their journey home as expected. Instead, they made arrangements for an extended stay that would last for nearly a year and a half. Their decision not to return home came as a result of Dedibaayaanimanook's (half) brother's illness. Minzhinawebines Sam Keesick's legs had turned dark and swollen to twice normal size even though the rest of his body remained emaciated. He was left with little mobility, and he suffered from terrible pain. It was in order to be with Minzhinawebines and help care for him that the Dedibayaashes decided to stay in Obizhigokaang Lac Seul that winter. They shared accommodations with the Maashkizhiigan family in Kejick Bay. One evening, family members organized a special dance in order to entertain their ailing brother. Then just before Christmas, Dedibaayaanimanook and Aaniz (Minzhinawebines's wife, "Gookom" Alice Brisket Keesick) set out for a brief visit to Pelican residential school. They wanted to spend Christmas Day with Niksaandan,[4] Gichi Jôj and the others who were there attending school. Just a year previously, the Lac Seul Hudson's Bay Company postmaster had written a note in his daily log about a group of Lac Seul Anishinaabeg who were heading "off to Pelican School to visit their children - 25 sleighs!"[5] Dedibaayaanimanook and Aaniz did not take a sleigh, however. They walked the entire journey and stayed at the boarding school. After Christmas, they began their walk back to Kejick Bay. A short while into their journey, they became aware of being followed, and when they looked around, they saw three figures skating rapidly toward them. Taking advantage of the snowless ice, the skaters were community members on their way to Diitibisewinigamiing Hudson. The five then decided on a contest to see who would arrive home first, the two taking a direct route on foot or the three skaters taking a much more circuitous course. Not long after the skaters left, a vehicle drove up to Dedibaayaanimanook and Aaniz. Someone they knew, a person who purchased blueberries from the Dedibayaash family, offered to drive them as far as Gaagaki-iwemog.[6] The two felt a twinge of guilt, sure that they would win the bet with their friends. When they reached Kejick Bay, however, Dedibaayaanimanook noticed a circle with a message written in the snow. A stick was positioned upright in the center and a radius drawn on the circle similar to a clock. Dedibaayaanimanook and Aaniz read the note. "Amii'owe apii gaagii'dagoshinaan." The radius indicated the stick's shadow when the skaters reached home—several hours before Dedibaayaanimanook and Aaniz's. Nothing was ever a sure thing!

Although Dedibaayaanimanook and her parents did not go home to Namegosibiing that fall, other members of the family did. Her brother Jiins and her cousin Gwiiwish Isaac Keesick went as far as Gojijiwaawangaang where they harvested the potatoes Dedibayaash had planted that spring. Jiins and Gwiiwish had finished setting up camp and were readying their equipment for the coming winter when they were surprised by the sound of knocking one late afternoon. Wondering who could possibly be in the area at that time of the year—just before freeze-up—and at that time of day, Jiins opened the door. There stood Giigooyikewinini. He had come the distance across the rough stretch of water for food because the cook at Camp Island had apparently miscalculated when he wrote up their grocery order. When Giigooyikewinini explained that another plane was not due into Namegosibiing with fresh supplies until after freeze-up, the two cousins exchanged several pounds of potatoes for the lantern fuel Giigooyikewinini had brought along to barter. Jiins and Gwiiwish remained in Namegosibiing that winter, harvesting furs from the southern regions of the lake. They travelled to Ginebigo Baawitig Ear Falls and back to Obizhigokaang Lac Seul several times in order to keep in touch with Dedibaayaanimanook and other family members and friends. Then in March, 1940, Minzhinawebines Sam Keesick died. He had suffered from his illness for many long months.

One day in early spring, Dedibaayaanimanook joined her mother for a walk along the shoreline of Lac Seul Lake where snow had begun to recede in the season's warmth. The song of a bird caught their attention, and as Dedibaayaanimanook stopped to look up, she felt a stab of pain behind her eyes. Even though she was given several different natural medicines, she was unable to rest. Her mother kept all the windows covered, and one day, Dedibaayaanimanook's pain became bearable again. But it was several more days before the sickness relented enough for a complete night's sleep. Soon after, the lake opened, and the Keesicks canoed north, past Gojijiing, then Otawagi Baawitig and on to Ginebigo Baawitig Snake Falls on the Chukuni River. They reached Wanamani Zaa'iganing Red Lake where they remained for several weeks. With the municipality continuing to grow, more and more relatives began to spend time in the area, drawn by the prospects of employment. Mine related work was dangerous and very unpleasant, but people needed wages to live because their hunting and trapping activities no longer seemed sufficient. Employers simply had no interest in providing Anishinaabe people with what is known today as meaningful employment. And so the people lived clustered together in their little settlement that was located across the bay from downtown, making the most of their circumstances. When the Keesicks were in town, Dedibaayaanimanook, Niingaanaashiik Mary, Ishkwe, Ginôk Eliza and Bejii Betsy were occasionally allowed to attend the town's latest attraction, the picture shows. The young girls had become fans of an actor they called Gaaginôbikiingwej,[7] and as they hurried along the trail to town, they hoped they were lucky enough to see another Humphrey Bogart movie. The silver screen was such a popular form of entertainment, in fact, that even Dedibaayaanimanook's parents enjoyed an occasional show.

One day, Dedibaayaanimanook and her niece Bejii Betsy were on their way to town when a deer suddenly bounded into the water close by. As it swam away, the two girls raced home and launched a canoe quickly enough to catch up to the deer before it reached the shores of the island. Both were experienced canoeists, so it was without the least hesitation that Dedibaayaanimanook leaned over and proceeded to drown the animal, much like the man she once saw in Lac Seul who also caught a deer in the same way. That evening, Dedibaayaani-manook and Bejii did not go to the movies. Instead, they helped to distribute fresh deer meat to the villagers, and thanks to their fearless action, their parents were able to enjoy deer stew for the next few days. Dedibaayaanimanook would later learn that she and Bejii had been the topic of conversation among the Anishinaabe people of Red Lake. Several community members visiting together downtown had looked across the bay and watched as the remarkable event unfolded.

It was not until the fall of 1940 that the Dedibayaashes were able to return to Namegosibiing. Dedibaayaanimanook too was curious to see how Giigooyikewinini had been managing during their fifteen months' absence—one of the longest periods she was ever away. Because her brother Jiins and her cousin Jiimis James were working for Giigooyikewinini, the families took up a residence at Camp Island that winter. Early one morning, toward the end of March, they awakened to the exuberant calls of a crow. The bird's call signaling spring's return, it was time to begin preparations for the first phase of another journey down the river. Dedibaayaanimanook and her family were completing the last of their packing when her mother glanced out the window and noticed that Giigooyikewinini was out on the ice hitching his sled dogs. But she thought no more of it. When Giigooyikewinini came to the door asking for their luggage, however, she realized they were about to get help with their move. The convoy of sleds was nearly half way to Gojijiwaawangaang within a very short time because the warm temperatures had melted away the top layers of snow, allowing the metal strips of Giigooyikewinini's sled runners to glide effortlessly across the ice. Sitting next to her mother on one of her father's sleds, Dedibaayaanimanook could see Manidoo Minis, the island where her grandfather, father, uncles, some aunts and cousins had gone to find their life's vision as young children. Seagull Island, as it was now called by the wemitigoozhiwag, was a tiny speck to their right as they neared the southwestern point of Negiishkensikaang on Ma'iingani Minis. As they continued along, Giigooyikewinini periodically stopped to offer Dedibaayaanimanook's parents a few sips of the brew he had brought along. Her mother declined, but Dedibayaash accepted. They were continuing to make excellent progress when a small object appeared on the horizon toward the southeast. It seemed to be approaching. In fact, it was Dedibaayaanimanook's cousin Detaginang Frank Keesick, his wife Gichi Jen and their children.

"Haw, haw! Gee, gee!" They could hear Detaginang calling out, but because those who were travelling in Dedibaayaanimanook's group included her cousin Jiimis and his wife Jii, they could not help but wonder why he seemed to be calling out for Jii. As soon as the travellers cleared up the misunderstanding arising from Detaginang's dog commands, they resumed their journey together. The Keesicks reached their intended destination, and after thanking Giigooyikewinini for his help, they bid him farewell. But instead of leaving right

away, Giigooyikewinini paused for several long moments, as though waiting for something to happen. Finally, he took his leave and vanished toward the north.[8]

"Giigooyikewininiwag biizhaawag!" One chilly pre-freeze up morning, after about six months had passed, the large gray fishing boat from Camp Island came into view at Jiibayi Zaagiing where the Keesicks had settled upon returning from Obizhigokaang Lac Seul. They heared that Giigooyikewinini had dispatched the two men, Pete and the English cook, to find Jiins. Thinking that a facility close to where the Dedibayaash Keesicks were living made good sense, Giigooyikewinini apparently wanted Jiins and Jiibwaat to build a fish house at Jiibayi Zaagiing. It was not known why, but beyond a little patch that was cleared away near the mouth of the creek that trickles into the bay, his plans never materialized. Over the course of time, Giigooyikewinini began to hire others, including Scandinavians from Red Lake. Hjalmar Fridvald, Hans Emrikson and Ben Johnson were some of the individuals who worked at Camp Island with Dedibaayaanimanook's family members. Giigooyikewinini was also in the habit of hiring the occasional vagrant he came across while in town on business. This included a young wemitigoozhi by the name of Jack Machura. Although he was a heavy drinker, Jack was a reliable worker while he was in Namegosibiing, where there was no alcohol for him to consume. Nonetheless, people could not help but notice that something about Azhashki—the name they gave him—was not quite right. It may have been the effects of his addiction to alcohol that they saw. A couple of years later, they heard that Jack Machura had been hanged, but the story was hard to believe considering how harmless he had seemed.

Among Dedibaayaanimanook's relatives who took up work for Giigooyikewinini at one time or another were Jiins Charlie, Jiibwaat Edward, Niksaandan George, Aanig Alec Keesick, Gichi Jôj George Trout, Gwiiwish Isaac Keesick, Jiimis James and later on, Bezhigoobines Frank King. Dedibaayaanimanook's cousin Jôjens George Keesick worked once or twice, including a couple of days one spring when he helped to lift ice. He and his family lived across the bay with Jiins's family. During the winter months, Dedibaayaanimanook's cousin Detaginang Frank Keesick had a type of sub-contracting arrangement with Giigooyikewinini that was based at his home at Gaaminitigwashkiigaag. Detaginang used the fishing equipment furnished by Giigooyike Ogimaa, the name by which the Detaginangs referred to Giigooyikewinini, and from time to time, someone arrived from Camp Island with a dog team to pick up Detaginang's catch. But Giigooyikewinini himself came only once or twice. As for others of Dedibaayaanimanook's relatives, they found that working at Camp Island provided them with the opportunity to supplement their trapping income without having to leave Namegosibiing. The work needed doing, so taking it on themselves meant that fewer outsiders needed to be brought in. However, accepting paid work necessarily meant having to give up many customs, including the annual journeys to Lac Seul. In due course, treaty annuity payments were made available in Wanamani Zaa'iganing Red Lake, thus making the trips to attend Treaty Time less necessary.

The work at Camp Island required taking up ice during the early days of April in preparation for the coming summer season. The thickness of the ice determined what amount needed to be cut. First, Giigooyikewinini took measurements, then Jiins and Jiibwaat cleared away the snow. They manually sawed the ice into dozens of chunks approximately eight cubic feet in volume. With the use of a series of pulleys and Giigooyikewinini's dog team, the blocks of ice were drawn from the water and up a ramp into the ice house where they were arranged in rows several tiers high. They were then covered over with thick layers of sawdust. Later, when Giigooyikewinini was better equipped, taking up ice became less strenuous with the use of a motor that not only cut the ice with a circular blade but provided energy for hauling the blocks into the ice house. The entire task of taking up ice usually took four or five days, depending on the number of people working on the project. One year, a worker lost his balance and fell into the icy water. Although he was quickly fished out, the Englishman—whom Giigooyikewinini had hired on as a cook—was chilled to the bone. Dedibaayaanimanook's relatives recalled how

their grandfather Giizhik had once assured them that there would be
no drownings in Namegosibiing. Dedibaayaanimanook's two brothers also helped Giigooyikewinini to build an L-shaped dock on the
western shore of the bay where the fishing camp was situated. They
also constructed a fish house, a warehouse and the Little Kitchen, a
tiny cabin in which another hired cook, Hans Emrikson, prepared
meals. Jiins and Jiibwaat helped with the cabin that came to be
known as Little John House, or Jônigamigong. It was named after the
diminutive John Forslyn, another Scandinavian whom Giigooyikewinini employed. Since Giigooyikewinini had immediately noticed that
Dedibaayaanimanook's brother was a gifted wood worker, Jiins had a
hand in almost all the building projects at Camp Island. Other relatives were hired for tasks such as setting and lifting nets and dressing
and packing fish.

With Dedibaayaanimanook's family and relatives now spending
so much time at Camp Island, they were soon able to piece together
the story of Giigooyikewinini. They had good reason for their interest in who he was. As the first wemitigoozhi to settle permanently
within their midst, he fulfilled the prediction of Dedibaayanimanook's
grandfather. His arrival was therefore a historic event that, for better
or worse, marked the beginning of profound changes in the people's
affairs. A few years later, people would have another reason for caring
about who he was.

Giigooyikewinini's story began with the information that his father,
Anton Olsen, was born in Spydeberg, Østfold county, Norway, in
1848. Anton became a foreman at a textile mill known as Hjula
Væveri. On May 25th, 1919, he died of cancer at Ullevaal Hospital
in Oslo. Giigooyikewinini's mother, Karen (nee Larsen), was born in
1854 in Næss Romerik, Akershus county, Norway. She passed away
on January 3rd, 1929 at the age of seventy-five. People also heard
that Giigooyikewinini had five siblings. All of the Olsen children were
born and raised in Oslo. His sister Sigrid was born on October 25th,
1885; Alvilde, on August 23rd, 1887; and Margit, December 23rd,
1890. His only brother, Albert, was born in 1893. Giigooyikewinini's

mother was forty-five years old when he was born on May 2, 1899[9] and given the name Einar. Many years later, one of his daughters would travel to Norway and visit the ornate Lutheran cathedral in which he was christened as an infant and confirmed at the age of thirteen. He accompanied his father on overnight trips to pick berries when he was a child. When they returned home from one of their first outings together, his father unpacked his backpack, only to find that much of their fruit had been crushed during their walk home. However, his mother was able to salvage the berries by using them for juice that she served periodically throughout the winter. During grade school, Giigooyikewinini earned a tiny wage by working at a bakery where he was required to carry flour sacks up the stairs. Some of them weighed as much as fifty pounds. As was the custom for those who completed school but were not contemplating university, he left home to make his own way in life at the age of fourteen.

Giigooyikewinini joined a crew of whalers, travelling to different places around the globe to hunt and harvest the giant marine mammals. Later, he signed on with one of the world's largest fleet of commercial ships, the Norwegian merchant marine. He frequented exotic places and distant port cities that included South Georgia, the Canary Islands and Buenos Aires. By that time, World War I was nearing its final year. Germany had decided to gamble that Britain would surrender before the U.S. entered the war. With the aim to starve Britain into submission by cutting off all supplies into the island nation, the Germans announced to the world in January, 1917, that they would resume sinking all ships associated with Allied ports anywhere on the high seas. Accordingly, Germany began a concerted u-boat campaign on February 1st, 1917, attacking and destroying merchant ships in unprecedented numbers. Terror and havoc reigned over the North Atlantic. By the war's end in 1918, nearly half of the entire Norwegian merchant fleet would be obliterated.

The SS *Homer* was built in 1895 by Sir Raylton Dixon of Middlesborough, England, for the Lamport & Holt Line/Liverpool, Brazil and River Plate Steam Navigation Co. In 1912, the ship was sold to

Uribe y Eguiraun, Montevideo, Uruguay, and renamed the *Odila*.[10]
Olaf Fretheim Olsen of Bergen, Norway, then purchased the *Odila*
in 1915 and changed the ship's name to *Solbakkens*.[11] On January 3rd,
1917, the 310-foot *Solbakkens*, 2585 gross registered tonnage, set out
from the port city of Buenos Aires, Argentina. Destined for Cher-
bourg, France, the vessel carried approximately four thousand tons of
wheat. A Norwegian flag fluttered from the flagstaff. Among the crew
members was Giigooyikewinini Einar Olsen. As a stoker, his task was
to shovel coal for the steam turbines that powered the ship's engines.
The *Solbakkens* crossed the Atlantic in just over two weeks, making a
first stop at San Vincent to pick up a load of coal, before proceeding
on to Santa Cruz de Tenerife of the Spanish owned Canary Islands on
January 20th. For the next several days, the *Solbakkens* plied steadily
northward, beyond Portugal, Spain and the Bay of Biscay—well into
the North Atlantic. It had not been that long since the Germans'
dreaded declaration. Nearing its final destination, the Norwegian ship
would soon be entering the southwestern English Channel. A little
French island known as Ouessant lay just ahead. This entire area was
known to be treacherous and stormy to navigate, particularly during
winter.

Sunday, February 4th, 1917, was a clear day with high seas and
a steady wind. The *Solbakkens* was now approximately sixty nautical
miles from Brest. Around 1:00 p.m. the crew members were startled
by a warning shot. A German submarine prowling the region had
sighted the *Solbakkens*. It was the UC 24, one of nine submarines (UC
16 to UC 24) of the coastal minelayer class built by Blohm and Voss
of Hamburg. Other classes included ocean minelayers, u-cruisers,
merchant u-boats and coastal torpedo attack boats. The primary
function of these u-boats was to seek and destroy merchant ships,
particularly those supplying Britain. UC 24 had been launched nearly
a year earlier on March 4, 1916, and commissioned five months later.
Having completed a mission off the British coast, the u-boat had just

left Helgoland on January 31st for a second patrol and was now heading toward Bocche di Cattaro in the Adriatic. The crew numbered twenty-six men, including Kapitänleutnant Kurt Willich.

Upon heeding the warning to stop, the *Solbakkens'* crew members were told to take provisions, then ordered into lifeboats. The Germans confiscated all documents, then placed an explosive on each end of the ship's hull. Giigooyikewini and thirteen others climbed into one of the two lifeboats about to be towed by the submarine. The ship's captain and the rest of the crew were on board the other. At around midnight, UC 24 cut them loose. They estimated their location to be around twenty nautical miles from Brest. The sea was heavy and the air, bitterly cold. A strong wind was blowing from an east-north-easterly direction. Soon after he shouted out their course, the captain and those in his lifeboat disappeared into the darkness and were never seen again. The lifeboat in which Giigooyikewinini and his mates took refuge was so leaky, three men were required to bail continuously. Otherwise, all would have sunk within minutes. With no matches, they were unable to light the lanterns. The mast did not fit properly. The sail had rotted and was full of holes. Without a functioning sail, they were unable to continue shoreward. Instead, they drifted back across the Bay of Biscay. During their first day adrift, a hailstorm struck. Although Giigooikewinini had brought along blankets from the *Solbakkens*, they were soaked through and rendered useless. They and all other extraneous weight had to be thrown overboard.

During those days barely afloat in their lifeboat, the men endured unimaginable horrors as they attempted to cope with the distress of their plight. The death throes of mates; the harsh elements without protective gear, medication, food or fresh water; the stress of never knowing whether they would reach land before succumbing to the sea's dreadful embrace; exhaustion from continuous bailing; lack of sleep. But as each day passed, their greatest torment became their craving to drink. One man became deranged while another was so desperate to quench his thirst that he drank the salt water, despite efforts to stop him. He died an agonizing death. There was a time when Giigooyikewinini tried to assuage his thirst by attempting to drink his own blood. It was a nightmare with no means of escape. Then, on February 8th, 1917, Giigooyikewinini and ten other survivors landed on the beaches of San Lorenzo in Gijón, Spain. But their lower extremities were raw from the salt water, and they were not able to walk. Some crawled, others were carried ashore.[12] But another obstacle awaited them. Due to their appearance and because of their state of semi-delirium, the men were mistaken for derelicts, then—even more dangerously—for Germans. They had no papers to substantiate their story. Despite these odds, however, Giigooyikewinini and his mates managed to make themselves understood, and they were immediately taken to a nearby hospital.

In Kristiania (Oslo)[13] Norway, Anton and Karen Olsen received a telegram from Herr Olaf Fretheim Olsen, the ship owner in Bergen. The message, dated February 16th, 1917, informed them that the *Solbakkens* had been sunk. Although their son's condition was stated as unknown, the consul in Gijón had relayed the information that he was indeed alive. The Olsens could do little more than hope, as they waited for further news. At the cathedral where he had been christened and confirmed, they prayed. Meanwhile, the survivors were treated for exposure, severe dehydration, the effects of prolonged contact with salt water and other sustained injuries. But by March 5th, 1917, they were well enough to testify before General Consul Johannes K. Sømme at the Norwegian General Consulate in Bilbao. Four weeks after the first telegram, another one arrived at Kristiania. This one, dated March 16th, 1917 gave Anton and Karen Olsen the news that their son had been one of the most severely injured of the survivors. But they were greatly encouraged to read that arrangements were underway for his return to Norway. Giigooyikewinini and his mates learned functional Spanish during their stay in Spain. Two of his mates found Spain to their liking and decided to stay. Eventually, they married young women from the area. But Giigooyikewinini longed for his homeland. Thus, on May 20th, 1917, three weeks after

his eighteenth birthday and three and a half months after the sinking of the *Solbakkens*, he embarked on his journey home. The British
consulate in the Spanish port city of Bilbao issued him a ten day visa to
travel to Britain by way of France, and on May 21st, he received con-
firmation from the French vice-consulate for a layover at St. Lazare.
Five days later, Giigooyikewinini had his visa stamped by the Sûrété
Generale at the Gare St. Lazare in France, then on the 29th, the Norsk
Generalkonsulat in London provided him with validation to proceed
to Newcastle-on-Tyne. On July 9th, the young Norwegian embarked
upon the final phase of his quest for repatriation.[14] Giigooyikewinini's
wrist did not heal properly because of the nature of his injury. As a
result, he was never able to bend his left wrist. Although he made a
good recovery, due mainly to his youthful stamina, the effects of his
ordeal would surface in the form of various ailments throughout the
latter years of his life.

What became of Germany's UC 24, the submarine that had
inflicted so much suffering, is worthy of note. On route to Cattaro,
the u-boat sank the *Ellavore* of Farsund, Norway, and the *Havgard* as
well as *Solbakkens*. Its third patrol, between April 11th and May 1st,
1917 took place in the vicinity of Sicily. Then, while leaving Cattaro
on May 24th to begin its fourth patrol, the u-boat was torpedoed by
the French *Circé*. Twenty-four crew, including commanding officer
Willich, were killed. During its brief career, UC 24 sank four ships
(excluding warships) for a total of nine thousand five hundred-six-
teen tons.[15] By way of comparison, German commanding officer
Kapitänleutnant Walther Schwieger sank forty-nine ships, including
the *Lusitania*. As for the French submarine that was named after
the Greek mythological enchantress who lived on an island in the
Mediterranean and turned men into beasts,[16] the *Circé* was sunk by
Austria's U 47 (formerly UB 47 of Germany) on September 20th,
1918, while cruising for enemy u-boats in the southern Adriatic. The
U 47 was given over to the French in 1920, and scrapped.[17]

Ten years after the destruction of *Solbakkens*, Giigooyikewinini decided to follow his sisters' footsteps and emigrate. His third class ticket

B47413, valued at 568.50 Kr., was stamped with the date October 18th, 1927, for passage on the SS *Stavangerfjord*. His destination was Kenora, Ontario, Canada, via Halifax. By that time, Giigooyikewinini was a young man of 28. In compliance with the Canadian Citizenship Act, he became naturalized on May 31st, 1935, four weeks after his 36th birthday. Of the six Olsen siblings, only the eldest, Albert, remained in Norway with his parents. The four Olsen sisters, Alvilda ("Hilde"), Sigrid, Astrid and Margit all emigrated to Canada, but their reasons for doing so are not known. Sigrid and Astrid lived in Winnipeg. Hilde married a young man by the name of Eric Martinsen, and Margit settled in Kenora with her husband Fred Blair, who was from the U.S. Giigooyikewinini would eventually lose all four sisters to breast cancer. He maintained a close contact with Margit, the sister who lived the longest, visiting her and writing frequently, despite Fred's attitude about Anishinaabe people. Margit died of breast cancer in 1969. Giigooyikewinini was employed with the railway for a period of time. After that, he took up commercial fishing on Shoal Lake and Lake of the Woods near Kenora in Northwest Ontario. While he was at Shoal Lake, he became friends with a certain Anishinaabe man who thought well enough of him that he offered him his daughter to marry. Giigooyikewinini, however, decided not to stay. Both lakes were becoming too crowded for his liking.

For a short while, he and his business partner, Gus Forslyn, fished in Wanamani Zaa'iganing Red Lake. It was during his time in Red Lake that Giigooyikewinini lost his balance and fell backwards as he attempted to loosen a fish box frozen to the ground. The fall damaged disks in his lower spine and he had to be transported to the hospital in a stretcher. From then on, Giigooyikewinini suffered from episodes of severe back pain. The two fishing partners applied for and obtained a commercial license that gave them entitlement to the fish in Namegosibiing Trout Lake.

By no means did Dedibaayaanimanook's people refuse to accept the wemitigoozhi into their community. Language, however, seemed to be a significant barrier against a closer relationship. Giigooyikewinini's speech carried a pronounced enough Norwegian accent that even those who spoke functional English found communicating with him difficult. In fact, some people first referred to him as Gaamayagi-taagoozij, the one who sounds foreign. For anyone not understanding the reason, it may have seemed odd that Giigooyikewinini would live among the people of Namegosibiing for nearly forty years without speaking any Anishinaabe beyond one or two words. When he first arrived, however, he made efforts to speak the people's language, but what they heard was so amusing they were unable to contain their laughter. There was no intent to belittle him, but Giigooyikewinini mistook their mirth for ridicule. From that time on, he gave up any further attempts at learning to speak the language, even though he came to understand it to some extent. A related aspect about Giigooyikewinini that people noticed was a hint of remoteness in his manner and a preference for solitude. His infrequent junkets to social-ize with community members were usually precipitated by home-made brew, but as time went on, he began to make more frequent jaunts across the frozen lake to visit with the Dedibayaash family at Jiibayi Zaagiing. Whenever other community members living at the Zaagiing heard that Giigooyikewinini had arrived, they hurried over and joined in the get-together. Dedibaayaanimanook's sister Gweyesh Annie in particular enjoyed the informal little gatherings in which Giigooyikewinini led the sing-alongs and accompanied himself on Dedibaayaanimanook's mother's water drum. One song that became a favourite of Dedibaayaanimanook's was called, "You Are My Sun-shine." It was a popular tune, and every time someone requested it, Giigooyikewinini seemed to sing it especially for her!

"Geyaabina bezhigo gishiimenzh?" After returning home from a day's work at Camp Island one evening later that winter, Jiins casually mentioned that Giigooyikewinini had asked whether his sister was still single. Such a query about Dedibaayaanimanook's marital status did not come as a complete surprise to family members because others, including an elderly man from Lac Seul, had already approached her father expressing a wish to marry her. She had felt immense relief when her father rejected their proposals, and other than what may have been, had Erik Anderson lived, she was satisfied with being single. This time, however, when Jiins's statement raised the subject of her singleness, Dedibaayaanimanook's reaction was different. In fact, his comment made her realize just how frequently Giigooyikewinini seemed to be in her thoughts. Most of her impressions about him were influenced by favourable opinions expressed by members of the family. For example, she knew that it was quite evident to everyone that physical work did not daunt him, and that his willingness to take on the hardships of life in Namegosibiing had struck an empathetic chord. Although people realized he had already acquired a great deal of knowledge and experience living on the land, they noted his genuine appreciation for all the information and know-how they had shared with him. Moreover, they perceived him to be sincere and trustworthy, unlike so many of the other wemitigoozhiwag they had come across, and they observed his courteous manner. It was apparently characteristic of what he referred to as the Old Country. "Bizhishig zhooniyaa e'izhimikawiwaaj!" It had long been the observation of Dedibaayaanimanook's people that wemitigoozhwag in general seemed consumed with the pursuit of money and the accumulation of material goods. The fact that Giigooyikewinini, on the other hand, remained largely unaffected by that kind of obsession, was extraordinary. In that regard alone, Giigooyikewinini stood well above the others. He had generally earned the people's respect, and despite his obvious shortcomings, they tended to feel kindly toward him.

As for Dedibaayaanimanook's own observations, she knew that Giigooyikewinini was much older than she. In fact, he was 23 years her senior. But in spite of that, she was drawn to his sense of humour and the gentleness she saw in his manner. Importantly, he showed respect toward her people that was uncommon for most other wemitigoozhiwag. Dedibaayaanimanook was certain enough about her family's good opinions of him that she was inclined not to resist her growing affection for Giigooyikewinini.

The spring of 1943 was over four years since the man from across the ocean first landed in Namegosibiing. Dedibaayaanimanook's parents and relatives were ready to leave for their journey south. This time, however, Dedibaayaanimanook was not with her family. Moshish, Gichi Jôj and other companions soon noticed the void in their lives, having spent so much time with her since childhood. Practically every event had included her, but now all their activities reminded them of her absence. At the age of 21, she had decided to spend the rest of her life with Giigooyikewinini Einar Olsen, and in so doing, she fulfilled the prediction her grandfather had made during her infancy.

1. Bizhiwi Minis, literally, Lynx Lake, has been incorrectly translated as Cat Island; it is the largest island in Namegosibiing.

2. Giigooyikewinini means Fisherman.

3. Ikwezens was Dedibaayaanimanook's more informal name used by family members and close friends. For the purposes of this narrative, however, Dedibaayaanimanook asked that her ceremonially given name be used.

4. Niksaandan George Keesick was one of Minzhinawebines and Aaniz's sons. When he became older, Niksaandan too began to have problems with his legs.

5. B107/a/33, Hudson's Bay Company Archives, Winnipeg, MB.

6. Gaagakiiwemog was an old reference to Whitefish Bay.

7. Gaaginôbikiingwej means the one with a long, angular face.

8. Many years later, Giigooyikewinini would tell Dedibaayaanimanook about his great disappointment when he had to go back to Camp Island without her that spring day.

9. Digitalarkivet. 1900-telling for 0301 Kristiania. June 11, 2005. <RHD: 1900-telling for 0301 Kristiania Digitalarkivet>.

10. Information provided by D. Asprey about the *Solbakkens'* previous names originated from D. Haws's Merchant Fleets, vol. 34, published by Shield Publications Ltd., Gateshead, England in1998. It was posted on the ships forum located at <http://warsailors.com/forum/read.php?1,20594,20599#msg-20599> in June 17, 2005 01:55 A.M.

11. In both his telegrams to the Olsens, O. Fretheim Olsen spelled the name of his ship with an "s", i.e., *Solbakkens*.

12. Sjoforklaringer Over Kirgsforliste Norske Skibe i 1917 (Sjøfartskontoret, Department of Trade and Industry, Government of Norway: Kristiania, 1917-1918), vol. 2, 124-130. This information was provided by archivist Arne Reed of the Norwegian national archives, Riksarkivaren, who took the time to send copies of the testimony (via regular mail) to Anita Olsen Harper who then made them available for this story.

13. Oslo was known as Kristiania from 1624 to 1925 in honour of King Kristian IV.

14. Giigooyikewinini's passport was stamped with these dates and place names.

15. Helgason, Gudmundur. The U-boats of World War One, 1914-1918. September 1, 2005. <uboat.net>.

16. The French named their submarines after sea creatures, precious stones, scientists, months of the First Republic calendar, as well as mythological characters.

17. Smith, Gordon. Navies and Fleets, 1914-1918. September 1, 2005.

<naval-history.net>.

Fig. 1 Giizhik Sam Keesick, Dedibaayaanimanook's paternal grandfather, patriarch of the Namegosibiing Trout Lake Keesicks (Courtesy Dedibaayaanimanook Sarah Olsen)

Fig. 2 Dedibaayaanimanook's father Dedibayaash William Keesick and her brother Jiibwaat Edward Angeconeb, on Chukuni River, 1940s
(Courtesy Dedibaayaanimanook Sarah Olsen)

Fig. 3 Dedibaayaanimanook's eldest paternal uncle Mooniyaans Thomas Keesick and his wife Maajiigiizhigook Mary (Courtesy Virginia Keesic)

Fig. 4 Njôy Margaret Anderson and her family, Frenchman's Head, Lac Seul adults, *left to right:* Njôy Margaret, Njôy's parents; children, back row, *second from left:* Eric, Njoy's eldest son; children, front row, *left to right:* Njôy's sibling (in cradleboard); Jack Bull; Jack's sister Skoob Josie Bull, daughter of Gôkodoons and Giiwijech Charlie Bull; Njôy's son Lawrence "Archie" Anderson (hands in pocket) (Courtesy Virginia Keesic)

Fig. 5 Njôy Anderson's parents, Mitigoons "Maada'ookiiwinini" Alec and Aanii Annie Sapay (Courtesy Virginia Keesic)

Fig. 6 The Akiwenz family, possibly at Treaty Time or Midewinaaniwan, Obizhigokaang Lac Seul *left to right:* John Akiwenz's mother; his father; John Akiwenz; his wife Banôna (Banwaana), Akandoo Matilda's half sister; Banôna's father Ojashinaake (Courtesy Virginia Keesic)

Fig. 7 *Left to right:* Zhashagiins Edward, Dedibaayaanimanook's cousin; Aazhawaj; Robert Wesley, Edaw's husband; unidentified wemitigoozhi; Charles Thomas, Fred Thomas's father, and De'igan's husband; Amanisookaan David Angeconeb, Garnet's father; Jijens Edward Bottle, Omagakii's father (Courtesy Virginia Keesic)

Fig. 8 A Keesick camp site, western main shore, Namegosibiing, mid-1930s *left to right:* Gichi Ikwe; Ginôk Eliza; Dedibaayaanimanook (Courtesy Dedibaayaaninamook Sarah Olsen)

Fig. 9a Near Aagimaako Baawitig on Chukuni River *left to right:* Dedibayaash; Bejii Betsy; Niiyoo Leo; Gweyesh Annie (holding infant); Dedibaayaanimanook; Gaamadweyaashiik; Gichi Jôj George Trout (Courtesy Virginia Keesic)

Fig. 9b Moshish Mary Keesick, Dedibaayaanimanook's cousin/sibling, around the early 1940s.

Fig. 10 Giigooyikewinini fished on Lake of the Woods before coming to Namegosibi-ing Trout Lake. (Courtesy Dedibaayaanimanook Sarah Olsen)

Fig. 11 Giigooyikewinini before he came to Namegosibiing. (Courtesy Dedibaayaanimanook Sarah Olsen)

Fig. 12 Giigooyikewinini's "Little Kitchen," soon after his arrival at Camp Island. (Courtesy Dedibaayaaninamook Sarah Olsen)

Fig. 13 Early 1940s, Camp Island, *left to right*: Dedibaayaanimanook's cousin Jiimis James, her mother Gaamadweyaashiik and her brother Jiins (Courtesy Dedibaayaanimanook Sarah Olsen)

Fig. 14 Camp Island, Namegosibiing, early 1940s: "Little kitchen" (tent); Jônigamigong (Little John House); fish house (Courtesy Dedibaayaanimanook Sarah Olsen)

Fig. 15 Giigooyikewinini shortly after arriving at Camp Island. (Courtesy Dedibaaya-animanook Sarah Olsen)

Fig. 16 Namegosibiing, early 1940s: Giigooyikewinini Einar Olsen
(Courtesy Dedibaayaanimanook Sarah Olsen)

Fig. 17 At Giigooyikewinini's house, Camp Island, circa 1940 *left to right*, standing:
Moshish Mary; Dedibaayaanimanook; Gaani, Jiins's wife; Moshishens *left to right*,
seated: Dedibaayaanimanook's cousin, Jiimis James; Giigooyikewinini; Dedibayaash
(Courtesy Dedibaayaanimanook Sarah Olsen)

Fig. 18 Camp Island, early 1940s, *left to right* Dedibayaash, Moshish, Dedibaayaani-manook, Jiimis James, Gaani Connie, Giigooyikewinini, Moshishens (Courtesy Dedibaayaanimanook Sarah Olsen)

Fig. 19 Hjalmar Fridvall, hired hand, with a trout, Camp Island. (Courtesy Dedibaayaanimanook Sarah Olsen)

Fig. 20 Camp Island, early 1940s: Flying boat bringing in supplies and taking out fish. (Courtesy Dedibaayaanimanook Sarah Olsen)

Fig. 21 Hjalmar Fridvall and Hans Emrikson, Giigooyikewinini's hired hands, at Camp Island. (Courtesy Dedibaayaanimanook Sarah Olsen)

Fig. 22 Fishing friends at Camp Island, early 1940s: Hans and Giigooyikewinini. (Courtesy Dedibaayaanimanook Sarah Olsen)

Fig. 23 Giigooyikewinini holding another large trout. Fish of that size were common when he first arrived in Namegosibiing Trout Lake. (Courtesy Dedibaayaanimanook Sarah Olsen)

Fig. 24 Camp Island, 1940s: Dedibaayaanimanook and her brother Jiins holding some of Giigooyikewinini's fox furs that she processed for him. (Courtesy Dedibaayaanimanook Sarah Olsen)

CHAPTER 7

Dedibaayaanimanook & Giigooyikewinini

~

Sarah and Einar

April 11th, 1943, appeared to be an ordinary spring day in Namegosibiing. In fact, it was anything but typical for Dedibaayaanimanook and
her family, because that was the day she left her parents for a new life
at Camp Island. She had given a lot of thought to her grandfather's
statement that she would grow up and marry a wemitigoozhi, and when
she finished the last of her packing, she had to restrain her excitement.
Just before her departure that day, however, her father spoke briefly to
her. "Gego gichi wiidigeken." He did not give any reasons, but perhaps
he was thinking about her Treaty rights[1] when he counselled her not
to legally marry Giigooyikwinini. "Gego gaye wiijiiwaaken giishpin
giiwej Agaamakiing." When he advised her not to go with him if he
ever decided to move back to the Old Country, Dedibayaash probably
reckoned that such a move would be a permanent separation from her
family and homeland, and would result in terrible hardship for her.

Although Dedibaayaanimanook was filled with anticipation about
the prospects of her new life, at that young an age, she could scarcely
have understood the magnitude of what she had tacitly agreed to. She
had undertaken much more than a change in living arrangements or
even household membership. In fact, she had consented to become
part of the wemitigoozhi's world, a place where foundational values,
world views, belief systems and practises were largely in contradiction
to those in which she was born and raised. From infancy, she had lived
in the protective embrace of her devoted parents, enjoying a close
companionship with siblings and relatives no matter where they lived.

But as soon as she embarked on life at Camp Island, she had to put it all behind. Her new home was a permanent location, and the adventure filled journeys along Namegosi Ziibi with family and friends were now a part of the past, nothing more than a collection of fond memories. Undoubtedly most upsetting of all was the change in how some of her friends and relatives seemed to regard her.

One day, just before the end of the season's fishing that spring, Giigooyikewinini invited her to accompany him and Jiins on a trip across the lake to collect a load of fish that her cousin Detaginang Frank had caught at Gaaminitigwashkiigaag Keesick Bay. Looking forward to spending time with her cousins and being back to where she had spent much of her childhood, Dedibaayaanimanook put on the new pair of ski pants and parka that Giigooyikewinini had bought her. They arrived at Gaaminitigwashkiigaag where she got off at Detaginang and Gichijen's house while the others continued on. But as soon as she entered, Dedibaayaanimanook was struck by a coldness so penetrating she felt frozen. One of her relatives refused even to look in her direction, much less speak to her. She was crushed by their sudden rejection, and as she searched for what lay behind their behaviour, she wondered what had gone wrong. What she had probably not considered was that her status in the community had changed. Now that she was the wife of not just another wemitigoozhi, but the one who hired members of the community, her peers clearly perceived her in a different way. It may have seemed to some that she was no longer interested in being part of the Anishinaabe community, or that she now thought of herself to be above the rest. Perhaps they even saw her as disloyal for having married a non-member. Without doubt, however, her siblings were reacting to these new realities, and Dedibaayaanimanook had not anticipated this possibility. Her sense of ostracization was but one example of the hardships about which her parents had once cautioned her.

After family members left Namegosibiing for Lac Seul during the latter part of that first spring at Camp Island, Dedibaayaanimanook found herself to be the only Anishinaabe person on the entire lake.

The loneliness of being without her family was beyond anything she had ever experienced, and the knowledge that they would eventually return did little to assuage her sense of desolation. Since no one at Camp Island could converse in her language, she had many opportunities to be alone with her thoughts. She began to reflect on the teachings of her parents and grandfather. The memory of their words were becoming a source of comfort and inspiration, helping her to deal with the task of adapting to the new circumstances of life on Camp Island. A mitigating factor during that time of adjustment was the fact that Dedibaayaanimanook's new home was in Namegosibiing. It was where her father, uncles and Giizhik himself had all been born and raised, and it was the place of her own birth and childhood. Namegosibiing was not only her beloved homeland and heritage, it was part of her character and her sense of self. That her permanent residence was in Namegosibiing was itself a form of consolation. Another effective method for dealing with the dispossession of her family's closeness was to keep busy, and with so many tasks to master and accomplish, she learned to put aside that yearning for the past.

The pace seemed especially hectic during Dedibaayaanimanook's first summer at Camp Island. On days when a plane was expected to arrive for a load of fish, the alarm clock's noisy clamor wakened her even before there was enough light to see. *"Sarah! Are you up?"* Giigooyikewinini's voice from out of the darkness shattered her desire to stay snuggled under the covers. Those first few occasions when she heard herself being called by her English name was a strange experience because she now had to think of herself in a different way. Dedibaayaanimanook got up and got dressed, then lit the fire. As she went about preparing breakfast and packing lunches, she realized that she now had the responsibility of running a household. She recalled her mother's instructive words about putting Giigooyikewinini's needs first and ensuring that he had the best of whatever was available. Remembering that she should listen to him and follow his instructions, she set to work. She began by hauling pails of water and filling a large metal tank as soon as the men left for the lake. After that, she gathered enough fire wood to heat the water. It was how the Olsens' cotton fish nets were washed and dyed during the height of the summer's fishing season. The remainder of Dedibaayaanimanook's day was taken up with a plethora of other tasks, and when the afternoon drew to a close, she prepared dinner for the men who always came home from the lake in a ravenous state. Hans Emrikson, a one-time cook, was one of the hired hands when Dedibaayaanimanook first arrived at Camp Island. One day, when the supply of groceries had run low, she decided to serve muskrat. Hans peered into the roasting pan, then announced that it was a goose they were about to consume. But he was unable to explain why the goose had four legs! Then one of the hired hands began to complain that Dedibaayaanimanook was not doing her full share of the work, insisting, for example, that it was her task to provide his cabin with fire wood. But Giigooyikewinini disagreed. Finding his expectations about Dedibaayaanimanook unreasonable, he fired the man when he persisted with even more complaints. Another man had a different kind of grievance. He threatened to leave because he thought that Dedibaayaanimanook did not like him enough.

It did not take very long for Dedibaayaanimanook to become familiarized with the many details relating to commercial fishing because she already possessed a wealth of knowledge acquired from watching and participating in her parents' activities. She found much of that know-how was directly relevant to fishing. For example, her first hand knowledge about the lake was invaluable. This included familiarity with Namegosibiing's physical features and the weather conditions typical for the region. Dedibaayaanimanook knew how winds affected the lake during different seasons of the year and which were most commonly associated with what type of weather. During the summer months, for instance, a condition described as waabaninoowe ondaaniman could be expected to bring cooler temperatures with increased chances of rain. Dedibaayaanimanook was also familiar with the different cloud formations and what they signified. Patterns of rapidly swirling clouds during a hot summer day indicated extreme instability, so to plan a trip on the lake at such a time was highly inadvisable. Having said that, however, Dedibaayaanimanook made the observation that the weather underwent changes since the time she was growing up in Namegosibiing. Another area about which she was well versed was the lake's various fish species, including what regions they inhabited and what they ate. With her extensive experience acquired on canoe trips to catch fish along streams and rivulets with her mother, she was knowledgeable in the use of fish nets and the functioning of anchor rocks, floats and bridle sticks. She had watched her mother on many occasions as she mended damaged meshes with a wooden shuttle. In fact, she helped by filling her mother's shuttle with cotton twine.

But there were also many new experiences that came with life at Camp Island. Using the large fishing boat with its inboard engine was one example. Dedibaayaanimanook was pleasantly surprised to find that learning about the boat engine was actually to her liking. As a result, she was soon familiar with cylinders and pistons, the crankshaft and grease cup, batteries and spark plugs, circuit cables, gaskets and much more. Both she and her brother Jiins helped to find mechanical ways for decreasing the chances of engine failure and for improving its operation. They devised a method for applying the choke without having to lift the engine cover and reach down into the hot engine. The risk of burning one's hand was eliminated. If Jiins was unavailable, Giigooyikewinini relied on Dedibaayaanimanook to assist with engine repairs. She reached into areas that Giigooyikewinini was unable to due to his wrist injury. As for boat outings themselves, Dedibaayaanimanook began to take the occasional turn at steering. Giigooyikewinini had hired a Scandinavian named Einar Nielson to build the large craft even though Morris Thomas (Tom Keesick's father-in-law) of the Obizhigokaang Lac Seul region was a renowned boat builder. Unlike Morris Thomas's design, the drive shaft angle on the Olsens' boat allowed room to fit the larger propeller unit they needed for handling the boat more easily while setting and lifting nets. Better maneuverability was an important feature for commercial fishing.

Dedibaayaanimanook developed a feel for navigating the boat in both fair weather and foul, and she learned how to ride the large waves. Although it was an entirely different way of thinking about travel, she concluded that using higher speeds across the lake could be quite an enjoyable experience!

Dedibaayaanimanook accompanied Giigooyikewinini on boat trips during slack periods in the season in order to become better acquainted with the details of lifting and setting nets. "Sarah, can you see that tall tree?" She looked in the direction he was pointing and she searched the horizon for the various landmarks he used to identify the exact location for setting a net. While Giigooyikewinini ensured that the net dropped unimpeded into the water, Dedibaayaanimanook's task was to keep it free from snags, tangles and knots. To do this properly, she needed to keep a constant watch on the net itself while it was still in the box, but due to the monotonous nature of the task, she occasionally lost her concentration. Her thoughts drifted away, and a gull swooping low in search of food drew her eyes from the net. At that precise moment, one of the threads snagged on a sliver in the wooden box, then another caught on one of her buttons.

"Can you beat that!" was Giigooyikewinini's favourite expression of exasperation, and this was the first time Dedibaayaanimanook heard it. Although no damage was done to the net itself, Giigooyikewinini had to hold it tightly as she hurried to free the web. Since the boat was in a constant forward motion, the entire net was dragged from its intended location. Distances of a few feet could make a significant difference in the size of their catch, so Dedibaayaanimanook learned the importance of staying focused. She also learned to avoid wearing clothes with prominent buttons, pins or zippers whenever she went fishing. Similarly, wearing watches and rings was not advisable. Throughout the time she was learning new skills and experiencing different situations, Dedibaayaanimanook was grateful that Giigooyikewinini was generally patient and appreciative of her efforts. He took care to give her tasks that were within her ability to carry out. It was also true, on the other hand, that Dedibaayaanimanook had a great deal of contextual knowledge. Giigooyikewinini could have hardly wished for a more capable and reliable partner. An incident that showed Dedibaayaanimanook's degree of dedication to doing the work at hand occurred during one of her first outings on the lake with Giigooyikewinini. They were in the midst of setting a net when black and yellow shapes began suddenly to form in front of her eyes.

Gaawiin inga gibichiisii onzaam inga gichi wanishkwechige. Trying to blink away the images, Dedibaayaanimanook silently resolved to finish their task in order to avoid interrupting the activity flow. The entire lake swirled slowly around her, but any disruption would serve only to intensify the distress of her pain, so resisting an overpowering urge to collapse, Dedibaayaanimanook leaned against the large net box and fought to control her growing nausea. When they finally arrived home, she went immediately to bed and slept for several hours. Only with an extraordinary force of will did Dedibaayaanimanook suffer in utter silence that day on the lake without Giigooyikewinini's awareness of what she had endured. As mentioned previously, Dedibaayaanimanook had been suffering from migraines long before she ever came to Camp Island. They were precursed with images of yellow and black shapes that obscured her vision. She became weak and sick with dizziness, nausea and terrible pain. Her only recourse was to lie down and try to sleep. Even though she had brought a small amount of traditional medicine—a gift from her mother intended as a remedy for the sickness that plagued her—when she first arrived at Camp Island, she never used it because there was no one to administer it to her. Instead, it became a kind of symbolic keepsake that provided her with a sense of connection with her parents and everything they had taught her. The tiny packet was in effect her sacred medicine bundle that would remain intact in her suitcase beneath her bed for many years.

Dedibaayaanimanook thus began to make sense of all the bustle that took place at Camp Island, and she was soon familiar with the entire routine. Summer fishing required that the gas tank be filled and all the equipment properly in place onboard. Boxes, tubs, hooks, knives, extra rope and other items were all loaded into the boat the evening before a trip. At the first light of dawn, the water was pumped from the boat, then protective gear, lunches, matches and boxes of chiselled ice were put into place. The route for the day's outing depended on wind strength and direction during summer. That concept was familiar for Dedibaayaanimanook, since canoe travel depended almost entirely on wind conditions. At times, it was necessary to follow a circuitous course to avoid the large waves. When nets were being lifted or set, it was important to position the boat in a way that avoided having the webs get caught on the boat propellers. That was best accomplished by lifting and setting the net against the wind. Each of the fish had to be removed without damaging either the fish or the net. Sometimes a crayfish—or even a loon—was caught, and it was capable of creating tight, complicated knots, but every tangle had to be thoroughly undone. During summer, it was possible to have much of the day's catch dressed by the time the fishers returned to Camp Island. Blocks of ice from the ice house chiselled into fine chunks were used for packing the fish in carefully arranged layers in two large wooden bins that Jiins helped to install in Giigooyikewinini's windowless fish house. There, the fish remained cold until a plane flew them out. The reason that taking up ice was a vital off-season activity during spring was because Giigooyikewinini needed to ensure that the amount of ice stored in the ice house would last until the cool weather of autumn set in. During winter, the fresh fish market demanded that fish be kept from freezing. For that reason, they were removed from the net and placed immediately in a large covered box in which the heat from a kerosene lantern ensured ambient temperatures of just above freezing. As soon as they returned to Camp Island with their catch, the "boys," i.e., hired helpers, dressed the fish, then wrapped them in burlap sacks and buried them under mounds of snow to keep them unfrozen until the plane's next arrival—usually no longer than a day or two. When the plane came to Camp Island, the fish were packed in boxes or tubs, then flown directly to Bowman in Hudson or to a dealer in Kenora. Later, Giigooyikewinini would fly the fish into Red

Lake and from there, have them trucked to the Kenora Fish Market. Dedibaayaanimanook was familiar with the use of a net, but the notion of continuously catching thousands of pounds of fish required getting used to, and she wondered whether enough people actually existed to consume such large quantities!

Over the years, many pilots came and went. Harold Farrington, Rex Kitely, Barney, Fraser Johnson, Gunner, Bill Miller, Bud Parsons, Bill Green and Bob Urquart were only a few who flew into Namegosibiiing to bring groceries and supplies for the Olsens and haul out their fish. Some of the pilots understood the need for reliable service and were committed to keeping to schedules as much as the weather allowed. Taking a personal interest in Giigooyikewinini and Dedibaayaanimanook's well-being, they helped in small but meaningful ways, such as making the occasional phone call on their behalf or posting an important letter. They were the pilots who became close friends. At other times, the Olsens had pilots who were disinterested and unreliable. They came in without supplies or broke schedules for no good reason. When that happened, fish spoiled and the Olsens had to absorb the losses in the form of wasted effort, fuel, labour and time. Namegosibiing's fish were needlessly squandered.

While she kept up with the household responsibilities and continued to be fully involved with fishing related activities, Dedibaayaanimanook began to learn basic English. As a result, she and Giigooyikewinini were able to communicate more effectively. This was necessarily a work in progress, since Dedibaayaanimanook understood and spoke very little of the language at the beginning. Among all of her siblings, in fact, Dedibaayaanimanook was one of the few who had not acquired any formal training in reading, writing or speaking English. Her parents had determined not to send her away to school due to the headaches she suffered. Why the state agents did not force her attendance is unkown, although the fact that the Dedibayaahs Keesicks were so frequently on journeys may have made their whereabouts difficult—but not impossible—to locate. Whatever the Indian agent's reason, her parents had made the right decision in that

she was spared experiences often too traumatic and painful even for
conscious thought. She thus avoided what had devastated the lives
of many who eventually returned home. By way of describing those
who had come back physically, emotionally, culturally, socially and
spiritually changed, Dedibaayaanimanook used the English word
"spoiled."

There was an element of commonality between the observations
Dedibaayaanimanook expressed about the effect that schooling had
on the youth who returned to Namegosibiing and comments written
by the Superintendent General of Indian Affairs many years before, in
his 1890 annual report to Parliament. In accordance with the terms
of the 1873 Treaty, communities received schools for their children.
Indian agents wrote glowing reports about how well Lac Seul students
were progressing in learning the English alphabet during those early
years after the treaty was first signed. By 1890—thirty-two years
before Dedibaayaanimanook was born—wemitigoozhi bureaucrats at
Indian Affairs began to see things in different, more sinister ways, as
became apparent when they put forth the opinion that schools teaching
literary subjects without any practical training would actually leave
children worse off than if they received nothing at all. Not having had
the opportunity to learn from their parents because they were away
at school, the children would be deprived of the hunting, fishing and
trapping skills needed to survive in their home communities. On the
other hand, having no "industrial" training, they would be unable to
find paid—presumably manual—employment, no matter how well
they could recite Shakespeare. Implicit in that logic was the assumption that no other type of either further training and education, or
employment, would ever be attainable for Anishinaabe people. Not
being able to speak functional English was the price that Dedibaayaanimanook paid for having escaped such a fate.

Giigooyikewinini's Anishinaabe language usage, on the other hand,
was even more limited than Dedibaayaanimanook's use of English.
When he leaned close to her one day and began counting in Anishi-

naabe, she was greatly amused by what she heard. He began auspiciously enough with *bezhig*, but when he followed *niinzhin* with a nonsensical *nishishin, gaawiin*,[2] he was veering completely off course. Seeing her reaction, Giigooyikewinini must have realized that he had gotten off track with his numbers. But he soon abandoned any concerns about derailment as he became more interested in eliciting her laughter than learning to count in Anishinaabe. Although Giigooyikewinini refused for the most part to speak the language, each acquired enough understanding of the other's language for a workable exchange of meaning. As well, Dedibaayaanimanook learned most of the words associated with commercial fishing. All the while, she continued to follow the examples her mother taught her, and she shouldered all of her responsibilities willingly. There was, however, one job that seemed too daunting for her even to consider. From the time she first arrived at Camp Island, she observed that Giigooyikewinini spent a considerable amount of time immersed in paperwork. He wrote down numbers in long columns, counting up the totals aloud as he went along. This he did on a daily basis. In the midst of one of his sessions, Giigooyikewinini removed his reading glasses and stood up. He paced around the kitchen a few times, mumbling to himself in what must have been Norwegian since Dedibaayaanimanook could not make out the words. Presently, he cleared his throat and turned to her.

"Sweetheart, how would you like to learn about this work?" he asked as he gestured toward the heaps of paper on the table. "Indawaasa gaawiin!" Dedibaayaanimanook surprised even herself by the emphasis with which she shook her head and declined his suggestion without hesitation. The very idea that she would spend time deciphering important scraps of paper was inconceivable. Sufficiently content with her proficiency with Anishinaabe syllabics, she had no desire whatsoever to learn to read and write the English language. Not many wemitigoozhiwag were interested in becoming versed in the use of her language, so it was true that business would always be conducted in their language rather than hers. But she had enough chores to keep her busy, so she thought it best to leave the paperwork to Giigooyikewinini's expertise. When he accepted her decision without comment, Dedibaayaanimanook was quite relieved, and she felt more determined to carry on with her own daily tasks as skillfully as possible.

One of the rewards she earned for her efforts was more time for personal interests. Unlike that of her more adventuresome siblings who desired to go into town for frequent visits, Dedibaayaanimanook's disposition was well suited for the sequestered life on the island. Her interest in the many life forms that existed around her had begun as a child when she and her nephew Gichi Jôj searched for tiny fish, water nymphs and other aquatic creatures. Now she could begin to familiarize herself with the island of her new home. The camp itself faced toward the rising sun. Backdropped by a mixed forest of tall boreal trees, it was well protected from the northerly winds. On a typical summer's day, Dedibaayaanimanook was surrounded by the soothing sounds of gently rustling leaves. Robins, white throated sparrows and other song birds along with the ubiquitous gulls were some of the birds that provided a musical note to the daily fare. One evening during the latter part of spring, she even heard the squawks of a fledgling owl as it looked down from atop Giigooyikewinini's radio antenna. Many other forms of stimuli presented themselves to a keen observer such as Dedibaayaanimanook. The fuzzy underside of a Labrador tea leaf, spongy textured sphagnum mosses, the menthalic flavor of an elusive snowberry snuggled beneath its cover of leathery leaves and the sight of tiny red pixie-cups reaching upward from the forest floor were some of them.

By way of acquiring a more direct acquaintance with Camp Island, Dedibaayaanimanook decided to take the well trodden portage trail to the other side of the island one day. She found herself on the south facing side of the island within a short time, and as she stood on the little beach facing the south, she could feel heat rising from the sand. A softly blowing wind transformed the water into countless mirrors that seemed to magnify the sun's brightness. Arriving at the spot where she stood, the breeze sent a series of gentle ripples through the hem of her cotton dress. Dedibaayaanimanook scanned the horizon for Manidoo Minis, the island where members of her family had gone to seek out their life's path many years before. Seagull Island, as it was now being called by the wemitigoozhiwag, was a small dot she could barely see, consumed as it was in the sun's meridian radiance. Dedibaayaanimanook found a suitably shaped rock and sat down; viewing Namegosibiing from this location on Camp Island was an experience that required time to absorb. After several minutes, she continued with her exploration by following along the rock strewn shoreline toward the west. A large boulder was perched tentatively at the upper end of a flat rock formation that stretched from the edge of the tree-line down several metres into the water. Dedibaayaanimanook surmised that massive ice chunks had pushed the rock into its current location during spring breakup. Just beyond the boulder, a patch of hearty little strawberries nestled among the clumps of grasses and other plant growth. She picked the delicate berries. They were so tiny and few that she barely had enough for a mouthful, but their size belied their sweetness. Further along, she gathered what amounted to little more than half a cup of purple ozigôkominan from a lone saskatoon bush. Nature had crammed them full of flavor as well.

On another walk, Dedibaayaanimanook decided to visit the north-west shoreline of Camp Island where a broken series of cliffs faces toward Animoshi Minis Dog Island. There, she came across the berries of a low growing evergreen shrub that lurked inconspicuously among the mosses. Mats of small shiny leaves that produced a type of tart, red berry shared their domain and were closely related. Although the two are barely distinguishable, Dedibaayaanimanook had no difficulty identifying the one from the other. Another kind of berries was plentiful enough where poplars grew along the banks of Namegosi Ziibi on the canoe route to Obizhigokaang Lac Seul, that her sister Gweyesh Annie was able to make several jars of jam using the red fruit mixed with cranberries. Dedibaayaanimanook and her travel companions often broke off branches of these berries and snacked on them as they travelled up the river. Now, she continued to search for some signs of the aniibiminaanan, but she was not successful. Another fruit Dedibaayaanimanook looked for during one of her walks in the forests of Camp Island were dewberries. She and her mother were once on a canoe trip near Gojijiing Goldpines with her nephew Gichi Jôj and her cousin De'igan when they came upon a small quantity of the delicious berries. However, Dedibaayaanimanook concluded that none existed anywhere on Camp Island. Instead, she found creeping masses of yet another evergreen toward the nethermost regions where spruce trees abound. From the time she was a small child, Dedibaayaanimanook took great pleasure in hunting for the diminutive white snowberries, or *bineminan*, as her father called them. Their cool, wintergreen flavor was most unforgettable. Halfway along the trail that led around the bay, she found herself knee deep in thick growths of an evergreen bush the stems and leaves of which her uncle Jiiyaan Donald used for making tea. She was equally pleased to discover that wild mint grew here and there along the shoreline of the bay. Dropping two or three sprigs into a pot of tea always provided a fresh, minty infusion.

On yet another foray, Dedibaayaanimanook ventured up the hill behind the house in search of raspberries. However, the hunt was futile. In fact, she would have to wait a few years before the bushes produced enough fruit for preserving. By that time, she and Giigooyikewinini would have a little girl to accompany her as she harvested the berries. Several young pincherry trees grew at the top of the hill. When Giigooyikewinini transplanted some of the smaller ones to the north side of the house, Dedibaayaanimanook contemplated the possibility of using the pincherries for jam at some future time. She was not in the least surprised to see that skunk currents grew in abundance beyond the hill toward the spruce forest. *"Baamaa giin, miishiijiimin!"* Dedibaayaanimanook recalled how her parents and other adults, alluding to the skunk currants' invariable habit of appearing before any of the other berries of the season, admonished the young ones not to push ahead of their elders.

Having thus made a successful start at familiarizing herself with some of the more readily accessible areas of Camp Island, Dedibaayaanimanook thought about another matter that interested her. Gardening would soon become a favourite pastime when she discovered the flower beds that Giigooyikewinini had built up around the house. They studied the seed catalogues that arrived at Camp Island in their mail bag in advance of the planting season, and together, they decided what seeds to order. She chose the flowers while Giigooyikewinini decided on which vegetables to grow in the gardens. Tomatoes and beans were started indoors. In their eagerness to get an early start one year, Dedibaayaanimanook and Giigooyikewinini began sowing in mid February. The shoots grew so long and thin that Dedibaaya-animanook needed to stake each and every one of them carefully, but by the time the risk of frost had ended, the plants were too spindling and weak to survive transplanting. It was a tragic sight to watch them flop over and slowly expire, considering all the attention she had given them. Giigooykewinini's raised garden built beneath the screened kitchen window was ideally located for the vegetables because it faced the southeast and was protected from the wind. By mid summer, it brimmed over with tomatoes, lettuce, green onions, radishes and climbing beans. Dedibaayaanimanook took time each day to tend to the plants, keeping them meticulously weeded and well watered. As for the flower beds, zinnias, monkey faces, marigolds and cosmos bobbed to the rhythm of summer's gentle breezes. Their mixture of vibrant colors and honeyed scent drew a steady stream of bumble bees, butterflies and other nectar craving insects. On occasion, a hummingbird was liable to hover briefly among the petals before disappearing from view. Then there were times when a delicate creature visited the blossoms. One day, Dedibaayaanimanook found it lying dead on the ground. She discovered, on closer examination, that it was covered over with fuzzy hair rather than the fine feathers she had anticipated. According to an insect handbook, it was a type of hawk moth that had been frequenting her gardens. It seemed all too soon when the growing season drew to a close, but just as autumn's colours began to set in, Dedibaayaanimanook's morning glories provided a final flourish of summer gaiety.

Camp Island was beginning to feel more like home by the time a year had passed. Still, Dedibaayaanimanook missed the company of family members once so near at hand. One day, she decided to mention her longing to see her parents. Giigooyikewinini agreed that she take a plane to Lac Seul and spend some time with her parents and relatives as soon as the fishing season began to slow.

Others in her family, including her half-sister Gweyesh Annie, had already flown in a plane. When her half-brother Jiibwaat Edward was employed with mine related work and tree cutting at Ikwewi Zaa'igan Woman Lake, for example, Gweyesh (who was married to Jiibwaat) flew to Lac Seul from Woman Lake to give birth to their son Anôy Roy. Even Dedibaayaanimanook's niece Bejii Betsy, Gweyesh's only daughter had flown. But Dedibaayaanimanook herself had not yet had this experience. As she climbed aboard for her first flight and seated herself on something suitable, she felt both excitement and trepidation. A few moments after the noisy take-off, she peered out the window and noticed what appeared to be a wooden egg crate nestled among the trees below. But why someone would want to leave it there was puzzling. Dedibaayaanimanook arrived at Lac Seul, and for nearly a month she re-lived the carefree days of her youth. But inevitably, her visit came to an end and it was time to return to Namegosibiing. Only a short segment of her trip home would be by plane, however.

Dedibaayaanimanook accompanied her parents, her sister Gweyesh Annie, Gweyesh's son Isaac and other family members north on Obizhigokaawi Zaa'igan Lac Seul Lake by canoe. They followed the familiar old canoe route of her childhood as far as Maadaawaang, and from there, Dedibaayaanimanook and her father continued northward, while the rest of the family remained behind to harvest wild rice. Staying with relatives along the way, father and daughter proceeded along the Chukuni River system. They passed through the regions of both Gullrock and Two Island Lakes, where Dedibaayaanimanook's mother had spent part of her childhood, before finally arriving at Wanamani Zaa'igan Red Lake. They were there for only a few hours when they came upon Giigooyikewinini, who had by coincidence arrived earlier on business. Immediately, he chartered a plane, and he and Dedibaayaanimanook left for home. As the plane became airborne, Dedibaayaanimanook looked out the window, watching how quickly their climb seemed to shrink the houses and trees beneath them. A thought suddenly struck her, and with sheepishness, she realized what she had seen on the flight to Lac Seul had been a trapper's cabin. Flying would need getting used to.

A little over a year after moving to Camp Island, Dedibaayaanimanook suffered a miscarriage. Then, during the first of week January, 1945, as the expected date of their first child's birth drew near, Giigooyikewinini agreed that she stay with her parents. Before departing, however, she took a few moments to instruct him on where to find the food staples and other various household items he would need during her absence. She also made it a point to show him where the broom, dustpan and scrub brush were located, hoping he would remember to use them on occasion. Soon she was seated on the sled with a woolen blanket tucked around her, heading on a northerly course across the channel with the dog team, escorted by Giigooyikewinini. As the long shadows of late afternoon stretched ahead of them, they reached her parents' winter camp site on the northeastern main shore of Namegosibiing. It was located near a point of land a few miles west of Jiibayi Zaagiing Jackfish Bay. Following along the Keesicks' snowshoe trail, the dogs strained into their harnesses, and with a final effort they scrambled up the incline to the cabin. Dedibaayaanimanook took her time to disembark and was careful not to slip. She was thankful the journey had been uneventful. Just as she reached the door, it opened before her and there stood her mother. *"Indaanisens!"* Gaamadweyaashiik was overjoyed to see her. But Giigooyikewinini did not stay. He knew that Dedibaayaanimanook and their unborn child were now safe, and with dusk descending rapidly over the lake, he wanted to return immediately to Camp Island. Dedibaayaanimanook sat down by the warm stove and sipped her mother's hot tea. Already she felt cared for, and taking several deep breaths, she tried to relax.

It had not been many hours since Dedibaayaanimanook first arrived from Camp Island. Her mother hovered close by, smoothing away creases in the blankets while her sister Gweyesh Annie stood in front of the stove, stoking the fire. As she propped herself slowly against the pillows, Dedibaayaanimanook was aware of how stiff and exhausted she was. She held her new born daughter closely, stroking the tiny face with her finger tips.[3] Its texture was as smooth as silky ribbon! Drawing the soft blanket gently around little Aaniz, Dedibaayaanimanook watched her sleep. She savored the cozy ambiance of her parents' cabin. Jiins had helped her father build the little addition in order to accommodate the family's needs. As she had done so many times as a child, she gazed at the flames flickering lazily behind cracks in the wood stove. Her mind went over the reason why she needed to come at such a time. In keeping with tradition, Dedibaayaanimanook wanted to be with her family for the birth of her first child. Aaniz's arrival was one of six for the Namegosibii Anishinaabe community during that twelve month span. In Namegosibiing itself, Jiijii'oo (a daughter), Aaniz Olsen and Jôj George Angeconeb were born to Gwejech, Dedibaayaanimanook and Gweyesh Annie respectively. The three others, Ogin Jennie Keesick, Gwiishkwa'oo Mayaawibiikwe Eliza Angeconeb and Gaanitaawe Jim Keesick were born in that order to Ja'iinsi, Gaanii Connie and Gichi Jii at Wanamani Ziibiing,[4] northeast of Red Lake.

By now, Dedibaayaanimanook was well adjusted to life at Camp Island. Even though her relatives all came to accept her partnership with Giigooyikewinini, her once close relationship with some of her sisters and friends had gradually diminished. Other changes had been taking place as well. The original Namegosibii Anishinaabe community started to unravel as social, economic and other reasons drew members away. Many no longer lived in Namegosibiing at all. Dedibaayaanimanook's youngest (paternal) uncle Jiimis James, for example, had settled permanently in Obizhigokaang Lac Seul in order to allow his children to attend school. Aanig Alec and his brother Gwiiwish Isaac were the exceptions in this family. Mooniyaans Thomas had passed on; Naadowe Robert lived at Oshkaandagaawi Zaa'igan Nungesser Lake; and Kiiweyaashin William and his wife now lived in and around Gull Rock Lake. Over the course of time, the grandchildren of Dedibaayaanimanook's uncles, having been born elsewhere, did not have that same sense of connection with Namegosibiing. Only a few, including Dedibaayaanimanook's parents, her Angeconeb brothers, her uncles Jiiyaan Donald and Netawibiitam John, along with their wives and some grown children, still lived in Namegosibiing. Despite everything, these community members remained tightly knit, and to the extent they were able, they held onto the old activities that included hunting, trapping and harvesting, activities that had once been sufficient for survival.

The driving forces behind these upheavals were the continuously proliferating activities of wemitigoozhiwag. Much of Dedibaayaanimanook's community vacated the homelands in the face of these intrusions. One April day, Dedibaayaanimanook and Giigooyikewinini's routine was interrupted when a plane crammed with supplies and equipment landed in the bay at Camp Island. A middle aged man emerged from the craft, and referring to himself as Albert Cook, he announced that he was setting up his fishing business on the island. "You can use this plane to remove your belongings!" he declared with an assuming air. Both Giigooyikewinini and Dedibaayaanimanook were astounded by what they had just heard. It was as blatant a case of arrogance as Giigooyikewinini had ever come across. Although all of Namegosibiing was now classified as provincial crown land, there were innumerable islands—not to mention the main shore—where others might settle. Why Cook thought he could simply displace the Olsens was strange, but as they later discovered, very much within character. Giigooyikewinini soon recovered from his shock, and before the pilot was able to unload any of the equipment, he ordered the man back on board and he told the pilot to return him to Red Lake. Then he took the next plane to town to ensure that neither Cook nor anyone else could legally appropriate the Olsens' fishing camp. Eventually, Cook returned to Namegosibiing, and this time, he chose another location. He decided to settle on an island just across the channel from Camp Island.

For the relatively few of Dedibaayaanimanook's people who were still in Namegosibiing in the latter 1940s, the arrival of Albert Cook—Goginini, that is, Cook Man, as they called him—was not such a great shock because Giigooyikewinini's appearance had already set the precedent. Nonetheless, it was just as daunting, because of the blatancy of the dismissive, indifferent attitude this individual showed toward community members. In fact, the manner in which he went about his daily business and interacted with the people of Namegosibiing seemed even more extreme than the typical mindset prevailing among the wemitigoozhiwag, and for that reason, his behaviour was worthy of note.

People never learned a great deal about Albert Cook's background, even though he spent a number of years in Namegosibiing. His wife Vivian, an elementary school teacher in Red Lake, came to Trout Lake a few times for brief visits. She brought along their only child, Bill. Dedibaayaanimanook remembered Bill Cook from a few years before, when she was still with her parents. The Dedibayaashes once travelled to Wanamani Zaa'iganing Red Lake to sell their blueberries locally. Some of the produce was purchased by an independent trader, Ken McDougall, and the rest was sold door to door on behalf of the Keesicks by a friend of mixed heritage who was able to speak English. While in town, the Keesicks decided to do some shopping, so they secured their canoe to the shoreline nearby. They completed their shopping, but when they returned to their canoe they found that it had been completely filled with water. They discovered that two young wemitigoozhi boys were the thoughtless pranksters, and Bill Cook was one of them. During his trips into Namegosibiing, the youngster seemed to show little interest or aptitude when it came to his father's fishing business. Instead, he completed high school and went to university in southern Ontario. Bill Cook graduated, then became a teacher at Lakewood Secondary School in Kenora. One of his students would be Giigooyikewinini and Dedibaayaanimanook's eldest daughter, Aaniz. Bill's wife Maureen taught Latin classes which the Olsens' second eldest, Enan, would attend.

The Olsens' neighbor across the channel went about doing his work in a manner that left community members wondering why he had ever decided to become involved with fishing. Many of the difficulties he experienced seemed to be the result of a serious case of stubborn pride, as he habitually pooh-poohed people's advice on best practices. Despite recommendations against bringing horses into Namegosibiing, for example, he was convinced that he knew best. Goginini had procured a small caboose-like shack with a potbelly stove. He nailed the shack onto a sled to which he hitched his horse. Anyone happening to look out across the lake at certain times during the day was liable to spot the caboose, puffs of smoke billowing from its chimney, as the horse transported Goginini and his hired help, Dedibaayaanimanook's nephew Niksaandan George, from place to place to lift nets in this very unusual manner. But large domestic animals require an agricultural setting to work best, being unlike the boreal creatures, such as moose or deer, who thrive in the free conditions of the natural environment. It therefore came to no one's surprise when they noted that Goginini's experiment with the use of a horse in Namegosibiing did not continue for long. Eventually, he decided to resolve his winter transportation problems by confining his fishing activities in Namegosibiing to the summer season. Still, it was apparent that his expertise, whether nautical or otherwise, was greatly lacking. Goginini had a fishing boat large enough for an inboard engine, much like that of the Olsens'. While tending to his nets on choppy waters one day, he failed to notice that the boat's tilt was allowing water to enter through the exhaust pipe. The boat filled quickly, but Goginini was oblivious to the disaster about to take place. By the time he noticed that he was sinking, it was too late. However, he managed to save himself by grasping onto floating objects and swimming to a nearby island where he was eventually rescued. That the incident did not end in his drowning was miraculous. Upon hearing of the episode, people once again recalled that Dedibaayaanimanook's grandfather Giizhik had given the Namegosibii Anishinaabe people his assurances that none of his people would ever drown in Namegosibiing.

Although he survived the misfortune, Goginini lost his large fishing boat along with the inboard engine, a load of fish and various equipment. He was forced to use a smaller, flat-bottomed wooden row boat to which he attached an outboard motor. However, his lack of know-how led to another misadventure. Goginini chose to ignore Dedibaayaanimanook's nephews who advised him repeatedly to chain his outboard onto the boat itself since constant vibrations eventually loosen the attachment mechanisms. Predictably, the motor became loose and slid into the water on an outing near Trout Lake Lodge. Goginini managed to row himself to the Lodge where the owner, Sarah Yates, loaned him one of her motors. Unbelievably, however, the same thing happened again when Sarah's motor loosened and sank to the bottom of the lake. By that time, even Sarah's compassion was beginning to wear thin.

Dedibaayaanimanook's nephew Simeon Angeconeb—Gweyesh Annie's son who was born at Ear Falls—accompanied Goginini in his flat bottom one gusty day to help lift his nets. Goginini was at the helm while Simeon sat at the bow, each ostensibly doing his utmost to locate the buoys. Goginini was so intent in his quest to find the marker that he seemed entirely unaware of the large waves. Suddenly, Simeon spotted the buoy, but for safety's sake, he decided to remain silent. After making several circles, Goginini seemed to realize for himself that it was best to stop the search and return to camp. His decision to get off the lake was prudent, but for him to have embarked on a trip in his flat bottom under those weather conditions was itself an act of extreme recklessness. When they arrived at Goginini's dock, water sprayed and cold, Simeon and his family were all gratified.

The time Albert Cook set out to walk into Red Lake just before freeze-up, he did so against the better judgement of community members. Having heard about Dedibayaash, Jiins and others who made a regular habit of walking into town and back convinced him that he could do likewise. In fact, he could probably do so in less time! Approximately half a day into his walk, however, it began to snow. With the skies overcast, Goginini soon lost his sense of direction. The number of days he wandered in wide circles far exceeded the number for which he had packed provisions.

Planning to remain at Namebinibagida'waagan[5] until Christmas that autumn, Dedibaayaanimanook's sister Gweyesh Annie and her family had just moved to the beach located on the northwestern main shore of Namegosibiing. This choice of location was in contrast to the preferences of her parents, who found it a nuisance to live where they were in constant contact with sand. Gweyesh Annie, who had become a single parent of seven children when her husband Jiibwaat Edward died in an automobile accident, had no choice but to adapt to her new circumstances. No longer having the luxury of following conventional rules about gender roles, she quickly learned to make decisions and perform tasks traditionally associated with men. The fact that she built a cabin for her family at Jiibayi Zaagiing one winter was an example of her commitment to the well-being of her children. Even though she faced enormous odds, Gweyesh was able to keep her family intact with the help of her family and relatives and with much courage and resilience. Her strengths and also her foibles were evident in the circumstances of the birth of Edward, the second youngest of her children, when the family was travelling along Namegosibi Ziibi one autumn. "Wiinge dash ingii' agaj." Gweyesh explained how keenly she felt her embarrassment when her husband Jiibwaat and his brother Jiins had to carry her on a stretcher as they portaged around a set of rapids. Having to rely on others to that extent was a kind of helplessness that was very difficult to endure for someone as self-reliant and proud as Gweyesh. Later, she found herself in another situation of vulnerability when she was in the woods felling a tree. Her snowshoe, unexpectedly hit by a branch, struck her as it flew upward. In this case, Dedibaayaanimanook's mother had special medicine that helped her to heal. It was true that there were moments when Dedibaayaani-manook was exasperated by her sister's proclivity for pretentious airs, but she deeply respected her resourcefulness and strength of will. Remaining close throughout most of their adult lives, the two sisters shared many personal experiences and visited frequently.

That autumn when Goginini decided to walk to town, Gweyesh Annie Angeconeb and her children were horrified when a disheveled figure stumbled into their camp. His clothes were ragged and filthy, and his grey hair was matted down with twigs and other bits of debris. Scratches covered every inch of his sunken, bearded face and a look of desperation filled his hollow eyes. Family members were shocked and incredulous when they realized that the spectre upon whom they were gazing was the wemitigoozhi fisher, Goginini, Albert Cook. Goginini would likely not have survived had Gweyesh decided to spend autumn elsewhere that year and whether he ever acknowledged it or not, he owed a debt of gratitude to the Gweyesh Angeconebs. In another incident that exemplified a serious discrepancy between activity and ability, Dedibaayaanimanook and Giigooyikewinini's neighbor was in the midst of dyeing his fish nets. He was about to pour a bucket of hot water over the nets when he lost his footing. The steaming liquid spilled into one of the rubber boots he was wearing.

Perhaps it was because Giigooyikewinini was aware of Goginini's clumsy ways that he arranged to share planes with him when he esti-mated that he did not have sufficient fish for a full load of his own. Under these arrangements, the pilot alternated his trips, landing either at the Olsens' or across the channel at Goginini's. One day, it was Goginini's turn to bring his fish to Camp Island. As soon as he was in the bay, he grabbed a tub full of fish and began to lift it onto the dock. However, he should have first taken time to secure his craft to the dock post. Knowing intuitively about the mechanics of Newton's second law of motion even before she had ever studied about it, one of the Olsen daughters observed what was about to happen. Aaniz Alice rushed over to lend Goginini a helping hand. Goginini's reaction, however, was a surly, "Oh, go sit down!" And with that, the tubful of fish landed in the water in a tremendous splash. Dressed whitefish lay scattered at the bottom of the lake, fit only for the Olsens' sled dogs. Suffice to say, innumerable similar incidents happened almost on a daily basis, but fortuitously, most had only mildly drastic consequences.

Goginini was far from the last of the wemitigoozhiwag to come to Namegosibiing. A few years after his arrival, in the summer of 1947, a young non-Anishinaabe woman landed at Camp Island. Introducing herself as Sarah Yates, she declared her intent to set up a tourist/commercial fishing camp on the lake. Giigooyikewinini inquired what location she had in mind, recalling the Albert Cook incident of a few years back. Once again, it was with amazement that the Olsens watched as the woman pointed across the bay, and again, Giigooyikewinini stated that such a proposition was out of the question. Sarah Yates immediately returned to Red Lake, but as Goginini had done before her, Zena[6] came back to Namegosibiing. This time, she came with her partner, (Hu)Bert Tyrell, and her father. The three set up what came to be known as Trout Lake Lodge in a south facing bay of a large island approximately a mile northeast of Camp Island. In their younger days, Dedibaayaanimanook's uncle Jiiyaan Donald and his wife had stopped on that very same beach as they journeyed south one spring.

Zena and her partner Bert hired various of Dedibaayaanimanook's relatives and Anishinaabeg from other regions, providing them with a temporary livelihood. Periodically, Wemichigoozhiikwe,[7] as she was alternately called, came to Camp Island to visit Dedibaayaanimanook and the two Sarahs shared household and other types of suggestions for making their work easier. But the presence of Sarah Yates, Bert Tyrell, and their commercial activities further displaced Dedibaayaanimanook's people from their homelands.

1. It was true that Dedibaayaanimanook and Giigooyikewinini did not take out a marriage license, nevertheless, Indian Affairs struck her name from their Treaty annuity paylists and she lost her Treaty rights.

2. Giigooyikewinini mispronounced the word "onizhishin," which means "beautiful," but he should have said "nisin," which means "three."

3. For her own reasons, Dedibaayaanimanook did not wish to share the details of the birth of her child. That is why none are included.

4. Wanamani Ziibiing is East Bay.

5. Namebinibagida'waagan is a term that refers to setting nets for suckers.

6. Zena is the Anishinaabe version of Sarah.

7. Wemichigoozhiikwe means white woman.

CHAPTER 8

The Olsen Family of Namegosibiing

The sun shone brightly and the winds blew lightly as a sturdy little flatbottom glided effortlessly over the gentle waves. Two small children peered cautiously into the water from where they were seated within the boat. They were both fascinated and repulsed by the fluid forms moving beneath them. Dedibaayaanimanook's oars dipped into the water, then sent it spinning into whorls that gurgled and frothed for a few brief seconds. When she lifted them, a series of drips left squiggly lines trailing on the water as the boat moved forward.

"Nashke ogo!" Dedibaayaanimanook nodded toward a school of careless minnows bursting into hundreds of tiny streaks just beneath the water's surface. The girls were enthralled by the spectacle. Further along, they strained for a better view when a crayfish suddenly scooted tail first into a cloud of green murkiness. The sight elicited squeals of delight. Dedibaayaanimanook continued to row. Just then, the elongated shadow of a jack fish lurking craftily among the water weeds came into view. The girls shuddered. Dedibaayaanimanook manoeuvred the craft to deeper water. As a monstrous boulder shrouded in a mantle of green algae began to loom menacingly from the fuzzy depths where the sunlight barely soaks through, the children shrank back with dread. "Gego gosaakeg." In soothing tones, Dedibaayaanimanook assured them not to fear. The outing continued for a while longer, then it was time to return home. Before heading the boat toward Camp Island, however, Dedibaayaanimanook sat motionless for an idyllic, fleeting moment.

Each of her trips on the lake was a time to relax with the children. Using the boat that her brothers had helped Giigooyikewinini build, she took them on short excursions along Camp Island's shoreline or across the channel to neighboring islands. Sometimes they went in search of cranberries. At other times, the outings took them to family and friends. Staying in contact with family members was often more manageable during the summer. With different individuals working for Giigooyikewinini at any given time, two or even three households sometimes lived across the bay from the Olsens. Her uncle Jiiyaan and her aunt Maagii, a few first and second cousins, her niece Bejii and various nephews stayed in tents and the log cabin Jiins had built. Other relatives lived at Trout Lake Lodge island where they worked for Zena Sarah Yates. Cousins and nephews who were hired on at Goginini's during the height of the summer fishing season lived on the southwestern shore of Gogi Minis Cook Island with their families. From time to time, Dedibaayaanimanook's parents stayed directly across the channel at Anishinaabe Minis Indian Island.

One day, Dedibaayaanimanook and the girls rowed across the short stretch of the bay where the girls' grandparents were temporarily living. The Dedibayaashes were no longer going on their trips down the river. As soon as they touched land, the elder of Dedibaayaanimanook's two children, Aaniz Alice, scrambled out of the boat and up the embankment. Visiting was very much to her liking, and she wasted as little time as possible on the trail. Enan Helen, on the other hand, was content to remain close to her mother. When Enan was born, Aaniz Alice was one and a half years old. Her grandfather began to refer to her as Gete Wemitigoozhi,[1] while Oshki Wemitigoozhi[2] was the name he gave Enan Helen.

The events leading to Enan's birth had begun on a late afternoon during the early part of July, 1946. With Dedibaayaanimanook's parents and other close relatives away in Lac Seul for the summer that year, Giigooyikewinini agreed it was best for her to go to Sioux Lookout for the birth of their second child. Hours before the amphibian plane landed at Camp Island, Dedibaayaanimanook was ready for the trip. She remembered the cool mid-summer evenings in Lac Seul, so she wore a cardigan over her pale cotton dress. A favourite woolen tam kept her hair neatly in place. The suitcase and bags she had begun packing several days earlier stood waiting in a neat little row by the veranda door. When it was time to leave, Aaniz followed her parents to where the plane was waiting. She carried her own small bag. Holding onto Giigooyikewinini to steady herself, Dedibaayaani-manook climbed aboard the aircraft and settled into the seat the pilot had assembled for her. She drew Aaniz close. When the engine began to sputter, Dedibaayaanimanook felt a sudden surge of excitement. She took a deep breath to calm herself. Through the plane's window she watched Giigooyikewinini guiding the boat to its mooring. She would not see him again for several weeks, but her thoughts turned to the promise of visiting with her parents and all the old friends of Obizhigokaang Lac Seul. Some of them she had not spent time with in over three years. Suddenly she became uneasy. What if she could not find her parents in Lac Seul? What would she do, and where would she go? The hospital's location was unknown. How would she find her way there? She thought about mothering two children and all the work that would need doing. How would she ever manage everything? The plane's takeoff interrupted Dedibaayaanimanook's reflection. Hold-ing Aaniz tightly, she saw her parental role as the children's protector jolting into focus.

The travellers arrived safely in Lac Seul late in the evening. Aside from Aaniz's air sickness, the flight was incident free. *"Boozhoo, Jiimisens!"* Much to her relief, Dedibaayaanimanook saw her nephew Jiimisens waiting on the dock. He took the two visitors from Namego-sibiing to Baswewe's house, where they spent a comfortable night with the family's much loved friend and relative. Early the next morning, Dedibaayaanimanook and her nephew set out in search of her par-ents, asking various community members they met where they had last seen the Dedibayaashes. But as each lead became a dead end, her disappointment grew. Dedibaayaanimanook was not able to locate her parents before Enan's birth, so she left Aaniz Alice in the care of Gookom Aaniz, who was once married to Dedibaayaanimanook's half-brother, Minzhinawebines Sam Keesick. At the hospital, Dedibaayaanimanook's harrowing experience began when her wrists and ankles were bound to the bed frame when her labour pains became unbearable. Her torment ended as she descended into a murky abyss of unconsciousness after an ether mask was clamped down on her face. Dedibaayaanimanook and Giigooyikewinini's second child was born on July 25, 1946. Dedibaayaanimanook was twenty-four years old.

During her hospital stay, the whereabouts of her parents was finally established. Dedibayaash and Gaamadweyaashiik proceeded immediately from Gojijiing Goldpines to Lac Seul when they heard that their daughter had arrived from Namegosibiing. Upon her release, Dedibaayaanimanook returned to Aaniz Alice's for a joyful reunion with her parents and the introduction of their latest grandchild. During that time at Lac Seul, the Keesicks learned that rumors were being circulated about Dedibaayaanimanook, and even though she knew that the invention of falsehoods about others was one of life's on-going realities, she could not help but feel betrayed. But despite this incident, Dedibaayaanimanook took the opportunity of being in Lac Seul with her parents to enjoy a more leisurely pace, visiting with friends and relatives who no longer came to Namegosibiing. For their part, Dedibayaash and Gaamadweyaashiik were delighted to spend time with their two little grandchildren. Back in Namegosibiing Trout Lake, however, Giigooyikewinini had become concerned for his family's return. Several weeks after Dedibaayaanimanook left, he asked Jiins to write her a letter. He wrote Giigooyikewinini's message in Anishinaabe, then gave the envelope to the pilot to post. However, the pilot's next trip for the Olsens' was to Lac Seul to bring Dedibaayaanimanook, and so for whatever reason, she never saw the letter.

Dedibaayaanimanook now had two children, but in her mind, motherhood was as important as being Giigooyikewinini's partner and support. More than ever, she believed in what her mother had taught about the principles that govern good living and how to conduct oneself. The importance of getting up in the morning before sunrise was a daily case in point. "Na'awe niniijaanisens. Aazhaa madwe anokii." Always so vivid in her mind were the words of her mother, describing how the sun beamed down each morning with special pleasure to see the young child already on the trail gathering firewood and attending to her rabbit snares when the first rays of light began to illuminate the sky. These words now reminded Dedibaayaanimanook to always start the day early, so, while the rest of the family slept, she was outdoors chopping and stacking firewood. Giigooyikewinini too appreciated the virtue of an early start. During the fishing season, he was already on the lake pulling up nets before the summer sun became too hot or the winds of winter began to blow too strong.

It was on one such morning when Giigooyikewinini had left for his nets on the lake that Dedibaayaanimanook and the girls rowed across the bay at Camp Island to visit with relatives. Aaniz skipped happily along the trail ahead of them, while Enan clung to the safety of her mother's nearness. Holding tightly onto her bottle of milk, she snuggled against Dedibaayaanimanook's skirts. Soon they reached the little cluster of tents. As they passed one of them, Enan ventured a peek through the opening, and there, she caught a fleeting glimpse of her great-uncle Jiiyaan Donald Keesick. Being unwell, he had been spending much of his time in bed. Aaniz Alice referred to her great-aunt Maagii as Injoozhish, that is, "my Auntie." Injoozhish Maagii was now devoting most of her time caring for the ailing Jiiyaan. It was Jiiyaan and Maagii's daughter, Moshish Mary, who first worked for Wemichigoozhiikwe Sarah Yates at Trout Lake Lodge. But Moshish did not stay there for long. Instead, she worked at Camp Island, helping Dedibaayaanimanook with the children during times when fishing was especially busy. Moshish Mary continued at Camp Island whenever she was in Namegosibiing right up to when Dedibaayaanimanook and Giigooyikewinini's third child was born in the winter of 1950. Dedibaayaanimanook enjoyed her sister's companionship and was appreciative of her help.

Each time Dedibaayaanimanook took the girls to their grandparents, the three were greeted with much affection. Dedibayaash's alternate name for Aaniz was Bezhig Wemitigoozhi, meaning White Person Number One. The name, Niinzhin Wemitigoozhi, that is, White Person Number Two, was for Enan, and when Doris was born three and a half years after Enan, she would become Oshki Wemitigoozhi, New White Person. With these descriptive names, Dedibaayaanimanook's father expressed love for his grandchildren who were of mixed heritage. At the same time, the names readily acknowledged that Dedibaayaanimanook's children were different from the Dedibayaash Keesicks' other grandchildren. They shared the same Anishinaabe genes, but being part wemitigoozhi, their share was not equal. This difference was not regarded as a negative, and in itself, it had no influence on how the children were perceived. It did not result in a diminution of the people's fondness for them. The important difference was how the children's father chose to raise them and the affects of those choices.

Giigooyikewinini's specific wish was to instill a western based socialization in each of the children. From the time of Aaniz's birth, he had made it plain to Dedibaayaanimanook that they needed to be raised in ways he judged would help to increase their chances of fitting into the Canadian mainstream (white) society of the day. Accordingly, Aaniz was barely two years old when he made arrangements for her to spend three months with Elsie and Joe Johnson at McKenzie Island, Red Lake, where she would begin to learn English and acquire the social mannerisms deemed acceptable within the non-Anishinaabe milieu. On the morning of Aaniz's departure, Dedibaayaanimanook folded her little daughter's clothes and placed them neatly in a suitcase. She dressed her in a set of newly sewn clothing, then after carefully combing her long dark hair, attached a silk ribbon onto each braid. Finally, she bundled Aaniz in a pair of woollen ski pants and a fur trimmed jacket. It was a typically cold day in Namegosibiing as blustery winds reduced visibility with blowing snow. When the plane arrived, Giigooyikewinini lifted little Aaniz in, then climbed aboard after her. Soon the engine sputtered to life, and the aircraft began lurching down the runway Giigooyikewinini had tramped with

his snowshoes. Gaining speed, the craft began to lift. Dedibaayaanimanook stood mesmerized as it soared above the trees of Animoshi
Minis. She waited for one last glimpse before the tiny dot vanished in
a cloud of swirling snow. A final drone faded into the wind. "Amiisi-
inzan i'i." Dedibaayaanimanook began to shiver when a fresh billow of
snow swooshed round her. But as she brushed her tears aside, all she
felt was the heavy emptiness that threatened to choke her.

Early the next morning, Dedibaayaanimanook's brother Jiibwaat
Edward dropped by Camp Island for a brief visit. He described how he
had gone to check some traps and had come upon Gigooyikewinini's
plane sitting on the ice not far from Esiban Point. It had apparently
stopped so Gigooyikewinini could give instructions to the hired hands
who were lifting several nets in the vicinity. Jiibwaat then peered into
the back window of the plane. There was little Aaniz lying face down
on the floor of the craft. Between her sobs, Jiibwaat could hear her
crying for her mother.

Even though the arrangement was only for a few months, Dedibaayaanimanook found it hard to accept that the safekeeping of her child
was now in the hands of strangers. Whoever they were, they would
decide what Aaniz was about to learn, and Dedibaayaanimanook knew
that none of it would include the wise teachings of the old people. But
then, she had given her consent to the setup. The decision had to do
with how she understood her parents' teachings to apply to her. She
believed that it was her responsibility to support Giigooyikewinini
in this kind of situation, therefore she needed to trust that his judgement was somehow in the best interests of their children, no matter
what the affects might be for her and for Giigooyikewinini. Through
this separation from her little Aaniz, Dedibaayaanimanook began to
discover that the hardships alluded to by her grandfather, parents and
uncles would be much more than physical.

Dedibaayaanimanook's relatives tacitly respected Giigooyikewinini's views as it became more apparent that he intended to actively
discourage the children from interacting with them. Furthermore,
they understood that this lack of free access would to some extent

extend to Dedibaayaanimanook herself. But since connection among family members continued to be greatly valued in what remained of the Namegosibiing community, people immediately recognized the need to find ways for maintaining contact. In no way would they simply abandon Dedibaayaanimanook. This was made evident by the fact that those who came to work at Camp Island always tried to include a social component to their business related activities. Family and relatives also took advantage of times when Giigooyikewinini was in town on business. Dedibaayaanimanook's parents, in particular, took every opportunity that presented itself to come to Camp Island to be with her. One winter's day, people heard that Giigooyikewinini would be going into town for several days. Being concerned that Dedibaayaanimanook and the children would be alone, Gaamadweyaashiik decided to spend some time at Camp Island. Evening set in, and as she reposed comfortably in the soothing warmth of her daughter's wood stove, Gaamadweyaashiik began to nod off. In her reverie, someone slowly approached and placed a small piece of ice in her hand. "Wegonen!" Gaamadweyaashiik awoke with a start, surprised to find little Enan clutching her hand with icy fingers. Opportunities to spend time with her two grandchildren were limited, and Gaamadweyaashiik cherished even the smallest incident.

Despite the best efforts of Dedibaayaanimanook and her parents, however, the general lack of people's presence in the children's day to day lives existed even when relatives lived as close to them as across the bay. The children began to seem unsure of what to make of their unfamiliar visitors, and as a result, they often ran off into the woods when relatives happened by, even though they were happy to include cousins in their play whenever any came to Camp Island with their parents, and even though it was true that Dedibaayaanimanook and the other adults were free to visit in relative peace and quiet when that happened. Perhaps one of the most damaging ultimate effects of their father's imposed disconnect was that some of the children began to think of the relatives of their flesh and blood as though they were strangers to be avoided. They did not understand their relationship with them or even realize who some of them were until the children were well into adulthood. By then, of course, the great-aunts, great-uncles and even cousins had long passed on. It was only much later that they came to comprehend their loss in not having had a closer connection with various members of their Namegosibii Anishinaabe kin. Knowing that their own loss was by far greater than that of the old people was probably more bearable, however, than the associated sense of guilt had the reverse been true.

Giigooyikewinini's plans for the youngsters also espoused a formal education, and when the time came, each of them would need to leave home to attend school. He reasoned that acquiring a Western education was the likeliest way for someone of mixed heritage to thrive in the dominant culture. That was the underlying reason why Gooyikewinini forbade the children to speak Anishinaabe even though it was what they naturally learned to speak first since Dedibaayaanimanook communicated with them in her language. Discouraging them from interacting with their relatives since he knew they would tend to speak the language in their company was part of that larger objective of Western culturization. In his Norwegian accented English, Gigooyikewinini scolded them each time they used Anishinaabe within hearing.

To the best of her understanding, Dedibaayaanimanook complied with Giigooyikewinini's wishes. Nevertheless, she continued to hold onto her own strong belief in the veracity of the old ways in which she had been grounded since birth. She was therefore much inclined toward sharing the heritage of her peoples' teachings with the children, even though necessity dictated that she exercise discretion in how she went about sharing those teachings. Storytelling was one method that she employed with success because the girls were as fond of listening to her narratives as she was of telling them. But the right set of circumstances had to present themselves first. Long winter evenings proved most suitable because that was when Giigooyikewinini was usually engrossed in his own kind of bedtime stories. With an array of American signals coming in clearly, Charlie McCarthy, Amos and Andy, Fibber McGee, Molly, and other types of shows kept him too preoccupied to take much notice in Dedibaayaanimanook and the girls.

The girls, too, had several options from which to choose. One account they never seemed to tire of dealt with Gaagashkiigiiwaaj, the Ones Who Shroud Themselves in Blankets. It was about the non-human people who habitually draped themselves in blankets in order to hide from others. Although they were not considered to have malevolent intentions, catching a glimpse of them disappearing behind an island or into the forest bushes made people uneasy, since their sighting was so uncommon an occurrence. Dedibaayaanimanook's Gaagashkiigiiwaaj narratives consisted of descriptions rather than stories because the beings were so elusive that no story lines existed about them. One evening just as dusk was settling over the lake, Aaniz and Enan were sent outdoors to bring in their blankets. Dedibaayaanimanook always gathered the blankets in the morning and took them outdoors after everyone was up. She draped them over a horizontal pole along the play pen that Giigooyikewinini had gotten Jiins to build for the children. From the time she was a child, Dedibaayaanimanook's mother had taught her to give the blankets a daily airing. It was a traditional health promoting practise the validity of which was recently confirmed by scientific research.[2] The two girls, who had been told to bring in their blankets, paused momentarily on the flat rock next to their playpen. As they peered into the darkness across the channel, several indistinct forms moving slowly from behind Anishinaabe Minis Indian Island toward Animoshi Minis Dog Island caught their attention. "Nashke Gaagashkiigiiwaaj!" Having forgotten all about their blankets, they rushed into the house, exclaiming that Gaagashkiigiiwaaj were out on the lake. Several days later, Dedibaayaanimanook heard that some relatives had gone into town for a visit, and that their route had taken them just north of Camp Island. But the girls were not convinced. In their minds, they had definitely seen Gaagashkiigiiwaaj that night, not the relatives!

Another of the girls' favourites was about the diminutive Memeg-weshiwag, a kind of non-human people who lived in rock cliffs. Aside from their size and appearance, their most distinguishing characteristic was their reluctance to show themselves. Most Anishinaabeg had never seen their faces because they never looked directly at anyone, and in order to keep hidden, they too were shrouded. The Memegweshiwag never risked venturing far from home and when Anishinaabeg on rare occasions came upon them, they maneuvered their stone boats into the cliffs and quietly vanished. While canoeing along a narrow peninsula, Dedibaayaanimanook's relatives once heard the elusive people talking and singing. The canoeists sat quietly for a long time, spellbound by the strange sound of their voices. As soon as the Memegweshiwag realized that they had been discovered, however, they abruptly ceased their activities and melted into the rock crevasses.

The account of an unusual old woman named Zhiigawiish was one of Enan's favourite stories. Apparently, Zhiigawiish had lived out her life without children of her own. Once she reached her latter years, however, she came to understand with much regret that she would never experience one of life's greatest blessings. Zhiigawiish had no family and she led a solitary life, but the yearning to hold a child in her arms persisted. One day, a group of young mothers out to pick blueberries happened into the area with their little ones. Zhiigawi-ish crept close and watched hopefully from her hiding place in the bushes. The women were in the habit of propping their cradleboards in a shady spot where the infants could breathe the fresh air and take in the scenery. Even though the mothers were only a few feet away, Zhiigawiish was able to come right up to one of the babies that had fallen asleep. She snatched it, cradleboard and all, and slipped nimbly into the forest. A few moments later, the unsuspecting young mother stopped to feed her infant, only to discover her terrible loss. She screamed, and even though her companions were instantly at her side, they were too late. Her child had disappeared. Young parents were cautioned by their elders always to protect and stay close to their children, particularly the infants, those who were most cherished in the community. One never knew whether Zhiigawiish was lurking behind the nearest thicket.

Another—true—story that Dedibaayaanimanook shared was about the betrayal of a little Pikangikum girl who was raised by her grandmother. When fall arrived and it was time for the family to move to their winter camp, she was simply left behind. She watched by the water's edge as the last canoe disappeared behind the point of land, but she was not aware that Gookom did not intend to return for her. That winter, a wemitigoozhi who arrived in the area to open a Hudson's Bay Company post was taken aback when he spotted what appeared to be a small, two-legged creature bundled in tattered bits of rabbit fur. In fact, it was the abandoned little girl. Against all the odds, she had managed to survive the harshest season of the year. The child possessed enough knowledge to keep herself alive, as her grandmother had probably known. Using whatever she was able to find—old tin cans and other pieces of metal, bits of string and wire, scraps of cloth and the like—she made herself a lean-to in which to live and she caught small animals for food and fur. Of all her implements, however, the one most valuable to her was a rusty needle she found where the family's tent had stood. The post manager and his wife were so amazed by her resourcefulness and courage that they took her into their home. One day, a conscience-stricken Gookom could barely believe her eyes when she recognized her granddaughter, alive and well, at the Hudson's Bay Company.

Both of Dedibaayaanimanook's girls asked her to repeat a story that dated back to the time when Anishinaabe people were at war with Bwaanag, the Lakotas. As the members of one group fled from the advancing fighters, they stopped for the night. But they knew that the success of their flight required that they remain absolutely silent. One young mother was able to keep her toddler quiet by spreading some sweet substance on the child's face. Too preoccupied tasting the jam that stuck to her fingers as she tried to wipe it away, the child remained quiet and she soon fell asleep. Another group of Anishinaabeg took refuge in a deep forest. Hearing no sounds of the enemy after waiting for several hours, one woman prepared to boil water over a camp fire. She looked into the pot where, to her horror, she saw the reflection of a Lakota warrior. He was watching intently from a tree above. Despite her terror, the woman was able to keep her composure long enough to enter the tent and inform her brother of the foe's presence.

Dedibaayaanimanook used these types of narratives to share the Namegosibii Anishinaabe traditions and historical stories that her parents, aunts and uncles had given to her. But another form of teaching she used was to tell the girls what she had heard whenever people gathered for feasts and visited. She listened to the knowledge keepers of the community as they talked about personal insights that came from life's experiences. As it was the duty of all children and youth, she paid attention to the words of her seniors, whether their words were intended for the entire group or for her individually. The practise of providing advice and instruction to the youth existed because it was the duty of the Gichi Anishinaabeg to hand down their wisdom and knowledge to the community's younger generations.

Some of the information of which Dedibaayaanimanook heard her father and uncles speak were the challenges and difficulties that now lay at their very doorstep. They stated that wemitigoozhi activites in the region were increasing so rapidly that finding a safe place in which to live was becoming more and more problematic. Soon, the time would come when there would be nowhere on the entirety of the earth in which to live safely and in good health as Anishinaabe people. Shortly after the untimely death of his infant daughter, Dedibaayaanimanook's brother Jiibwaat Edward Angeconeb had paid her a distressing visit. He described how he had sat alone by the shoreline, looking across the water toward Jiiyaani Minis. As her brother spoke about the overwhelming anguish of his loss, Dedibaayaanimanook detected a sense of hopelessness in his voice.

"Awiyawishag gidinendaagoozimin." He went on to mention a widespread historical attitude among wemitigoozhiwag that sub-humanized Anishinaabeg, and he warned that they were now in such close proximity that people of Namegosibiing would begin to experience, in direct and terrible ways, the kind of treatment arising from a belief that Anishinaabeg were not human beings, but wild animals. As a result of that attitude, increasing numbers of family members would die, not from natural causes, but from those related to the sickness of alcoholism and other destructive impacts. *"Gaawiinidash niin inga waabamaasiig."* These were the chilling words that alarmed her the most, that she would see his surviving children reach adulthood, but that he himself would not be a witness as they grew up to live under so much adversity. When Jiibwaat extended her his hand in farewell that day, Dedibaayaanimanook was deeply disturbed by the finality in his manner. It would be the last time she ever saw her brother. Not long after, she received word that he had died in hospital after being struck by a vehicle. Dedibaayaanimanook rarely spoke his name after that. Instead, she referred to him as Insayenziban gaa gii' bichibizoj, that is, my late brother who was hit in an automobile accident. Whenever that kind of traumatic news reached her, Dedibaayaanimanook found it best to be alone with her thoughts, because that was when she heard the words of her grandfather, providing her with comfort and with guidance on how best to proceed with her own life. This type of incident and how she dealt with it was what she shared with her children, even though they were still very young.

For Dedibaayaanimanook, retaining a deep conviction about the integrity of all things Anishinaabe meant continuing to live out those Anishinaabe values and ways of thinking. That was why, as an Anishinaabe woman with a wemitigoozhi partner, she considered one of her responsibilities as loyalty to Giigooyikewinini. The other was to teach the children, because in her mind, the two were not mutually exclusive. As well as storytelling and talking about what the leaders said, Dedibaayaanimanook taught the girls by having them watch as she did her work. She herself had learned to sew from her mother during her childhood, then later on, she was able to advance her skills immeasurably when her father purchased a sewing machine for her. It was therefore understandable that Dedibaayaanimanook wanted to see her children acquire the same skill. Initially, all new fabric and notions she used were gifts from her parents, but after they passed on, she needed to find a source for her materials and she needed to teach herself how to make garments for the children.

The used clothing non-Anishinaabe friends in Red Lake sent the Olsen family in Namegosibiing provided the solution to both problems. To illustrate, if she had been given a second hand coat, she dismantled the entire garment into its constituent parts. Then she carefully removed all the pleats and darts and ironed the fabric flat. By applying patterns of her own making onto the fabric's opposite face, Dedibaayaanimanook constructed whole new pieces of outer wear that lasted until the girls outgrew them. She similarly unravelled used garments one stitch at a time until she learned the technique for decorative knitting, smocking and embroidery whenever she was especially intrigued by interesting patterns. Thus she was able to knit socks, mittens, gloves, scarves and sweaters, incorporating special patterns for the entire family while teaching the girls some of the simpler techniques. With few exceptions, the clothes she and the children wore were of her making. The garments were not only well suited to the seasons in Namegosibiing but were of a style and construction quality superior to most store bought items. One of the exceptions was a pair of green ski pants she had purchased on a rare outing to Red Lake with Giigooyikewinini.

But Dedibaayaanimanook also took on larger sewing projects such as winter outerwear for Giigooyikewinini. Fur trimmed parkas that kept him warm on fishing and trapping trips across the lake were products of her handiwork. In particular, a parka using generous quantities of fox trim on off-white canvas became Giigooyikewinini's favourite for visits into town. Sewing with beads was another favourite pastime that she wanted eventually to teach the girls. As a young teenager, she herself had made a pair of moose hide gloves with gauntlets that she decorated with glass beads. She also made several belts covered solidly in beaded designs which she sold for approximately three dollars each. As soon as she finished making a pair of ermine trimmed gloves embellished with floral designs in translucent red, green and gold glass beads, Giigooyikewinini wore them into town with his favourite parka. Many years later, after Giigooyikewinini passed on, Aaniz Alice would inherit the gloves as a keepsake of her mother's giftedness and her father's appreciation of those special talents. Her methods were labour intensive and they demanded a great deal of skill and patience, but she was blessed with both qualities in abundance.

Long winter evenings were especially suitable for Dedibaayaanimanook to teach the girls about sewing. After the dinner dishes were done, she began her teaching sessions by taking the kerosene lamps into the bedroom and placing them in sconces that Giigooyikewinini had nailed onto the wall. Then she turned on the radio, setting the dial to the kind of music she most enjoyed, country bluegrass—all of this, of course, she could only do when Giigooyikewinini was in town. Dedibaayaanimanook sat the two girls beside her on the bed and showed them how to transform bits of fabric scraps into skirts and blouses for their homemade dolls. In much the same way that her mother had done for her when she was a child, she began the process of transferring her sewing skills to her children.

Dedibaayaanimanook had also learned how to take advantage of the fact that commodity items such as rice and flour were still being shipped in cloth sacks. Her mother had shown her how to use the cotton fabric for making blouses, skirts, pillow slips and tea towels. Included with her mother's instructions was the method for removing any printing stamped on the material as well as how to keep white cotton towels and clothing stain free and bright. Anishinaabe women had long used a process they called "onzaanan bingwi," that is, boiled ashes. After being boiled, the ashes were strained away and discarded. The items to be bleached were then put into the clear liquid and boiled. Later, lye was used. Then, household laundry bleaches replaced the old method for keeping whites white because commercial products were more convenient to use. But it was Dedibaayaanimanook's experience that the bleaches failed to outperform the natural method her people had once used. As well, the effects of bleaches on the natural environment were non-benign. Although Dedibaayaanimanook taught the children about the use of cotton sacks and natural bleaching, it was not long before paper bags and plastics came into use for packaging.

The fact that Dedibaayaanimanook succeeded so well in mastering the art of sewing became evident when friends and acquaintances in Red Lake noticed the two girls' attire on occasions when they accompanied their parents into town. Quick to express their admiration for Dedibaayaanimanook's workmanship, non-Anishinaabe women seemed both amazed and fascinated by the notion that a young Anishinaabe mother actually knew how to sew. In fact, it seemed that Dedibaayaanimanook's reputation as a seamstress had spread among the Olsens' circle of wemitigoozhi friends and acquaintances in Red Lake because whenever she was in town, they presented her with their broken zippers and sagging hemlines.

There were other aspects to teaching the children. In terms of the more spiritual content of Anishinaabe thought, Dedibaayaanimanook usually let the children's natural sense of curiosity determine the extent to which she provided them with an explanation. Mindful of Giigooyikewinini's opinion, however, she generally answered their questions to their satisfaction without further elabouration. For example, Dedibaayaanimanook kept a small cloth medicine bundle in her suitcase beneath the bed. The mixture and instructions for its use had come from her mother. When she opened the suitcase one day and the two children inquired about the packet, she simply emphasized the sacredness of the medicine. Another teaching that came up had to do with honouring the memory of those who had passed on. After a main meal, Dedibaayaanimanook cautioned the children about not throwing the bones of certain animals into the fire. "Ashamaadaa sa Nookomiban." She told them, however, to burn other types of food as a gift offering to her departed grandmother. Once the food tumbled into the stove and was consumed by the flames, Nookomiban's acceptance of their offering was assured. During such a learning session, one of Dedibaayaanimanook's younger children once lifted the stove lid and tried to peer inside. "Niwii' waabamaa Nookomiban!" she exclaimed, expecting to see her great-grandmother appear among the glowing embers. In another incident, Dedibaayaanimanook's children were playing in the woods when they looked up and noticed what appeared to be a bundle of rags tucked among the branches of an evergreen. From their mother's admonition, they understood it to be of a special significance and, obeying her words, they never disturbed it. Her teaching the children about such matters continued for as long as they lived with her on Camp Island in Namegosibiing.

With her situation unique in the community, Dedibaayaanimanook had no one to emulate. Those early years with Giigooyikewinini had been a period of immense adjustment and learning, but it was also true that she came to Camp Island with a vast amount of knowledge. Without her perseverance, the fishing operation would not likely have achieved the same degree of success, and wemitigoozhiwag who came to know the Olsen family of Namegosibiing were well aware of her dedication. Some even reminded Giigooyikewinini about her diligence, devotion and hard work. Their acknowledgment and recognition that she in fact achieved full and equal partner status at Camp Island was itself a remarkable tribute to her.

1. Gete Wemitigoozhi means Old White Person

2. The fact that one's general health is positively affected when blankets and pillows are given regular airing outdoors was well known among Dedibaayaanimanook's people. Particularly during winter, the practice serves to kill bed mites, thus reducing mite droppings in one's sleeping area and decreasing the chances of developing respiratory problems.

CHAPTER 9

Niwii' Biminizha'waa Nimishoomis

~

I Will Follow My Grandfather

"Ginoondawishim ina?" Dedibaayaanimanook tried to make herself heard, but the howling wind and the roaring breakers swallowed her words. As seething waves crashed unrelentingly against the boat, she tried to keep the flashlight pointing toward shore. Its beam of light barely penetrated the night's blackness. Bracing her knees against the wooden net box helped her stay balanced until a spray of icy water flung itself across her face. Dedibaayaanimanook gasped for breath. Merging with her tears, the freezing water trickled down into the net box. "Gego gotaajikeg!" Straining to keep her voice from quavering, she reassured Aaniz and Enan not to fear. They were still warm and dry beneath the canvas.

"Wegonen!" Suddenly a faint cry rose above the storm's din. Dedibaayaanimanook could barely see the tiny beacon of light appearing from beyond the shoreline, but as a figure came running along the trail toward them, she felt the pounding in her chest begin to subside. It was her faithful brother Jiins. Only a few days earlier, Dedibaayaanimanook had come over to see how her parents were keeping. Her mother had been having problems with her heart and feeling unwell, so she decided to bring her back to Camp Island with her. Now she was back here with the girls to inform the family of her mother's death.

As they always did for the passing of a community member, people gathered at the traditional cemetery at Gojijiwaawangaang for the interment of Gaamadweyaashiik Emma Keesick. But circumstances at Camp Island did not allow Dedibaayaanimanook herself to attend.

Although she realized that her mother would one day leave them, she did not anticipate how profoundly she would grieve her departure. Then a year later, Dedibaayaanimanook's beloved father died. Dedibayaash William Sam Keesick was buried beside Gaamadweyaashiik at Gojijiwaawangaang. Keeping busy was never difficult for Dedibaayaanimanook, and for her to continue doing so helped her to cope with the devastation of losing both of her parents so quickly. She was now twenty-eight years old and the mother of three young children.

By now, the woman who lived just east of Camp Island was a well established presence in Namegosibiing. Dedibaayaanimanook discovered that she and Zena Sarah Yates had much more in common than just their names.[1] Giigooyikewinini, on the other hand, shared the same birthday with Zena, but there were few other ways he wished to be associated with her. Being from the Old Country, it may have been that his notions about a woman's place did not match Zena's role at the lodge. She seemed to know about his views, and so she usually timed her visits to Camp Island when he was out on the lake or in town. As a result, their paths rarely crossed. When she came over during the summer, Zena often arrived in her large fishing boat. About the same size as the Olsens', the *Sally* was also painted in a battleship gray but was trimmed with a distinctive red stripe down its length on both sides. Zena came escorted by one of her staff or her business partner, Bert. At other times, she came alone in one of their smaller boats, since she knew how to operate an outboard motor. She stayed long enough to share cooking suggestions, favourite recipes and gardening techniques with Dedibaayaanimanook. Coming prepared with various utensils and ingredients, she carried out one or two demonstrations. One summer afternoon, Zena brought along a camera after hearing that an orphaned moose calf had been adopted by the Olsens.

Her visits were less frequent during winter. Driving a team of prancing huskies, she pulled up in front of the Olsens' cabin just before Christmas one year. She brought along gifts for each of the children and a vial of perfume for Dedibaayaanimanook.

Even though Giigooyikewinini seldom visited Trout Lake Lodge—
for the above mentioned reason—he made certain that the door of
neighborliness remained open just a crack. He made his infrequent
forays for the purpose of using the phone for an important call and
usually during the quietude of winter because summertime at the
lodge was much too "topsy-turvy" for his liking. Whenever little
Aaniz and Enan were lucky enough to accompany their father, they
followed him eagerly on skis of their own. As soon as they reached the
lodge and opened the door, they were greeted by a delightful aroma
that came wafting from Zena's kitchen. Derived from a mixture of
freshly grated vanilla, nutmeg, coconut and cinnamon, it was a characteristic feature of Zena's domain, especially during winter when she
experimented with and expanded upon her cooking repertoire. When
the girls looked around, their eyes grew wide with fascination at the
sight of all the wooden racks lining the kitchen walls. The shelves
were laden with glass jars of chocolate jimmies, rainbow sprinkles,
glossy nonpareils and silver dragées. Further up were several glitter-
ing coffee pots. Tucked just beneath the rafters, they were enveloped
in clear, shiny plastic. Inverted mixing bowls of various sizes and
decorative designs nestled nearby. From another grouping of shelves,
white enamel cooking pots with red handles gleamed down upon the
children's upturned faces. The counter top was closer to eye level. It
was where a crystal candy jar sat, crammed with assorted bonbons
ready to be raided. Even years later, Aaniz and Enan would recall
the delicate bouquet of Zena's kitchen whenever they came across a
particular blend of spices and cooking sweets.

The community knew Zena to have a compassionate side to her
nature. In fact, it was said that she could not bring herself to go fishing
because she pitied the fish and cried when she saw them struggle to
escape. However, she was also known for pragmatic decisions that
placed profit before the well-being of her staff. She was a shrewd entre-
preneur. The largest documented trout to come out of the waters of
Namegosibiing was the one caught in one of Giigooyikewinini and
Dedibaayaanimanook's nets one summer in the early 1950s. The

creature weighed 54 pounds.[2] For many years, the lodge made reference to the Olsens' trout by way of promoting the business without, of course, divulging that it had been caught in a gill net by commercial fishers. Zena and her partner Bert hired Dedibaaayaanimanook's relatives as well as Anishinaabeg from other communities as their tourism business grew. During the 1950s and 1960s, Dedibaayaanimanook's nephews Niiyoo Leo, Isaac, Simeon, Anôy Roy and Ed all worked at the lodge. Having put schooling behind them, Jiibwaat and Gweyesh Annie Angeconeb's sons were very young when they first began to work. They performed whatever work needed doing, helping with the commercial fishing, cabin building, taking up ice, guiding guests, cutting fire wood, and so on, at Trout Lake Lodge. During their employment, the Angeconebs lived on the Trout Lake Lodge island, off private property with their mother, Gweyesh. By that time, their father had lost his life in an automobile collision.

When Isaac married Tina Rae and Simeon married Tina's sister Agnes, the young wives worked for Zena before starting their respective families. Others of Dedibaayaanimanook's relatives who worked at Trout Lake Lodge included her brother Jiins and his daughter Kwiishkwa'oo Eliza. She too had stopped attending residential school. Irene Keesick, whose younger sister Cecilia married Ed Angeconeb, returned to Trout Lake Lodge every summer for many years before Zena and her partner sold the business. Since Trout Lake Lodge was open for business only during the summer, however, Dedibaayaanimanook's nephews were free to help with the fishing at Camp Island throughout the winter months. They also came during slow periods when the lodge had no guests, often living across the bay.

As she had done when her cousins and brothers were employed at Camp Island, Dedibaayaanimanook rose early each morning to make breakfast and pack lunches for her nephews. They arrived for breakfast and left for the lake while it was still dark. When they returned in late afternoon, Dedibaayaanimanook had a hot dinner for them, and if a plane was scheduled to pick up the fish, she helped them finish dressing the day's catch. Working with her nephews allowed her to share in the latest community news and thus maintain a sense of connection with her relatives and kin, of whom most of the younger generations were no longer living in Namegosibiing due mainly to the lack of employment. There were also times when Dedibaayaanimanook was now able to enjoy an occasional carefree moment to relax with her relatives. One summer afternoon when the fishing chores had all been finished, Dedibaayaanimanook sat down on an upturned fish box next to her nephew Niiyoo Leo. They watched in fascination as massive schools of minnows swam past. Numbering in the thousands, they formed dark undulating ribbons that stretched from the shallow regions of the bay all the way to the deep waters beyond the point.

"Gonige ogikendaanaawaan e'inawendiwaaj." As they sat mesmerized by the astounding sight, Dedibaayaanimanook wondered aloud whether the tiny creatures were aware that they were all related to one other. Then two minnows came into view, swimming some distance from the rest. "Ganabaj wiin ogikendaanaawaan ogo," Niiyoo replied to his aunt. He reckoned that the two to which he was pointing probably knew that they were related. Although Dedibaayaanimanook always took the business of fishing seriously, she retained an innate sense of appreciation for those meaningful but brief moments that life provided, such as the break she shared with her nephew that placid afternoon on the dock.

Giigooyikewinini, too, had an appreciation for things other than fishing. When he first came to Namegosibiing, for example, he was heard to mention an interest in raising a bear cub. It was not long after he made his comment that Dedibaayaanimanook's brother Jiibwaat and her cousin Gwiiwish Isaac Keesick were out hunting and came across a tiny cub. They slowly approached the animal, but it scrambled up a small tree as soon as it heard them. All the while it squealed noisily with fright. "Daga miinaadaa Giigooyikewinini." Gwiiwish then recalled Giigooyikewinini's wish for a cub, so he decided to retrieve it. He shook the tree vigorously until the little animal tumbled to the ground. Immediately, he reached down and scooped it up in his arms, but it struggled and growled so fiercely that he had to release it. Later, Dedibaayaanimanook expressed her relief when she heard about the failed attempt. "Wiinge iidog daagii'mindido!" Reminding them that the cub would grow into a very large size, she shuddered at the thought of living on Camp Island with a fully grown black bear.

Dedibaayaanimanook herself had considered raising a wolf pup, but that did not come to fruition either. Instead, she and Giigooyikewinini found themselves adopting and raising baby moose. Remaining with them for several years, their first was a male whose reputation extended throughout the Red Lake region as a result of a vastly exaggerated story that was published in the local paper. Based on Pete Moose's supposed (mis)adventures in Namegosibiing, the article amused everyone but Giigooyikewinini. Then the Olsens rescued a pair of calves so small that they needed to be fed milk from a baby bottle. As she held the calves and felt their helplessness, Dedibaayaanimanook wanted to help them live.

During their first winter of life, the twins remained on the island and stayed close to the Olsen family. Elsie and Ferdinand fed on a diet of deciduous twigs and oats mixed with birch sawdust from Giigooyikewinini's chain saw cuttings. Elsie, who was slightly smaller than her brother, was extremely timid and easily frightened. Depending on Ferdinand for her security, she never let him far from her sight. One day the veranda door was left open, so the children coaxed Ferdinand all the way into the house. Elsie, in the meantime, stood watching as her brother disappeared through the doorway. With great agitation, she circled around the house several times, all the while crying pitifully. Only when Ferdinand reappeared was she consoled. Ferdinand, who clearly sensed his sister's need, was protective of her and was careful not to leave her for long.

As time went on, the two moose ventured further afield. Compelled by their natural instincts, they began to stay away for longer periods until eventually, their infrequent appearance at Camp Island became a cause for celebration. One day in June, when the twins were two years old, Elsie gave the Olsen family a pleasant surprise by stopping at Camp Island for a short visit. The yellow collar that Dedibaayaanimanook had made her still hung around her neck. But Elsie seemed anxious to leave. She waded into the water and swam northwest, toward the distant Aanizi Minis Alice Island. That evening, Dedibaayaanimanook and Giigooyikewinini thought about Elsie and they both realized that something about her behaviour told that they should take a boat ride to Alice Island. The next day, they took their youngest child, Irene, and set out across the lake with a pail of oats and a camera. They arrived on the eastern side of the island and turned off the engine. It was not too long after calling Elsie's name that they heard rustling sounds from the bushes nearby. Suddenly Elsie appeared on the rocky shoreline. As she stood proudly before them, a wobbly little calf nudged shyly against her thigh!

Late one evening toward mid-autumn, Dedibaayaanimanook thought she heard banging on the veranda door. She got up to see what had caused the thump, and as she slowly opened the door, she was filled with joy to see that it was Elsie once again. Standing nervously in the shadows just behind Elsie was her young calf, Elferd. Dedibaayaani-manook leaned toward Elsie and gave her a gentle embrace. When she went back to bed, she had a vivid dream. "Nimaamaa, ingigishkigan gi miinin." In the dream, Elsie referred to Dedibaayaanimanook as her mother, then she took off the garment draped over her back and gave it to her as a keepsake. The Olsen family waited with much anticipation during the next several weeks, expecting that Elsie and Elferd would return. Dedibaayaanimanook even went for walks in search of the smallest sign of their presence, but there was none.

As for Ferdinand, he too dropped by Camp Island to see his parents. His visits, however, occurred only during winter and early spring before break-up. One day, he arrived with a partially healed wound on his underbelly. Giigooyikewinini did his best to apply ointment on the lesion. Ferdinand stayed at Camp Island for almost a month. When Giigooyikewinini had to go to Trout Lake Lodge one afternoon, Zena Sarah Yates found the sight of Ferdie trotting across the bay behind him amusing. She took photographs of the moose as he stood waiting patiently to return to Camp Island with his father. Then some months later, one of Dedibaayaanimanook's nephews mentioned that a tourist in the area had shot a bull moose. It had a faded yellow collar around its neck. Elsie and Ferdinand were the last moose that Dedibaayaanimanook and Giigooyikewinini ever adopted.

The time had now come for the older Olsen children to attend public school. The three eldest boarded with an older Christian couple who lived on a picturesque little farm just east of Kenora. Their guardians, the Goulds, belonged to an obscure, almost secretive, fundamentalist group that subscribed to honest work, regular church attendance and a great deal of prayer. Although she never actually met Elizabeth "Auntie Lizzie" Gould, Dedibaayaanimanook highly regarded the woman who cared for her three eldest children. She noted that Mrs. Gould sewed many of the girls' clothes and that they always presented a neatly groomed and well dressed appearance. When they returned for the holidays, they seemed reasonably happy and were in good health. Overall, Dedibaayaanimanook was satisfied with Mrs. Gould's guardianship, given that nothing was ever ideal and that far worse situations existed for children of Anishinaabe ancestry. Toward the end of August each year, it was the same routine for Dedibaayaanimanook and Giigooyikewinini. They stood on the dock together and waved to the children as the plane flew them into town. Depending on circumstances, they might see them for Christmas. Whenever Giigooyikewinini was able to go into Red Lake and take the bus to Kenora to bring Aaniz and Enan back for the Christmas holidays, the family was briefly united. Dedibaayaanimanook put up window wreaths made from fresh cedar boughs, and she hung crêpe paper streamers across the kitchen ceiling while Giigooyikewinini and the children went in search of the perfect holiday tree. Everyone had a hand in loading down its branches with shiny glass bulbs and blankets of glistening tinsel. The radio played sprightly carols, and the roasting turkey sizzled. It was all part of how the family celebrated together.

Usually, however, Dedibaayaanimanook and Giigooyikewinini had to wait for up to nine and a half months before the children returned. But whichever way it happened, the children always had to leave again, and Dedibaayaanimanook was left to endure the desolation of a house, recently so alive with happy voices, that now seemed so soundless and still. Dedibaayaanimanook turned to her many chores for the distraction she needed while time's passage drew her through the days of emptiness.

It had now been many years since she first came to Camp Island. With the exception of the paperwork that always came attached to everything, she had mastered all aspects of their commercial fishing operation. Her sense of self continued to be as deeply grounded in the Anishinaabe teachings of her parents and grandparents as it had been during childhood. The quiet pride of her deportment demonstrated the power of the old teachings more forcefully than any words she could have ever spoken about herself. As alluded to before, sharing her life with a wemitigoozhi meant that she was often in situations where she was the only Anishinaabe present. It was a time when racism and sexism were prevalent and overt, and politically and socially acceptable.

Impressed by the genuineness of her character, wemitigoozhi visitors from town often tried to express their regard for Dedibaayaanimanook. Sometimes, however, their best efforts sounded more like backhanded compliments. This happened during conversations in which a particular word, meant specifically to be offensive yet very common at the time, was mentioned. Wemitigoozhi friends were pleased to declare that they did not think the term "squaw" properly applied to Dedibaayaanimanook, implying that it was her exceptionality as an individual—plus their insight and generosity—that elevated her from the "squaw" status of the others. In another type of conversation, an interesting exchange took place just after the Indian Act provided some measure of recognition to Anishinaabe people. "*Sarah* is the true Canadian!" Alluding to the commonly held notion that Anishinaabe people had only very recently advanced enough in their civilization to be citizens of the country, a wemitigoozhi visitor who had dropped by at Camp Island was attempting to point out that it was Dedibaayaanimanook and all the other Anishinaabeg who were the *real* citizens of the country. The speaker, referring to himself and the rest who were sitting around the kitchen table with him, stated that they were actually the second class Canadians because Anishinaabe people were already living in the country when the Europeans arrived.

Yet a different kind of attitude presented itself to Dedibaayaani-manook one winter's day when a plane loaded with wemitigoozhiwag from Red Lake landed at Camp Island. As soon as Giigooyikewinini invited the men in for a few beers, Dedibaayaanimanook went out-doors. One of the Olsens'dogs had recently had a litter of pups and now a little one cavorted close to where Dedibaayaanimanook stood chopping fire wood. She had already finished a sizable pile when one of the wemitigoozhiwag came swaggering out the door. Even though she saw him approaching, she continued with her work. But when he reached for the axe, she handed it to him and moved aside. She wondered how many blocks of wood he planned to chop. Instead of a piece of wood, however, the man grabbed the puppy, and with a swing of the axe, he chopped the innocent creature in two. How the wemitigoozhi could conceivably believe that such an act of barbarism would impress Dedibaayaanimanook was unimaginable. Whatever the intent, the behaviour had to be taken for what is was, an unfathom-able act of a warped mindset. Then there were times when wemiti-goozhi visitors to Namegosibiing sat at the Olsens' kitchen table for no other reason but to leer at Dedibaayaanimanook in vulgar ways that served only to display the depth of their ignorance. Their sense of pleasure seemed to thrive in their own crudeness.

Even wemitigoozhi women who were the Olsens' friends[3] uninten-tionally violated Dedibaayaanimanook's Anishinaabe sensibilities. In one incident, Dedibaayaanimanook and Giigooyikewinini were out on a boat ride with friends while visiting in Red Lake. It was a warm afternoon, but Dedibaayaanimanook did not react when she looked over and noticed that one of the women was undoing the top buttons on her blouse. When her friend suggested that she too might con-sider peeling back some of her clothing to enjoy the sun's rays more fully, Dedibaayaanimanook simply declined. While it was true that she appreciated the good intent of those who wanted to help her navigate successfully within white society, there were limits to the sort of advice she accepted! Dedibaayaanimanook certainly shirked the kind designed to attract the attention of men because her mother had taught her about the importance of modesty and morality. Rather, it was Zena Sarah Yates's practical kind of helpful hints, those that related to ways for improving day to day work, that she readily embraced. While wemitigoozhiwag felt free to offer her their advice, Dedibaayaanimanook never tried to impose her beliefs or ideas on anyone other than her own children, even though she maintained an unshakable faith in the authenticity of what her parents had taught her.

Dedibaayaanimanook had learned through two basic forms of teaching. By first observing her parents and others of the family, then by emulating them, she learned how to set snares, skin fur bearing animals, make moccasins, set muskrat traps and numerous other tasks related to physical survival. The other type came in the form of exhortations. She had already internalized the teachings of her parents and grandparents in early childhood. Helping to shape the essence of who she was, the instructions handed from the senior Elders of the community were invaluable.

"Gego wiikaa miikinji'aaken awiya gaa aakozij." As a child at play, Dedibaayaanimanook was admonished never to belittle, revile or ridicule anyone in pain or afflicted with age related debilities. This teaching instilled an attitude of respect and deference toward all fellow humans, and provided Dedibaayaanimanook with an outlook that helped her to live in harmony with members of the larger community.

"Gego wiikaa majenimaaken awiiya." The expression referred to an inner human dignity that every individual possessed. To show an attitude of disrespect or disregard toward another person was in fact to disdain or scorn one's own self. Adherence to this teaching helped to ensure good relationships and protect against the use of evil medicine.

"Gego wiikaa dazhimaaken awiya." Dedibaayaanimanooks' mother cautioned against saying negative things about others, that is, gossiping. To do so was to invite the same situations upon yourself and even your children and grandchildren. Beyond that, friends talking together in public needed carefully to avoid loud laughter. Persons within hearing distance might inadvertently think themselves to be the object of a joke and thus become offended. Dedibaayaanimanook would always become reflexively uneasy whenever her children laughed too loudly in the presence of anyone not of the immediate family. The latter two admonitions also helped to prevent individuals from falling out with community members. Cohesiveness and unity were too vital for survival in the Anishinaabe world for fractures to happen easily. The threat of expulsion or isolation was therefore an effective way for encouraging a general state of harmony.

Another admonition governed deferential behaviour when conversing with another person, particularly a visitor into the community. Dedibaayaanimanook's father told her not to look directly at someone speaking to her. To do so was an invasion of the person's privacy and was highly offensive.

The fact that Dedibaayaanimanook retained the old ways was evident by her habit of averting her eyes. Given the context of mainstream Canadian society that placed so high a value on direct eye contact, those who were unfamiliar with this tenet historically misunderstood traditional people who avoided looking at someone during conversation. Another norm associated with humility taught against boastfulness, bragging and loud behaviour. Even though one was extremely well served by a subdued demeanor within the context of traditional culture, its effects in the contradictory world of the wemitigoozhi was to give an impression of weakness and vulnerability.[4] "Mii' geniin enaadiziyaan." In conversations with Jii, the widow of Dedibaayaanimanook's cousin Jiimis mentioned that her parents' teachings were similarly evident in her mannerisms.

In yet another set of instructions, Dedibaayaanimanook's mother taught her that the behaviour of a young girl needed to be different from that of her brothers. Even the way she played had to be different, especially as she approached pre-adolescence. For example, Dedibaayaanimanook's brothers used slingshots to catch small game such as spruce grouse and squirrels while she was allowed only to throw rocks or set snares. Later on, however, after Dedibaayaanimanook came to Camp Island, she became proficient with the use of not only a .22 rifle but with Giigooyikewinini's .3855, even though her first experience with his .3030 resulted in being knocked backwards into the shrubs and getting bruised on the right side of her face. Her brother Jiins had forgotten to warn her about holding it tightly against her shoulder. When she once inquired about his shotgun, Jiins refused to let her use it, explaining that it had an even more powerful recoil. Over the course of time, Dedibaayaanimanook became an exceptionally skillful hunter. In fact, she was able to shoot more accurately than Giigooyikewinini. She shot both caribou and moose, although she never caught a bear, and whenever a duck swan into the bay at Camp Island, she had no difficulty shooting it with a .22.

Another of her parents' teachings required her to remain seated in a corner at the far side of the stove, well away from male members of the household at certain times. Once a woman married, she was expected to leave her parents because her life now focussed on building a union with her partner and being supportive as he took on a leadership role. Her partner, however, made final decisions only in areas in which men were expected to have expertise. It was just as shameful for a man to attempt to make decisions in areas where women were expert as it was for a woman to attempt to overrule her mate's decision. Although roles were gender based, women's contributions to the well-being of a family and community were recognized and valued. In fact, it was said that the death of a woman had a greater negative impact upon a family and its community than that of a man.

Both girls and boys were instructed not to stretch out their arms when they first awakened. The reason behind this traditional admonition was not clear. They were also taught not to sleep on their backs because to do so was to imitate the deceased. Furthermore, children were discouraged from being idle in order to prevent harmful messages and thoughts from entering their minds. Other voices of discretion mingled with those of her parents. Dedibaayaanimanook remembered hearing her mother's and father's conversations with aunts and uncles about the teachings and stories they had all received from Giizhik Sam Keesick. She learned about how her grandfather had an austere upbringing, and that he had assimilated the lessons of living in the same kind and peaceful way taught by the one Europeans referred to as Jesus. It was from Gizhe Manidoo, the Loving Being, that Giizhik learned the powerful and liberating lesson of unconditional forgiveness. This way of life was known as minobimaadiziwin, and as it was practised by her grandfather, it excluded card playing, dancing, drinking, the totem system and celebration of the *Midewiwin* of the grand medicine society. Nonetheless, Dedibaayaanimanook knew that her father did not forbid her mother's attendance at *Midewinaaniwan*. In fact, whenever her mother took her and Gichi Jôj to Lac Seul for the celebration, her father went on a trip of his own or simply stayed home. Dedibaayaanimanook recalled that the event was held on a high sandy embankment not far from Adikamego Zaagiiing Whitefish Bay. "Gii' zhawendaagozi nimishoomis." Toward the end of his life, Dedibaayaanimanook's grandfather was said to have achieved Gizhe Manidoo's love. Dedibaayaanimanook herself remembered some of his words, and most of what she heard and retained began to take on its fullest meaning after she grew up and needed inspiration during times of adversity.

"Niwii' biminizha'waa nimishoomis—I want to follow my Grandfather," was how Dedibaayaanimanook explained her resistance against efforts of well intentioned friends, both Anishinaabeg and wemitigoozhiwag, who wanted to see her embrace mainstream Christianity. However, she was determined to adhere to what she had learned from the example of how her grandfather had lived his life guided entirely by the strength of his inner convictions. These had been based on an integration of basic Christian principles into Anishinaabe teachings rather than church attendance or fellowship within an institutionalized form of the Christian religion. That was why Dedibaayaanimanook found guidance and strength whenever she meditated on her grandfather's teachings about love and forgiveness, and as she strove to live out those principles, her efforts became her spirituality. Considering that others of Giizhik's grandchildren had also received his instructions, there was the question of why the teachings served her so particularly well. Perhaps the single most important factor was that she was able to avoid residential school. Had she gone, she too would have had to face daily attacks directed against all aspects of who she was as an Anishinaabe human being. The clothes she wore, the food she ate, the language she spoke, the parents who loved her, the blackness of her hair, the brown of her eyes and her skin, and most significantly, the belief system of her people would have all been denounced and denigrated.

Despite the divergency of the worlds from which they came, Dedibaayaanimanook and Giigooyikewinini succeeded in forging commonalities and balance during their lives together. The early 1970s began to see Giigooyikewinini, now in his seventies, suffering serious health problems. Dedibaayaanimanook was in her fifties. All but the youngest of the six Olsen children had now left Namegosibiing to attend school and pursue lives for themselves. Eventually, even Irene needed to leave her parents to complete her schooling. Dedibaayaanimanook and Giigooyikewinini were now alone, and as they continued to fish commercially, the challenges and barriers became more and more daunting with time. One cold morning several weeks after freeze-up, Dedibaayaanimanook accompanied Giigooyikewinini to lift a net southwest of Camp Island. Having given up their dog team a few years previously, they now used a snowmobile. Giigooyikewinini drove the machine, pulling the sled on which Dedibaayaanimanook sat with the fish box of tools. They made their way toward the distant marker, the wind blowing briskly from the north. Then, so quickly that there was no time to think, Dedibaayaanimanook felt the massive weight of frigid waters encircling her, pulling her downward. Chunks of ice swirled everywhere. "*Sarah—grab the axe!*" She struggled wildly to stay afloat, but it was the urgency in Giigooyikewinini's voice that broke through her panic. She could see an axe in front of her.

The snowmobile had hit a large section of thin ice, and as the machine dropped beneath him, Giigooyikewinini had the presence of mind to reach behind and grab the axe in the fish box. With it, he pulled himself from the water. He then held it toward Dedibaaya-animanook as he lay stretched across the ice. With the last of her strength rapidly fading, Dedibaayaanimanook grabbed for it and held on. Slowly, he pulled her toward him as the ice beneath continued to crackle and sag. With their garments freezing solid, they began their laboured trek back to Camp Island. Only when they reached home and were able to start a fire did they think about just how narrowly they had managed to escape a terrible tragedy. Several months later, their son Harald came for a visit and retrieved their snowmobile.

The Olsens were now alone on the lake for much of the non-summer season because most of Dedibaayaanimanook's nephews and other relatives no longer spent winters in Namegosibiing. Some lived in Red Lake in search of work while others moved to the home communities of their wives. However, friends and relatives continued to drop by to visit at Camp Island throughout the year. Dedibaayaanimanook and Giigooyikewinini were appreciative of all such visits with one exception—the Ontario Ministry of Natural Resources (OMNR) officer. Aside from the quotas that Giigooyikewinini and Dedibaayaanimanook found increasingly difficult to fill and the fact that fish prices barely kept up with ever rising costs, the number of provincial rules regulating the industry was becoming onerous during those latter years of commercial fishing. Provincial focus continued to be environmental protection, but additional regulations were more and more related to health concerns. For instance, the use of wooden bins for storing fish no longer met the standards. The Olsens were required to purchase expensive stainless steel bins. Game wardens patrolled Namegosibiing closely in order to make sure that the Olsens were not dumping or otherwise wasting anything they had caught. With each visit, the enforcement officers seemed to come armed with a new set of decrees. The provincial OMNR imposed heavy penalties for any illegal activities, but Giigooyikewinini and Dedibaayaanimanook observed the regulations and codes meticulously. They were never charged with any infractions, even as rules and regulations became more burdensome with time.

An OMNR function that affected Dedibaayaanimanook directly had to do with the hunting of game animals in Namegosibiing. Only Anishinaabeg with Treaty status were permitted to kill animals for personal consumption without a license during the off-season. Since the Indian Act had wrongly stripped Dedibaayaanimanook of her Treaty rights when she partnered with Giigooyikewinini, all of her hunting, fishing and harvesting activities fell under provincial jurisdiction. The answer to why provincial OMNR regulations were enforced in Namegosibiing in so draconian a manner from the time of the 1950s, and why the regulations became so increasingly oppressive had to do with the growing number of commercial tourist businesses being allowed into Namegosibiing. Soon after their arrival, camp owners started to believe that Namegosibiing was theirs, and they saw all of the lake's resources, particularly the fish, as belonging to them exclusively. In their minds, the presence of Dedibaayaanimanook and Giigooyikewinini—the only commercial fishers on the lake after Sarah Yates relinquished her license—blocked their pursuit of unhindered access to the lake's usage. That was why the operators began to pressure the OMNR to remove the Olsens from the lake, even though no legal reasons existed for doing so. Earlier on, the Olsens were told to leave Trout Lake and fish just north of Memegwesh. Giigooyikewinini had sent Jiins and another man to assess the feasibility of such a relocation, but when they returned, his mind was already made up not to move. One camp owner was especially motivated to see Dedibaayaanimanook and Giigooyikewinini's departure. As a result, there were times during the summer when the Olsens' fish nets had been cut. At other times, nets were dragged from their location and left in a tangle of knots. It was said that the (original) owner of Sandy Beach Lodge bribed one of his guides to vandalize the Olsens' nets in the hope of discouraging their fishing activities.

Then, in the early 1970s, Giigooyikewinini became gravely ill. That was when, through false and coercive means, he was prevailed upon to sign away their commercial fishing license for a fraction of its actual worth. The buyer owned the local airline company as well as several fly-in tourist camps throughout the region. Having been clients with the airline owner for many years, Dedibaayaanimanook and Giigooyikewinini had given them a great deal of business. That Giigooyikewinini was approached to sign a document when he was suffering terminal illness and heavily medicated for pain could not be described in any other way than cowardly.[5] Not that long after, OMNR purchased the license from the individual for an undisclosed figure, and commercial fishing in Namegosibiing ceased.

Dedibaayaanimanook and Giigooyikewinini lost their commercial fishing license, but they refused to leave Camp Island. Instead, they decided to take up residence in Red Lake for the winter months. When the town's first senior's block was completed during the mid-1970s, they were among the first to move in, furnishing their new apartment with purchases from the local Hudson's Bay store and other retail outlets. It was Dedibaayaanimanook's first real experience with the amenities of urban living. Holding onto what was theirs, Dedibaayaanimanook and Giigooyikewinini continued to return to Camp Island every summer, and their grown children came to visit.

Dedibaayaanimanook was sixty-five years old when her life's partner died on September 18, 1987. Giigooyikewinini was eighty-eight. In accordance with his wishes, she ensured that he was buried at Gojijiwaawangaang. Dedibaayaanimanook and one of her daughters rode in the Otter aircraft with the casket. When they reached Namegosibiing, the pilot did not fly immediately south. Instead, he took a slight jog north and flew low over Camp Island. It was Giigooyikewinini's last plane ride to the island. His interment took place on a bronze autumn afternoon. Many of the birch leaves, having already fallen and turned brown, were strewn along the trail upon which pallbearers carried his pale blue casket to the top of the hill. Giigooyikewinini Einar Olsen is the only wemitigoozhi to lie at rest at the traditional Anishinaabe cemetery of Dedibaayaanimanook's people.

Eleven years later, Dedibaayaanimanook suffered yet another devastating loss when her only son, Harald, died in a hunting incident.

Many friends came to pay their respects and share her sorrow. Then, in 2002, she celebrated her eightieth birthday. This time, people from near and far came to join in honouring her special milestone.

"Amii' ewii'ani bezhigoyaan—gaawin awiya ji ganoonag." Dedibaayaanimanook recently commented that virtually all of the people with whom she grew up are now gone. There is no one left to speak the Anishinaabe language with her, to share the memories of old times and old ways. But she is assured that her life's story is available for descendants who do not speak Anishinaabe and for those who did not share a friendship. Furthermore, *her* story may help to revive an interest in those ancient ways, and motivate descendants to research, protect, preserve and reclaim the legacies of their forebears and their homeland.

1. Sarah Yates's partner Bert commonly referred to her as Sally.

2. Since Dedibaayaanimanook's people had already been catching large trout in Namegosibiing, it is quite possible that the commercially netted trout was not the largest to have ever been taken from the lake.

3. Due to her willingness to cultivate an attitude of friendship toward wemitigoozhiwag, Dedibaayaanimanook would ironically be accused of "loving" white people, presumably to the exclusion of Anishinaabeg.

4. See Chapter 4, Note 7.

5. The injustice that the Olsens experienced was acknowledged and discussed with Giigooyikewinini as he lay dying in the hospital. A mutually acceptable arrangement was made, and Giigooyikewinini was content that Dedibaayaanimanook would receive a measure of compensation. Since the time of Giigooyikewinini's death, Dedibaayaanimanook has indeed received some of what they ought to have obtained for their fishing lisence. This came about as a result of a sense of moral justice on the part of the eldest son of the original airline owner who, incidently, pre-deceased Giigooyikewinini by several years.

Fig. 25 Camp Island, early 1940s *left to right:* Gaamadweyaashiik, Dedibaaya-animanook's mother; Dedibaayaanimanook; Jiins; Dedibaayaanimanook's father, Dedibayaash. (Courtesy Dedibaayaanimanook Sarah Olsen)

Fig. 26 *left to right:* Gaamadweyaashiik; Giigooyikewinini; Dedibaayaanimanook; Dedibayaash. (Courtesy Dedibaayaanimanook Sarah Olsen)

Fig. 27 Camp Island, circa 1946: Dedibaayaanimanook with her first child, Aaniz Alice. (Courtesy Dedibaayaanimanook Sarah Olsen)

Fig. 28 Aaniz Alice, Camp Island. (Courtesy Dedibaayaanimanook Sarah Olsen)

Fig. 29 Camp Island, 1945: Dedibaayaanimanook holding Aaniz Alice.

Fig. 30 Camp Island, circa 1946: Dedibaayaanimanook rinsing laundry; Aaniz in a play pen built by Jiins. Relatives working at Camp Island lived in tents across the bay. (Courtesy Dedibaayaanimanook Sarah Olsen)

Fig. 31 Dedibaayaanimanook holding Aaniz Alice at Camp Island. (Courtesy Dedibaayaanimanook Saran Olsen)

Fig. 32 A load of sawdust for the ice house at Camp Island. (Courtesy Dedibaayaanimanook Sarah Olsen)

Fig. 33 Camp Island, 1947 *left to right:* Dedibaayaanimanook with Enan Helen and Aaniz Alice; her sister-in-law Gaanii Angeconeb, Jiins's wife, with Gwiishkwa'oo Eliza and Jaani Charlie. A tent can be seen across the bay behind them. (Courtesy Dedibaayaanimanook Sarah Olsen)

Fig. 34 Camp Island, 1950 *left to right:* Enan Helen; Aaniz Alice; Dedibaayaanimanook, holding Doris; Chiins Charlie Angeconeb; Jaani Charlie; Chiins's wife Gaanii, holding Zaagaate Josie; Gwiishkwa'oo Eliza. (Courtesy Dedibaayaanimanook Sarah Olsen)

Fig. 35 Dedibaayaanimanook holding a trout, Camp Island. (Courtesy Dedibaaya-animanook Sarah Olsen)

Fig. 36 Late 1940s: Aaniz Alice and Enan Helen.Goginini's camp on Cook Island can be seen in the background. (Courtesy Dedibaayaanimanook Sarah Olsen)

Fig. 37 Lifting a net near Duck Island, late 1940s left to right: Aaniz Alice; Enan Helen; Giigooyikewinini. (Courtesy Dedibaayaanimanook Sarah Olsen)

Fig. 38 Camp Island, early 1950s: Enan Helen and Aaniz Alice; Dedibaayaanimanook used rabbit fur to trim the girls' hats. (Courtesy Dedibaayaanimanook Sarah Olsen)

Fig. 39 McKenzie Island, Red Lake, late 1940s: Aaniz Alice and Enan Helen wearing the outfits Dedibaayaanimanook made them. (Courtesy Dedibaayaanimanook Sarah Olsen)

Fig. 40 Aaniz Alice helping her father Giigooyikewinini build Enisiiwigamig, the Elsie's House, circa 1948. (Courtesy Dedibaayaanimanook Sarah Olsen)

Fig. 41 Pete Moose, on the ice in front of Camp Island, early 1950s. Goginini's fishing camp is visible across the channel. (Courtesy Dedibaayaanimanook Sarah Olsen)

Fig. 42 Camp Island, early 1950s:
Pete Moose visiting the sled dogs.
(Courtesy Dedibaayaanimanook
Sarah Olsen)

Fig. 43 On the ice house, Camp Island: Dedibaayaanimanook feeding Pete Moose.
(Courtesy Dedibaayaanimanook Sarah Olsen)

Fig. 44 Camp Island, early 1950s: Dedibaayaanimanook's cousin Gwiiwish Isaac
Keesick, with unidentified person holding Olsens' 54 lb trout.
(Courtesy Dedibaayaanimanook Sarah Olsen)

Fig. 45 Trout Lake Lodge, 1957: Gweyesh Annie Angeconeb's son Isaac. (Courtesy Dedibaayaanimanook Sarah Olsen)

Fig. 46 Trout Lake Lodge, early 1950s: Gweyesh Annie and Jiibwaat Edward Angeconeb's sons, Anôy Roy and Ed (with Sarah Yates's father). (Courtesy Linda Prior)

Fig. 47 Trout Lake Lodge: Gweyesh Annie's sons Ed and Isaac Angeconeb with unidentified co-worker. (Courtesy Dedibaayaanimanook Sarah Olsen)

Fig. 48 Trout Lake Lodge, 1956 *left to right:* Gaamichaakojiizij Bert Tyrell; Isaac, Gweyesh's son; Niksaandan; Jiins, Dedibaayaanimanook's brother. (Courtesy Linda Prior)

Fig. 49 Gweyesh's second youngest son, Ed Angeconeb. (Courtesy Dedibaayaanima-nook Sarah Olsen)

Fig. 50 Trout Lake Lodge, 1950s: Niiyoo Leo Angeconeb, one of Gweyesh Annie's sons (Dedibaayaanimanook's nephew). (Courtesy Linda Prior)

Fig. 51 Trout Lake Lodge kitchen, late1950s: Gweyesh Annie's daughter-in-law Tina; Bert Tyrell; Wemichigoozhiikwe Sarah Yates. (Courtesy Linda Prior)

Fig. 52 *far left*: Gweyesh Annie Angeconeb's daughter-in-law Tina Angeconeb, watching guests at Trout lake Lodge. Dedibaayaanimanook's father's drum hung on the wall behind them. (Courtesy Linda Prior)

Fig. 53 Dedibaayaanimanook's father's handmade drum.

Fig. 54 Camp Island, early 1960s: Wemichigoozhiikwe Sarah Yates and Gaamichaa-kojiizij Bert with Elsie and Ferdinand. (Courtesy Dedibaayaanimanook Sarah Olsen)

Fig. 55 Camp Island, early 1960s: Dedibaayaanimanook with Ferdinand and Elsie Moose. (Courtesy Dedibaayaanimanook Sarah Olsen)

Fig. 56 Elsie's twin brother Ferdinand, waiting patiently for Giigooyikewinini at Trout Lake Lodge. (Courtesy Linda Prior)

Fig. 57 Ferdinand, with a wound on his underbelly, came to visit with only one of his antlers. He still wore Dedibaayaanimanook's yellow collar and he still enjoyed an embrace from his adopted father, Giigooyikewinini. (Courtesy Dedibaayaanimanook Sarah Olsen)

Fig. 58 Camp Island, early 1960s: Giigooyikewinini with Fredinand and Elsie. (Courtesy Dedibaayaanimanook Sarah Olsen)

Fig. 59 Elsie; Ferdinand; Giigooyikewinini; and Gweyesh Annie. (Courtesy Dedibaayaanimanook Sarah Olsen)

Fig. 60 Elsie, Ferdinand and Gladys (Anita), Dedibaayaanimanook and Giigooyikewinini's fourth child. (Courtesy Dedibaayaanimanook Sarah Olsen)

Fig. 61 Camp Island, Namegosibiing, early 1960s: Ferdinand and Harald Einar Olsen, Dedibaayaanimanook and Giigooyikewinini's only son. (Courtesy Dedibaayaanimanook Sarah Olsen)

Fig. 62 Ricing at Manoomini Zaa'igan: Soons Oojiiwasawaan with his grandson, Russell. (Courtesy Dedibaayaanimanook Sarah Olsen)

Fig. 63 Soon's wife Aaniz Alice visiting at Camp Island with her grandson, Russell. (Courtesy Dedibaayaanimanook Sarah Olsen)

Fig. 64 Trout Lake Lodge: Gweyesh Annie's son Simeon Angeconeb. (Courtesy Linda Prior)

Fig. 65 Namegosibiing, late 1950s: Dedibaayaanimanook with Irene, her youngest child. (Courtesy Dedibaayaanimanook Sarah Olsen)

Fig. 66 Namegosibiing, 1960s: Dedibaayaanimanook toured the shorelines of Animoshi Minis Dog Island. (Courtesy Dedibaayaanimanook Sarah Olsen)

Fig. 67 Mid-1960s, Dedibaayaanimanook visited the shorelines of Camp Island with her nephew Anoy Roy Angeconeb. (Courtesy Dedibaayaanimanook Sarah Olsen)

Fig. 68 Out on the lake, late 1960s: Dedibaayaanimanook and Giigooyikewinini. (Courtesy Dedibaayaanimanook Sarah Olsen)

Fig. 69 Fishing, late 1960s: Irene with her father, Giigooyikewinini. (Courtesy Dedibaayaanimanook Sarah Olsen)

Fig. 70 Camp Island, mid-1960s: Giigooyikewinini and Dedibaayaanimanook. (Courtesy Dedibaayaanimanook Sarah Olsen)

Fig. 71 Camp Island, early 1970s: Giigooyikewinini and Dedibaayaanimanook with visitors. (Courtesy Dedibaayaanimanook Sarah Olsen)

Fig. 72 Camp Island, late 1960s: Giigooyikewinini and Dedibaayaanimanook. (Courtesy Dedibaayaanimanook Sarah Olsen)

Fig. 73 Camp Island, late 1970s: Giigooyikewinini and Dedibaayaanimanook helping to dock the plane.

Fig. 74 Gojijiwaawangaang, Namegosibiing, September, 1987: The place of Giigooyikewinini's interment.

Fig. 75 Family and friends take Giigooyikewinini to his final resting place at Gojijiwaawangaang, Namegosibiing Trout Lake.

Fig. 76 Namegosi Ziibi, the river on which Dedibaayaanimanook and her family canoed to and from Namegosibiing Trout Lake (as seen from the Highway 105 bridge).

Fig. 77 Namegosi Ziibi.

Fig. 78 Jiibayi Zaagiing Jackfish Bay, Namegosibiing, 2002: Dedibaayaanimanook's granddaughter, Leslie Agger.

Fig. 79 Animoshi Minis Dog Island, as seen from Camp Island.

Fig. 80 Camp Island from a plane, looking toward the northwest. (Courtesy Dedi-baayaanimanook Sarah Olsen)

Fig. 81 Aerial view of Dedibaayaanimanook's home at Camp Island.

Fig. 82 Dedibaayaanimanook's trail to Gakiiw, Camp Island.

Fig. 83 Early freeze-up at Gakiiw, Camp Island (1960s). (Courtesy Dedibaayaanima-nook Sarah Olsen)

Fig. 84 Manidoo Minis Spirit Island, now know as Seagull Island, was where Dedibaayaanimanook's progenitors sought their life's vision.

Fig. 85 Dedibaayaanimanook and her granddaughter Leslie enjoyed a trip on the lake during a calm Namegosibiing afternoon.

Fig. 86 Camp Island, 2002: Dedibaayaanimanook showed her granddaughter Leslie how she made leaf dolls as a child. (Courtesy Dedibaayaanimanook Sarah Olsen)

Fig. 87 Hiking trail to Namegosibiing, 2001: Dedibaayaanimanook with her grand-daughter Leslie and friend R. Paul Rogers of Sweden.

Fig. 88 Red Lake café, 2003: Dedibaayaanimanook and her daughter Irene.

Fig. 89 August 21, 1993: Dedibaayaanimanook attended the wedding of her grand-daughter Donna in Red Lake. (Courtesy John Richthammer)

Fig. 90 Christmas dinner with family, Winnipeg, 2001 *left to right:* Garth Agger, Elijah Harper, Irene Olsen, Anita Olsen Harper, Dedibaayaanimanook, Sagate Josie Angeconeb, Helen Olsen Agger, Sarah Williams.

Fig. 92 Winnipeg, 2006: Dedibaayaanimanook with friend John Richthammer.

Fig. 92 Dedibaayaanimanook with family and friends, Winnipeg, 2006 *left to right:* Peggy Venables, Curt Sandulak, Leslie Agger, Dedibaayaanimanook, Helen Agger, Garth Agger, Marion Neufeld, John Neufeld. (Courtesy Marion Neufeld)

EPILOGUE

After her forty-five year partnership came to an end in 1987, Dedibaayaanimanook turned to her children for help in dealing with the challenges of life without Giigooyikewinini. This included the ubiquitous paperwork, underwritten as it was by the legalities that govern so many facets of life. But she and her children had continued to remain in close contact, and now they established an even closer connection. Dedibaayaanimanook began to share in more of their activities, especially when they involved visits to Namegosibiing Trout Lake.

Even though she kept the apartment in Wanamani Zaa'iganing Red Lake, Dedibaayaanimanook took every opportunity to spend time in Namegosibiing. Her son Harald regained legal trapping entitlement to much of the traditional homelands, so she accompanied him as often as she was able. During this time with Harald, she taught him about the old traditional ways that trapping programs of the day did not teach. For example, she included the component of living on the land that reiterated the importance of showing a respectful and thankful attitude during hunting, trapping and harvesting activities. She also discussed the practicability of his aspirations for living on the land, and pointed out all the changes that had taken place since the time of her childhood when people were still relatively free to pursue a traditional livelihood. Furthermore, she talked about his intent to inculcate the spiritual component of Namegosibii Anishinaabewiziwin into the various courses he delivered, pointing out that he had never gone on a vision quest journey and cautioning that he would need to wait until life's many experiences had given him wisdom before attempting to teach others about such matters. But otherwise, Dedibaayaanimanook welcomed her son's obvious interest in following after the footsteps of his Anishinaabe heritage despite his Western education. Over the course of time, they developed a partnership arrangement in which she helped with the purchase of rifles, tools and other materials, while he supplied the labour.

Dedibaayaanimanook also came to Namegosibiing with her daughters. Since summers were the best time for them to come, they worked together to cut the grass, pull out the weeds, plant seeds and, after Harald's passing, take care of the on-going repairs that needed to be done. Dedibaayaanimanook also went for boat rides with them and her grandchildren, visiting the different places where she had lived as a child. One summer, she took her granddaughter to where Aaniz Alice was born. On another outing, they went to Jiibayi Zaagiing Jackfish Bay, stopping for lunch on a rocky point that looked toward the east. Then they visited the island where Giigooyikewinini's cabin burnt to the ground. Dedibaayaanimanook enjoyed trips along the shorelines of Camp Island, just as she had done many years before when her daughters were little girls. In so doing, she helped to keep alive an interest in the old ways of the ancestors.

Other activities included Dedibaayaanimanook's continued visits to see her daughters. She had always gone on trips with them even before Giigooyikewinini's passing. For example, she joined them on a vacation to Hawaii in the 1970s, where she was mistaken for a native Hawaiian. But the person who inquired from which island[1] she came was somewhat mystified when he heard the name Camp Island! Then Dedibaayaanimanook flew to Florida with her daughter, granddaughter and son-in-law, where she walked along white, powdery beaches and gathered souvenir seashells. In the late 1990s, she spent time in Ottawa with another daughter and son-in-law. She toured the House of Commons and she sat down in the Speaker's chair to have her photo taken. During visits with her daughter Aaniz Alice, she went to pow-wows to see how other Anishinaabe people preserve their culture and celebrate their heritage. Her daughter Irene, who now lives in Red Lake, took her on many outings along logging roads and highways around the Red Lake area. As she viewed the slashing and gouging left by logging interests, she thought about the words of her own teachers, about an attitude of respect and deference toward the land, using its gifts in ways that left no footprints and reciprocating by putting down tobacco as an expression of gratitude. She remembered how her mother had told her that the trees were living beings who became anxious and wept whenever they sensed their impending demise. She reminded her daughters that it was in order to harvest them in a proper way, by honouring their covenant with them, that her people had included thanksgiving for the trees' gifts when they held their annual feasts.

Dedibaayaanimanook was also able to visit places not seen since childhood. A special outing took her to Ginebigo Baawitig Snake Falls on Chukuni River, to where she had canoed with her father up the river to Red Lake many years before. On yet another excursion, she went to the sacred Manidoo Baawitig, beneath Manitou Dam to listen as never ending volumes of water thundered down their incredible drop in a deafening roar. She was stunned by this spectacle of wemitigoozhi's invention. "Maamakaadizi a'a wemitigoozhi!" was her comment when she saw the hydroelectric structure with its enormous generating station for the first time. Dedibaayaanimanook could not help but be amazed by the wemitigoozhiwag who had the ability and capability to harness the energy of the mighty Baawitig. But there was only the faintest hint of admiration in her voice because ancient wisdom taught that there was always a negative side to that kind of exploitation. As she turned away, the sight of a juvenile eagle sitting atop a nearby tree helped to quell her dismay.

During a trip to Gojijiing Goldpines, located at the northernmost end of Lac Seul Lake, Dedibaayaanimanook stood in front of the Goldpines lodge. It was once the Hudson's Bay post/store where her parents, aunts, uncles and other relatives and friends had often shopped and sold furs when she was a small child in the early 1920s. Looking across the lake, Dedibaayaanimanook pointed to where she expected to see two small islands, the places where she and her parents had frequently stopped to rest for the night as they made their journeys and also where her mother had spent time doing laundry for one of the wemitigoozhi families living in Gojijiing. But Dedibaayaanimanook could not see the islands because the flooding that resulted from the Ear Falls dam had completely eradicated them. Deplorably, the inundation that had brought about so many noticeable changes to the once familiar landscape had also been very damaging in spiritual ways. For example, much of the Lac Seul community's traditional cemetery was ruined. Dedibaayaanimanook recalled hearing the voices of community members who described attempts to restore the damage but were sickened by the task of having to gather the bones and skulls of deceased family members when caskets disintegrated in the deluge. To this day, remains have continued to wash onto shorelines and beaches. With friends, relatives and acquaintances—in general, all Anishinaabeg were considered relatives—of Dedibaayaanimanook's family affected by the events of the flooding, the topic was too distressful to continue thinking about. The flood experience certainly confirmed a clear reality: Wemitigoozhiwag appeared to regard no action too disrespectful to undertake.

Dedibaayaanimanook also continued with her sewing activities for as long as she was able. Over the years, the products of her handiwork included hundreds of items, from parkas, mukluks, moccasins and mitts, to jewelry, miniature souvenirs and wall hangings. Up to very recently, she volunteered at the Friendship Centre, assisting in making quilts and blankets and teaching other volunteers in order to raise funds for the community. But when she began to experience health problems, her ability to execute the techniques she had refined no longer met the standards she came to expect of herself. Not being able to work with beads and leather was a particularly disappointing loss because she regarded it to be her lifelong calling. Dedibaayaanimanook therefore bequeathed the gift of her sewing skills to her daughter Irene, coaching her on how to produce the fine quality workmanship for which her own products were so well known. As well, Dedibaayaanimanook continued with summer visits to her beloved Namegosibiing because they were her form of medicine. She kept the same apartment to which she and Giigooyikewinini had first moved those many years ago, as a symbolic gesture to honour their forty-five year partnership. Increasingly having to rely on help with the day to day routine of living, Dedibaayaanimanook was fortunate that her daughter, Irene, was living in Red Lake, and that two granddaughters, both also living in Red Lake, were nurses who were able to keep a watchful eye on her health and visit frequently.

Many invitations came Dedibaayaanimanook's way to take an active leadership role during the years after Giigooyikewinini's departure, but she declined each of them, citing her parents' instruction not to do so. Furthermore, she had witnessed the unhappy spectacle of how other Anishinaabe people were being sought out and mined for their information, traditional knowledge and insights, particularly by prospecting academics seeking to advance their reputation while steeped in the old colonizers' precept about their entitlement to Indigenous knowledge and innermost belief sanctuaries. Dedibaayaanimanook noted how these Anishinaabe individuals were then discarded, after receiving a token payment in return. Rather, Dedibaayaanimanook remained committed to confining the sharing of her life's insights and teaching activities to her children. As adults, they now had a deeper appreciation for her as their mother and mentor, and a better understanding of her words and instructions. An example had to do with one sibling who had always imagined that she was not truly loved because she had no remembrance of ever receiving a hug when she was a child. It was only later in life that she came to appreciate the fact that Dedibaayaanimanook and Giigooyikewinini had been expressing their love toward her and her siblings all along, but in other ways. Led by the conviction, for instance, that education was the only way to achieve a reasonable life in mainstream society, Dedibaayaanimanook and Giigooyikewinini had worked long and hard during their lives together in Namegosibiing in order to afford sending the children away to school. The separation itself had been an immense sacrifice that only caring parents could make voluntarily. Another example of greater appreciation came with the realization that Dedibaayaani-manook had willingly taken on many hardships when she decided to stay in her partnership with Giigooyikewinini—who suffered from the sickness of severe alcoholism—in order to provide a measure of stability for the family.

Foremost in her instructions to her grown children, Dedibaayaani-manook reminded them always to remember the ancestors whenever they were at home in Namegosibiing. When they enjoyed a traditional meal, she told them to place a small quantity of the food on a birch bark plate and burn it in the fire in recognition of the ancient people's presence. She instructed them to pour a small amount of tea onto the fire or onto the ground close by because that was what her grand-father Giizhik had specified. "Asemaa bakobii' e'binesiiwang." She also reminded them to put tobacco into the water when it was thundering. Remembering to use tobacco in the proper way was what Dedibaaya-animanook emphasized the most.

* * *

The process of synthesizing Dedibaayaanimanook's oral narrative into written form was a daughter's eleven-year journey that came to an end near the eighty-sixth birthday of her mother. It was a unique experience that taught the meaning of appreciation, patience and understanding.

1. "What island are you from?" is generally one of the first questions that native Hawaiians ask when they meet a fellow native Hawaiian for the first time. With Dedibaayaanimanook wearing a muumuu and lei, the Hawaiian's question was a perfectly understandable mistake.

Genealogical Chart 1: Possible line of the descendants of Jiiyaan, Dedibaayaanimanook's great-grandfather

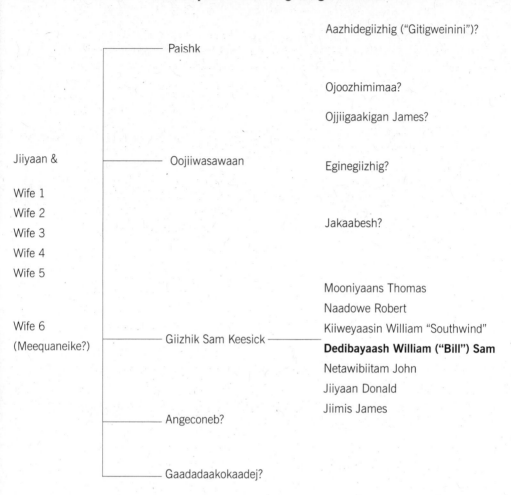

Aazhidegiizhig ("Gitigweinini")?

Paishk

Ojoozhimimaa?

Ojjiigaakigan James?

Jiiyaan &

Oojiiwasawaan   Eginegiizhig?

Wife 1

Wife 2

Wife 3   Jakaabesh?

Wife 4

Wife 5

          Mooniyaans Thomas

          Naadowe Robert

Wife 6   Kiiweyaasin William "Southwind"

(Meequaneike?)   Giizhik Sam Keesick ——— **Dedibayaash William ("Bill") Sam**

          Netawibiitam John

          Jiiyaan Donald

          Jiimis James

     Angeconeb?

     Gaadadaakokaadej?

Note: Which of the six wives of Dedibaayaanimanook's paternal great-grandfather Jiiyaan was the mother of which and how many children is not known. Also, the correct chronological order of his children and grandchildren (other than the children of Dedibaaya-animanook's grandfather Giizhik Sam Keesick) is not known. Judging from how people spoke, the assumption appeared to be that Giizhik was among the younger of the siblings. Other assumptions based on what people said plus the fact that Giizhik had seven sons who survived to adulthood and Dedibaayaanimanook's father Dedibayaash spoke of having many relatives, are that (1) some or all of Paishk, Oojiiwasawaan and Angeconeb may have been Dedibayaash's uncles and/or great-uncles and (2) the individuals listed in the third column-except for Giizhik's children- were Dedibayaash's cousins. The question marks indicate the uncertainty regarding the placement of these persons including Gaadadaakokaadej.

Genealogical Chart 2: Giizhik Sam Keesick's surviving children and known surviving grandchildren.

	Mooniyaans Thomas (1860-?)	Omooday Paul; Midaasogiizhigook; Naansii Nancy
	Kiiweyaas(h)in William Keesick "South Wind" (1863-1938)	Aatayaa John Keesick South Wind; Anama'egaabaw James Ashen; Oshkaandagaa Charlie Ashen; Jigoozhi Pat Keesick Kiiweyaasin; Baswewe's husband; Maashkizhiigan George Ashen; Diike
	Naadowe Robert (1870-?)	Namegosibiiwinini Sam; Nishki'aa Isaac ("Big Isaac'), or, Robert Isaac; Jiimis James; Niibidebiitam Alec; Jôjens George Nataway; Aayabiikwens;Ingwezhe; Jii
Giizhik Sam Keesick (1829-1929)	Dedibayaash William ("Bill") Sam Keesick (1875-1950)	Eliza (step-daughter); Waasegiizhik Donald (step-son); Minzhinawebines Sam William; Gweyesh Annie; Robert (step-son); Annie (step-daughter); Minogazh Agnes (step-daughter); Jeanne (step-daughter); Jiibwaat Edward Angeconeb (step-son); Jiins Charlie Angeconeb (step-son); Nancy(?); **Dedibaayaanimanook Sarah**
	Netawibiitam John (1883-194?)	John; Baabiijinigaabaw; Gwaage;?; Detaginang Frank; Meniyaan Mary Anne; Mazinigiizhik James
	Jiiyaan Donald (1877-1967)	Gikinô'amaagewinini Paul; Moshish Mary; Moshishens
	Jiimis James (?)	Gwiiwish Isaac; Zhashagiins Edward; Mooniga'igan; Ogimaakwens; De'igan; Naansii Nancy; Aanig Alec; Menjen; Sarah; Gaap; Gweshkiish; Shamaandi; Daisy

Note: The dates of birth are based on information provided by Treaty annuity pay lists for 1901 with the exception of that of Giizhik Sam Keesick, which is approximate.

Indizhinikaajigemin

~

Our Meanings

The following terms, within which so much of the peoples traditions were carried, were once common in Dedibaayaanimanook's
everyday conversations (the ô sound is that of the first part of the
diphthong in the English word "owe"):

aa'aasi(wag): Crow(s).

Aabitabiboonigiizis: January. This term refers to the fact that
winter was considered nearing half way at the time of this month.

aabitawaasige: The moon is in its first (or last) quarter.

aadasookaan: Specific type of story.

aadasookewin: The telling of special types of stories.

aagaskoo(g): Sharp-tailed grouse.

aagim(ag): Snowshoe(s).

aagimaak: Ash (tree).

Aagimaako Baawitig: Snowshoe Falls on Chukuni River.

aakoziwin(an): Sickness(es).

aaminikewag: The fish are spawning. Whitefish spawn around the
time of October's full moon. Namegosibii Anishinaabeg
caught the fish and hung them to dry just before freeze-up.
It was also when the first snow of the season covered the
ground, making rabbit tracks easily visible and easier for
Dedibaayaanimanook and her cousins to set snares along
the animals' trails.

aanak(oog): Vireo(s); warbler(s).

aandaaniman: A non-traditional Namegosibii Anishinaabe (i.e., incorrect), "new age" way of saying the wind is changing direction.

aanikoobidaagan(ag): Great-grandchild(ren).

aanjigwanewag: Refers to certain birds returning in spring with a new set of feathers. The name Angeconeb derives from this term and was probably a ceremonial name.

aanzig(wag): Merganser (fish duck).

aasaaganashk(oog): A tall grass-like plant of the wetlands.

aasamiingwe'igan(an): Moccasin vamp.

aazhidekozhesi: Pine grosbeak.

aazhogan(ing): (At the) bridge.

abinoonjiizhi mashkiki: A medicine made specifically for children.

abwe: S/he is cooking over an open fire (by holding the food over the fire with a stick).

achaak: A spirit (after death).

adaawewinini: A (male) retailer.

adikameg: Whitefish.

Adikamego Zaagiing: ("Zaagiing" for short) a place in Lac Seul First Nation where a woman named Majibinewish once lived.

adikwanazid(ag): Caribou hoof.

adis: Sinew.

agaamakiing: From/to (the lands) across the ocean.

agaamew: Across the bay.

agaaming: Across the water.

agwaagosin: It is moldy.

agwaashkaa mikwam: Waves are pushing the ice onto shore.

Agwingwis: A Swedish person.

agwôgwôbikisin: It is rusty (metal).

ajidaatigwesi(wag): Nuthatch(es). This term alludes to the bird's habit of creeping down a tree headfirst.

akadamoog: Pond lilies.

akakanzhesh: Black soot.

akii: The earth.

akiimazina'igan: Map.

Akiiwawbiikwe (Akiiw for short): Zhashagi's wife's (ceremonial) name.

akik: Pot, pail.

akikoons: A small pot/pail.

akiwenzi: An elderly man.

amanisowin: The experience of an event that cannot be explained by natural phenomena.

Amanisookaan: David Angeoneb (Garnet and Harry Angeconeb's father); Amanisookaan had a sister named Madeline Keeper.

amikogiba'igan: Beaver dam.

amikominan: Black currants.

Anamikodaadiiwigiizis: January. This term reflects the wemitigoozhi influence in that it alludes to the act of greeting one another.

andawaanzhide: Gathers evergreen boughs for bedding.

andawenjigewin: Big game hunting.

andobawaajige: (S/he) goes on her/his vision quest.

andobawaajigewin: The practise of going on a vision quest journey.

andomakwe: (S/he) has gone bear hunting.

andomanise: (S/he) goes for fire wood.

aniibiish(an): Leaf (leaves).

aniibiminaanan: A type of berry.

"animikiikaa": Dedibaayaanimanook once heard a man visiting from Grassy Narrows describe a thunder storm in this way.

animikiins: Battery.

animikoons(an): Seed(s).

animikoshin: S/he is lying face down.

animitaagoziwin: (The practice of) oratory.

animosh(ag): Dog(s).

Anishinaabe(g): Dedibaayaanimanook had two meanings, one referred specifically to the Ojibwe people; the other was a broader term referring to Indigenous peoples in general.

Anishinaabekwe(g): Anishinaabe woman (women).

Anishinaabemowin: The Anishinaabe language.

Anishinaabewaya'ii: Whatever pertains to being an Anishinaabe person.

Anishinaabewiziwin: All the elements that make up the Anishinaabe way.

anisib: Clear, cold water.

anisideyaagamin: The soup is clear of particles.

anokiiwin: Employment, work.

apicaneyaab: A leather strap positioned across the forehead for carrying goods.

apis: A piece of steel or iron against which flint was struck.

apishimon: Mattress.

asaa'we(g): Perch.

asabeyaab: Cotton twine.

asemaa: Tobacco.

ashaageshi: Crayfish.

Ashaageshi: The person to whom Niingaanaashiik Mary Keesick gave a ceremonial name.

ashigan: Bass (found only in certain bays).

ashkibwôk: An edible plant that grew in and around the region of Wabauskang First Nation.

Ashkibwôkaaning: An old name for Wabauskang, a First Nation community accessible from Highway 105. The name derives from the edible plant ashkibwôk that grew in the area.

ashkimaneyaab: Rawhide for snowshoe webbing.

ashkime: (S/he) weaves snowshoe webbing.

Asin: The paternal grandfather of Gaani (who married Dedibaay-aanimanook's brother Jiins). The descendants of Asin and his wife Joojoosh took on the surname Stone.

asiniikaan: A mine.

asiniimashkiki: A gray colored medicine for toothaches; it was derived from a type of rock.

ataagib: Green algae.

atawaa: Have a contest with someone.

Ayikwe: A sister (i.e., cousin) of Dedibaayaanimanook's father, Dedibayaash William Sam Keesick; Zhaaganaash was one of Ayikwe's grandchildren and great-nephew of Dedibayaash.

azaadi: (White) poplar.

azhashkiiwaagamin: The water is muddy (with clay, etc.).

baakwaayshii giizhizekwaan: French cooking.

baakwaayshiig: Frenchmen.

baamadaawe(g): Independent trader(s), historically, in competition with Hudson's Bay Company.

baapaase: Downy woodpecker; red-naped sapsucker.

baasa'iwiinaan: Marrow.

baashka'aawesi(wag): (Black-headed) gull.

baashkinebiisaan: A heavy mist.

baashkinegamaa'an: Steam is rising from the water.

baawitig: Rapids.

babiidikwe: (It) creates a deep, resonating sound.

babiikwaanakwan: There are cumulus clouds (i.e., the clouds are sphere shaped).

bachechiwish: Junco.

badakwaanawe: Just before the sun emerges from the eastern horizon, its rays rise up in the shape of a vertical column of light.

badakwane: A blazing fire rises in a tall column.

bagaan(ag): Black hazelnut.

bagesaaniminag: Prunes.

bagwaanegamig: Canvas tent.

Bajiish: Patricia, who married Wawiyetigwaanikwe's son Frank Williams.

bakewinaa: Leave (someone).

bakiniwanii'igane: Goes to pull up traps for the season.

bakwanj: Windfall.

bakwezhigan: Flour; bannock; bread.

bakwezhiganaabo: Stew thickened with flour.

banzwaa; banzwô: Refers to the custom of singeing off the
    feathers of ducks, loons, grouse, etc. as well as the quills of
    porcupine to make removal easier.

bapashki: Ruffed grouse.

bashkwegin: Leather.

bashkweginwekizinan: Moccasins, i.e., soft soled shoes.

bawaajigewin: The practise of dreaming dreams; special dream.

bawa'iminaanan: Pincherries.

bepegwajimishakwan: It is a sunny sky with broken clouds.

bepegwajizhaagigamiiwan: The lake is open here and there
    (along the shorelines). The bepegwaji part of this word
    relates to intermittency, zhaagigamiiwan is a complete sen-
    tence stating that the ice has broken up and the lake is open.

beshk: Common nighthawk (in Namegosibiing this bird was seen
    only in Jiibayi Zaagiing).

bezhig: One.

bigishkanjige: S/he is chewing something into small pieces.

Bigwadasim: Wiinsag's wolf dog.

bigwajaya'ii: In the woods (away from people).

Biinjidawaabikideng: A long narrow channel in northeastern
    Namegosibiing referred to as Long Channel in maps of the
    lake.

biinjidawigamaa: Relating to a bay.

Biinjidawigamaag: A long narrow bay in northwestern Namego-sibiing with several islands and points of land; wemitigoozhi maps now refer to it as Caskie Bay and Red Bay. The Keesi-cks trapped in Biinjidawigamaag but never lived there.

biipiigiwizens: A whip-poor-will like bird.

biishaaganaab: The old term for apicaneyaab.

biisweyiigin: Flannelette.

biiwaabik: Metal.

biiwaanag(oog): Flint (for making arrowheads and for starting fires).

biiwaanagoons(ag): Flint (intermingled with lead shot which people obtained during Diba'amaadim Treaty Time).

biiwegizhiganan: Left over scraps of material.

biiwide: A stranger; a foreigner.

bikojiisi(wag): Black fly (flies).

bikwaakwadanwiin: Pellets of lead shot.

bikwak(oon): Arrow (arrows).

bikwakooshib: (Golden eye) duck.

bimaagiweba'odizon: Bicycle.

bima'oodaasoowin(an): Flat-bottom (row)boat(s).

biminoowe: The advancing wind creates a path.

Bimose: The person Paddy married after he and Aananoons left each other.

bine(wag): Spruce grouse. Dedibaayaanimanook's partner Giigooyikewinini called them "spruce chickens."

binemizhiin: Dedibaayaanimanook's father's term for Labrador tea.

bineshiinzh(ag): Bird(s).

binesi(wag): Thunder.

binesiwidikomag: Large butterfiles or moths, such as the luna moth, that have feather-like hair covering their bodies.

bingoshiins(ag): Sandfly.

bingwaabo: Lye solution.

bingwi: Ash; ashes.

bizhikiweshkan(an): Cow horn(s).

bizhiwaatig: A specific type of evergreen shrub.

boonagoke/gondamaago: Fishes with a baited hook on a string tied to a pole that has been secured in the snow beside the ice hole (often leaving it overnight).

booshkegiin: Its up to you, whatever you think.

Bwaanii'odashawaabiwin: A hill from which the Bwaanag, the Dakotas, kept a watch for their enemies (the literal translation for Sioux Lookout).

Daawangishkang: Christopher Williams, Wawiyechigwaanikwe's eldest son.

dabinawaa: (It is) sheltered from the elements.

dabinooshkigewag: The trees provide protection. This one-word sentence is evidence that Anishinaabe people understood that trees play a key role in a healthily functioning ecosystem.

dagwaagin: It is autumn.

dagwaagshib: Ring-necked duck.

dakinaagan(an): Cradleboard(s).

dakinoowe: A cold wind is blowing.

dakobijige: S/he is having a great-grandchild.

dazhe: It has a nest.

dewe'igan: Drum.

dibaajimowin: Story, narrative.

dibaakonigewikwe: A woman lawyer.

diba'amaadim: Literally, the event or practice of receiving payment; Treaty Time.

dibikigiizis: Literally, the night sun, i.e., the moon.

diindiinsi(wag): Blue jay(s).

dô'ibaan(an): Water hole(s) in the ice from which to obtain water.

doonabii(g): Tulibee (a kind of fish Keesicks caught at Stiff Lake).

doowaakwe: A woodpecker drums on a tree.

doozis: Aunt.

e'dagwaagig: During autumn, when it is autumn.

Eliza the cook: A woman who lived at Otawagi Baawitig Ear Falls; her brother was Chief Akiwenz.

Enjashoo: A man from Lac Seul who married six times.

es(ag): Clam(s).

eshkan: Bar; antler.

esiban: Racoon.

ewii'ando naadagwej: As s/he prepares to go out and check the rabbit snares.

gaa izhibimishinowaaj: Cemetery.

Gaa Okosing: A name used by some people for Winnipeg. The word alludes to the idea of sitting piled together.

Gaa'aanzagoodeg: A constellation (the Little Dipper) that

Dedibaayaanimanook's father spoke about; another relative referred to this constellation as "Gaa Okagoodeg" (the idea of something piled together).

gaabimisemagak: Literally, that which flies; an airplane.

Gaadakwaasigej: Literally, the one who shines briefly, i.e., the moon of February.

gaag: Porcupine.

gaagaagiwaandag(oog): Juniper(s).

gaagens: Baby porcupine.

gaagigebagak: The plant with everlasting leaves, i.e., Labrador tea.

gaagigebagoon: Labrador tea. The term refers to the fact that the plant is an evergreen broadleaf, hence does not shed its leaves in autumn.

gaagigebimaadizi: Lives forever (an expression often inscribed on headstones). These were Dedibaayaanimanook's chosen words for both Giigooyikewinini's and Harald's headstones.

gaagii'gozaabandamowaaj: The dreams through which Gichi Anishinaabeg derived meaning for "shaking tent" ceremonies.

Gaagii'nisidizoj: The one who killed himself.

Gaaginwaasigej: The one who shines for a long time, i.e., January.

gaagitabiwaaj: Those who remain behind. This was an old term that referred to people who remained on the reserve rather than leave on migratory journeys.

gaagondaaseg: Absorbine Jr. (an ointment for stiff muscles).

gaakaabishii(g): Non-tufted owl(s).

gaakaawaskwaabik: A type of metallic substance found in the ground.

Gaamadwenowebiik: Gwejech's daughter, i.e., Dedibaayaanima-nook's niece.

Gaaminitigwashkiigaag: Keesick Bay (place of Dedibaayaanima-nook's birth).

Gaaminitigwashkiigaawi Ziibi: Bathurst Creek.

gaaminomaagobagak: Wild mint. The term refers to the plant's pleasant aroma.

gaamiskoningwiij jachakanoo: Red-winged blackbird.

gaanaajigôjigewaaj: Inchworms. This term refers to the inch-worms' reaching gesture.

gaanda'igôson: Thimble.

Gaaniinzhoogwonding: Two Island Lake.

gaanoosookaagonagizij: Soft snow.

gaaskaagonewadin: The snow freezes overnight to a crisp surface (during springtime).

gaaskiiwag: Smoked dry meat.

gaaway(ag): Porcupine quill(s).

gaawiin: No.

gaawiisagangej (gaawiisagangewaaj): Gray fly (gray flies).

gaawiminagazh(iig): Wild rose thorn(s).

gaawiminagazhiiwaatig(goog): Wild rose plant.

gaazanagak aakoziwin: Influenza.

gaazanagak (aakoziwin): Cancer.

Gaazhimikwamiiwaagamig: Literally, the place where the water is ice cold. This was a place on the northwest main shore of Namegosibiing where the water of a little creek ran icy cold even during the hottest days of summer.

gabesh: Spend the night (this meaning originated with the northern people, i.e., those from Pikangikum); stop for a prolonged stay (this was the usual Namegosibii Anishinaabe meaning, e.g., this meaning would apply to when Dedibaayaanima-nook moved to Camp Island where she spent the rest of her life in Namegosibiing).

gagaamikijiwan baawitig: (water)falls.

gagidowin: That part of a spiritual feast in which individuals verbally share their insights; speech.

gagiikwewin: Teachings, exhortations.

gagizhaabatenoowe: The first strong southerly winds affecting ice conditions have arrived; a hot wind is blowing.

Gajii: Waabachaanish's wife (who was a well respected midwife).

gakiiw: Where the portage trail leads.

gakiiwekana: Portage trail.

gakina awiya, gakina gegoon: Everyone and everything.

gashkadin: It is freeze-up, the lake has frozen.

gashkawan: It is foggy.

gashkawanibiisaan: A heavy fog (resulting in poor visibility) over the lake.

gashkibidaagan: A bag with drawstrings.

gashkigôsonaabik: Sewing machine.

gawaandag: Black spruce.

gete: Old; of the past; from before, e.g., gete waakaa'igan is an old house/building.

gete izhichigewin: The old ways; the traditional ways.

gibiiginige: S/he draws the curtains.

Gichi'anama'egiizhigan: It is Christmas.

Gichi Anishinaabe(g): The elderly people who are the community's traditional knowledge keepers and senior teachers.

gichi Midewinini: The man who leads in the Mide ceremonies.

Gichi Neyaabikaang: A place in Lac Seul where a person named Eliza lived.

Gichi Neyaashiiing: Treaty Point, Lac Seul.

Gichi Onigaming: Stiff Lake (east of Rice Lake).

gichi wakwi(in): The highest (cirrus) clouds. They were often seen as a harbinger of warmer weather.

gichibineshiinzh: Killdeer.

gichigami: Ocean, sea.

gichimaa'iingan: Gray/timber wolf.

gidoodaapinaawaswaan: The person you helped to deliver.

gii'gozaabandamowag: They held a shaking tent ceremony.

gii'oshkagoojin: There was a new moon.

giishkaatig: Cedar.

Giiwedin gidoojiimig: An expression stating that your ears are frost bitten (literally, the North kisses you).

Giiwedinanang: The North Star (Polaris).

giiwedinong: From the north.

Giiwegaabaw: A person who had many sons.

giiwese: The dark cloud is reversing direction.

giiwose: Goes moose hunting (in winter).

giizhig: Sky.

Giizhiganang: The Day Star (that accompanies the sun, but is only occasionally visible).

giizhoowinoowe: There is a warm wind.

giizis: Sun.

giizisomazina'igan: Calendar.

gijigaaneshiinzh(ag): Chickadee(s).

gimiwanoonsiwan: There is a fine rain.

giniiw(ag): Golden eagle(s).

ginoonzhe: Jackfish.

giyaashk(wag): Gull(s).

giyaashkwajishin: The snow is piled and looks like a gull.

Giyaashkwanaabikong/Giyaashkwanaabiko Zaa'igan: Gull Rock Lake.

Gizhe Manidoo: The kind, caring spirit; this being is know to Eurocaucasians as Jesus.

gizhewaadizi: S/he is kind, loving.

gizhoobike: S/he is making hot tea.

gojiskwa'ige: S/he tests the ice thickness (with a stick, axe, etc.).

gookominaan: An elderly woman.

gookooko'oo(g): Tufted owl(s).

goon: Snow.

goonikaa: There is a lot of snow.

gopa'am: (S/he) travels up the river.

gôshkwandaabizhiw(ag): Mountain lion(s), cougar(s).

gozaabanjigan: Shaking tent.

Gwejenjens: Jôniins's mother.

gwekaaniman: The correct Namegosibii Anishinaabe way of saying that the wind is changing direction.

Gwekabiikwe: Annie Neepin: Jiiyaan Donald Keesick's granddaughter; she was born at Gete Waakaa'iganing (Hudson's Bay Point) in Namegosibiing.

Gwekinoo: Sam Southwind's father.

gwekinoowe: Dedibaayaanimanook's father's expression for saying that the wind is changing direction.

gwiigwiishi(ag): Whiskey jack(s), gray jay(s).

gwiingwan: Meteor.

gwiishkwa'oo(g): Robin(s).

gwingwa'aage: Wolverine.

ikwe niimi'idim: Woman's dance.

(od)inaabamaan: S/he alone sees (someone); s/he dreams of him/her in a special way.

indakikwaabik: My kettle metal, i.e., my (metal) kettle.

indoodaapinaawaswaan: The person I helped to deliver.

indoozhim: My nephew (i.e., my sister's son).

indoozhimikwe: My niece (i.e., my sister's daughter).

ininaandag: Balsam fir.

inini(wag): Man (men).

ishkô bimaadizi: Dies (in reference to humans, rather than animals or plants).

ishkode(n): Fire(s).

ishkôndenaabik: Doorknob.

ishkonigan(an): Literally, whatever is left over, i.e., reserve land(s).

ishpadinaang: Where there is an elevation or hill.

Ishpadinaang: The higher land at Lac Seul (Keejick Bay) were the Ojiiwasawaans lived.

iskigamizigan: Tree sap harvested for consumption, but not yet boiled into syrup.

jaaginewaaj: As all the people die.

jachakanoo: Blackbird. The term mimics the bird's chirp.

jiibay: Ghost. The term was sometimes used as an (irreverent) exclamation. Using it to refer to a human was considered highly insulting, to say the least because it could imply either a death wish or that the person being thus referred to was already dead. As with some other forms of profane language, however, people would sometimes use the term in a more joking manner.

jiibayazaanjigo: (A dog) buries its bone. This verb refers only to a dog, but to everyone's amusement, one of Dedibaay-aanimanook's relatives was once heard to say, "Amii' gii' jiibayazaanjigoyaan." It was his way of saying that he had finished caching his equipment for another season.

jiichiingwaaskwadin: This term, related to spring, alludes to the jagged edges of ice that form when slush freezes overnight.

jiichiishkishii: Sandpiper.

jiigibiig: Along (close to) the shoreline or water.

jiimaan(an): Canoe(s), boats(s).

Jiimaani Ziibi: Canoe River.

jiiweganaabizhiish(ag): Dragon fly(ies).

Jiiweganaabizhiish: (Jiiwe for short) Soons Oojiiwasawaan's mother.

maa'am: (S/he) goes for groceries.

maadaawaang: The place where two rivers meet.

Maadaawaang: Mattawan, where the Chukuni and English rivers converge. A Hudson's Bay Company post was once located there.

maada'iganzhib: Northern shoveler (a type of duck).

maada'ige: Scrapes the skin off an animal hide.

Maadinawegiizhigan: (today is) Saturday.

Maaganad Margaret: Bôy's wife.

maamaagwegin: A thick, canvas-like fabric. This was Mooniyaan-sikweban's favorite.

Maamawichigewigamigong: To, at, in the Hudson's Bay Company store/trading post.

maanadoobaatig(wag): alder(s).

maanataanag: Harvested furs.

maanazaadi: Black (balsam) poplar.

maang(wag): Loon(s).

maangodikom(ag): Pond strider (literally, loon's lice).

Maangogiizis: The loon's month, i.e., May.

maanitam: (S/he) perceives to have heard something negative being said.

madaabii: (S/he) comes down from the woods; (s/he) comes down to the water's edge.

madaawa'am: S/he travels down river.

madogaan: A temporary tepee-like dwelling which used canvas in latter years.

madoodswaan: Sweat lodge.

madoowokaadaak(wag): A type of non-edible plant somewhat similar to a carrot.

madweskwadin: The ice is rumbling.

madweyaakodadin: Branches and twigs are snapping in the cold temperatures.

magoojebizhosh(ag): (Water) nymph(s).

ma'iingan(ag): Wolf (wolves).

ma'iinganens: Coyote; young wolf.

Majoojshwanaawagan: John Angeconeb's relative; the name alludes to the fact that this person had a bent back.

makade: Black gunpowder.

makadeninshib: American black duck.

makadeshib: White-winged scoter (type of duck).

makakoons(an): Small container(s)/box(es).

makakoshkwemag(oon): Birch bark container(s) for storing dried food.

makizinikaan(an): Hand made shoe(s), i.e., moccasin(s).

makizinike: (S/he) makes moccasins.

Makoke Minis: An island off Hudson's Bay Point where Dedibaay-aanimanook's father prepared and dried bear meat and fish. At times her uncle Jiiyaan also went to the island for the same purpose.

makominaatig: Mountain ash.

makominan: Mountain ash berries.

Mako'Odaaminike: Where a small creek trickles into Namego-sibiing and black bears once caught fish during spawning season.

makoonsiminan: A type of cranberries.

makwa(g): Bear(s).

mamaandaawizi: (S/he) possesses extraordinary powers.

mamaandaawiziwin: Use/practise of special power to perform extraordinary feats.

mamangaashkaa: (There are) large waves.

mandaamin: Corn.

Manidoobaawi Zaa'igan: A lake located down the English River beyond Manidoo Baawitig.

manoomin: Wild rice.

manoominike: (S/he) is harvesting wild rice.

mashkiigobagoon: Labrador tea leaves.

mashkiigominan: (A type of) cranberries.

mashkiigwaabo: Swampy water.

mashkiigwaatig: Tamarack.

mashkiigwakiing: Swampy lowlands where Canada geese nest/live during summer.

mashkiigwemojaash: A type of pitcher plant.

mashkiki: Medicine.

mashkikiiwazh: Medicine bag/bundle.

mashkikiwaabo: Medicinal tea.

mashkikiwaatig(oog): Medicinal plant(s).

Mashkodeng: An alternate name for Winnipeg used by Dedibaaya-animanook's people.

mazina'iginwemashkimodens: Envelop.

meme: Pileated woodpecker.

Memegweshiwag: A type of Anishinaabeg who were small, lived in rock cliffs and travelled in stone vessels.

meniganaakokande: It is made to be shaded from the sun (for sitting).

meniganaakoons: A crib like structure that defines the boundary of a grave.

meniganeyaab: Mesh (fencing).

mewinzha: A long time ago; before the influences of the wemiti-goozhi's religions, economic systems, etc.

michiskwaa: There is no snow on the ice.

michiskwa'igan: A sled with runners that allows for usage on bare ice (rather than in deep snow).

Mide: The ceremonies of what is known in English as the grand medicine society.

Midechige: S/he is conducting a Mide ceremony.

Midewinaaniwan: There is a Mide ceremony taking place.

miginokii: (The dog) has the task of running ahead in order to chase an animal.

migizi(wag): Bald eagle(s).

Migiziwi Giizis: Bald Eagle Month, i.e., March.

migoos: Awl (a tool used for making holes in leather).

miigisens(ag): Bead(s).

miijim: Food deriving its protein from an animal (i.e., fish, fowl, venison, etc. rather than beans, nuts and other plants).

Miishiij: Bessie Simard's mother.

miishiijiiminan: Skunk currants.

mikinaak(wag): Snapping turtle(s).

mikindaagan(an): Bundle(s) of fur pelts.

mikwam: Ice.

mikwaminaana'an: It is hailing.

mina'ik: White spruce.

minikwewin: The sickness of alcoholism and its associated negative/destructive behaviours, consequences, etc.

minis: Island.

minobimaadiziwin: The practise of living a meritorious life.

minookamiing: In late spring (when new growth begins to appear).

Minziwegwanebiik: Majoojshwanaawagan's wife. The name refers to a type of butterfly with a feather-like covering.

minziweyaanakwan: The skies are completely overcast.

mishi: Big, large, grand.

Mishi Baawitig: Grand Rapids (Manitoba).

mishoomisiban: late grandfather (the _–ban_ suffix indicates that the person has died when referring to a person).

misigiwaam: A teepee like structure.

miskazhe: S/he has measles.

miskomin: Raspberry.

miskominikesi(wag): Song sparrow(s).

miskwaabiimagwaatig(oog): Red dogwood.

miskwaadesi: Painted turtle.

Miskwaagamiwi Ziibi: The name for Winnipeg once used by the Keesicks of Namegosibiing.

mitaawang: Sand.

mitadim(oog): Horse(es).

mitig(oog): Tree(s).

mitigomizh: Oak.

mitigwaab(iig): Bow(s).

mitigwakizinan: (Store bought) leather soled shoes (the *mitig-* prefix, in reference to wood, contrasts with the soft moccasins people usually made and wore).

mitigwanii'igan: wooden trap (used in the olden days).

mooningwane: Northern flicker.

moonzhôgan: Scissors.

Moonzhonii John: Joe Paishk's (paternal) grandfather.

moonzobiiway(an): Moose hair(s).

moonzogazh: Moose hoof.

Moonzogazh: Titus's father.

moonzokan(an): Moose bone(s).

moonzowiiyaas: Moose meat.

moonzweshkan(ag): Moose antler(s).

Mooshka'oshi ("Crane"): Gaadadaakokaadej's second wife, whom Dedibaayaanimanook saw in Lac Seul (this person died in either 1939 or 1940).

mooska'osi: (Great blue) heron.

naabe: Male (deer, moose, etc.).

naajiwanii'igane: S/he goes out to check the trapline.

naanzhakiise waasigan: Lightning is striking.

nabagijiimaan: Scow; flat bottom boat; rowboat.

nagaadibikwe: A term that refers to advancing clouds that then turn back at the end of the day.

nagaazide onaak: A horizontal piece of wood at the bottom of a cradleboard that helps prevent the infant from sliding down when the cradleboard is in a vertical position.

nagajichigewag: They are very adept.

nagwaajigan: Snare.

namaangan: Shuttle (for snowshoe webbing, etc.).

name(g): Sturgeon(s). These fish are not found in Namegosibiing.

namebin(ag): Sucker(s).

namebino zow(an): Sucker tail(s).

namegos(ag): Lake trout.

Namegosibii Anishinaabeg: the Anishinaabe people who have descended from the Anishinaabe people for whom Namegosibiing was home since before memory.

Namegosibii Anishinaabewiziwin: Those essential attributes, beliefs, characteristics, practices, qualities and traits that set the Anishinaabe people of Namegosibiing apart from other Anishinaabeg.

nameteg(wag): Fish that are (sliced widthwise and) hung to dry

Nechaawaabikook: A person to whom Dedibaayaanimanook referred as her aunt. Nechaawaabikook's second husband was a wemitigoozhi.

negiish: Close to shore.

negimo: It snarls (i.e., a dog or wolf).

nengaw: Sand (the word used by Dedibaayaanimanook's father).

nenookaasi(wag): hummingbird(s).

neyaabikaang: Where the shoreline forms a smooth rocky point.

Neyaashiing: Treaty Point, Lac Seul.

nibi: Water.

nibo: dies (in reference to animals or plants, etc., but not humans).

nigiigwanikadin: There is hoarfrost.

Niingaanibinesiik: (Niingaan for short) one of Dedibaayaanima-
    nook's long deceased (female) cousins.

Niinge: My Mother (also vocative case). The term was used by
    Dedibayaash and some other Namegosibii Anishinaabeg.

niinzhin: Two.

niinzhoode: A twin.

niisiiwezigwadin: There are icicles.

nika(g): Canada goose (geese).

nimidaawa'aamin: We are travelling down river.

nimisenz: My elder sister.

nimishoomis: My grandfather.

ninandawaanzhidemin: We are out searching for balsam
    branches.

ningaabii'anong: In/at/from the west.

ningizo: The frog (or fly) is hibernating.

ningôwanise: Powdery fine snow particles are falling (when it is
    clear and exceptionally cold).

niningwan: My nephew (my brother's son).

ninshib(ag): Mallard duck(s).

nita'am: S/he is paddling her/his canoe against the river's current.

nooka'igan: Smoked moose meat pounded into a fine consistency.

nookom: My grandmother.

nookomiban: My late grandmother.

noons: My dad, my father (a term once used by some Namegosibii Anishinaabeg, including Dedibaayaanimanook's father).

noonzhe: Female animal.

Obiyaasaaganashkokaang: Post Narrows.

odaabaanaak(wag): Toboggan(s).

Odaadawaa'amoog: Orion's Belt.

odaanikoog: Great-grandchildren.

odaapinaawaso: S/he is a midwife, s/he practices midwifery.

odaapinaawaswaan: The person whom someone helped deliver.

Odaminowigiizhigan: (it is) Canada Day (or other day of celebration).

odatagwaagan: Backbone.

odazheboyesi: Water boatman (a type of water bug).

odedikos: Kidney.

ode'iminan: Strawberries (literally, heart berries).

Odeshkan: Another name for the constellation Gaa'aanzagoodeg.

odesimiigan(ag): Breastbone(s).

odinaajimowin: Her/his narrative, story.

odoodem: Her/his clan.

ogaans(ag): Pickerel(s).

Ogaansaaminikaan: The mouth of a creek in the eastern part of Namegosibiing where black bears sometimes feasted on spawning pickerel.

ogabanjiigosh: Wren.

ogiishkimanisii(g): Kingfisher(s).

ogimaakaan: A chief according to the system set up by the federal department of Indian Affairs.

Ogimaawish: One of Dedibaayaanimanook's relatives on her mother's side.

ogin(iig): Rose hip(s).

Ogojichan: Gweyesh Annie's puppy.

ogonjoonaagan(an): Fish net floats. Dedibaayaanimanook's parents made theirs from cedar wood.

ogwiimenzan: The person associated with a ceremonial name (a possessive noun). Dedibaayaanimanook honored the Namegosibii Anishinaabe custom in which a person's ogwiimenz name cannot be appropriated without the express permission of the name giver.

ojiig: Fisher.

ojijaakogaadaashk(oog): Fiddlehead(s). These were not eaten by Dedibaayaanimanook's family.

Ojijaakoons Paishk: An Anishinaabe man whose mother's name was Bizhiw and whose father was a wemitigoozhi; Ojijaakoons drowned at Gojijiing Goldpines.

ojikomishi(wag): redpoll (*mishi* refers to wood).

Ojiniigan: an individual who married into the Keesick family.

Ojoozhimimaa: Gichi Jôj's grandfather.

okik: Jack pine.

okikaandag(oog): Jack pine bough(s).

okoozh: Bird's beak/bill.

omaamaamaa: Motherhood.

Omagakiiwigiizis: June (the frog's month).

ombisijigan: Baking powder.

ombizinagens: Yeast.

omiimii(g): Pigeon.

omiimiisi(wag): Fish fly(flies).

omisenzan: Her/his older sister.

omiskoziis(ag): Water bug(s).

onaabiiginige: S/he plays a (specific) game using a piece of string.

onashkinachige: (S/he) fills a gun with gun powder.

oniijaanisan: His/her child.

onjigawa'ibaan: Birch sap as it is being collected.

onzaaminaajimo: S/he is exaggerating.

onzaawizhooniiyaawasin: Gold (the metal/ore).

oodenaang: (to, in) town.

Oojiiganang: The Big Dipper.

oojiigayaashk(wag): Type of tern/gull smaller than the gulls of Namegosibiing. The *—oojii* part of this term is a reference to the relatively small size of a tern, in the same way that a fly (oojiins) is small.

oojiigayaashkowaaw(an): The egg(s) of an oojiigayaashk.

opôganasin: The type of stone used for making a pipe.

Opôganasiniing: Pipestone Bay (Red Lake).

oshimis: Her/his niece (brother's daughter).

oshkagoojin: There is a new moon (i.e., a waxing crescent).

oshkiinzhigomin: Dewberry.

osigane: S/he pulverizes animal bones to extract the fat.

ososodamaapinewin: Tuberculosis.

owiibidii(g): A small fish that resembles a whitefish, but has teeth (not found in Namegosibiing Trout Lake).

ozhibii'iganak: Pen(cil).

ozhiininaganjige: S/he bites the shot to re-shape it.

ozikaansi: Rail (a marsh bird with a short tail and short wings).

ozikonaanaabo: Soup base made from ozikonaanibimide.

ozikonaanibimide: The fatty substance derived from finely crushed (bear or moose) bones.

ozow: His/her/its tail.

shkwaayaasige: The moon is waning.

sib: A reference to clear, pure water, such as the water that was once characteristic of the Namegosibiing of Dedibaayaan-imanook's childhood. Not many lakes are referred to as sib because very few were clear as was once the case with spring fed Namegosibiing. Most are referred to as zaa'igan (i.e., zaaga'igan) as in Wanamani Zaa'igan, Red Lake.

skaajimaniigin: A certain type of wool tartan fabric.

waabaagaminige: S/he drinks tea with milk (or cream), i.e., s/he adds milk to her/his tea.

Waabachaanish: Gichi Jii's paternal uncle.

waabaninoowe ondaaniman: Literally, the wind is blowing from tomorrow's direction, i.e., an easterly wind is blowing.

Waabashkiigaang: A particular place at the narrow channel between AanzigoZaa'igan (Otter Lake) and Namegosibiishishiing (Little Trout Lake) where Dedibaayaanimanook's parents and relatives always stopped for at least one night on their way to or from Lac Seul.

Waabashkosiiwagaang: An old name for Grassy Narrows.

Waabazaadiikaang: (White) Poplar Hill.

Waabigozhiishiwayaan: Aaniz (Gokom) Alice's mother (literally, mouse fur).

waabizheshi: Marten.

Waabizhingwaakokaang: The original name for Lac Seul.

waabooz(oog): Rabbit(s).

waabooz waazhaabaan: The production of rabbit fur strips for a rabbit skin blanket.

waaboozekon: Rabbit skin blanket.

waaboozekonemagood: Rabbit skin dress.

waaboozomiikana(n): Rabbit trail(s).

Waaboozoshimowin: the Rabbit Dance.

waaboozwôgon: Very fine snow that falls during certain weather conditions.

waadabiig: Tree roots.

waagikomaan: Crooked knife (for wood carving).

waagosh: Fox.

waakaasagibizon: The fabric portion in which an infant is bundled in a cradleboard.

Waakaashimowin: The Circle Dance.

Waanin: A man of mixed heritage (having one parent wemitigoozhi and another, Anishinaabe) who worked for the Hudson's Bay Company post at Lac Seul for most of his life. His wemitigoozhi father, Don McIvar, was known among the Namegosibii Anishinaabe people as Manidoo. Waanin spoke Anishinaabe and was a good friend of the Dedibayaash Keesicks. Dedibaayaanimanook last saw him when she was in Sioux Lookout for the birth of her second child.

Waaninaawangaang: The name for Sioux Lookout that makes reference to the sand.

waapijiibizon: A bunting shaped blanket in which infants slept during the night.

waasigan: Lightning.

waasikwegin: A smooth, cool fabric.

waawaashkeshi: Deer.

waawaashkeshiwimiijim: Meal made from deer meat.

waawaate: The auroras.

waawiyaazi: There is a full moon.

waazh: A burrow made by a small animal such as a mouse; a bear's den.

waazhike: It makes a burrow, such as when a rodent makes a burrowing nest.

waazooskodewa'am: A specific verb for the kind of canoe travel circumscribed by the areas of open water along the shoreline just before break-up.

waazooskodewin: That period in spring when the snow melts and freezes in characteristic ways.

wadenigwan: The snowflakes look like feathers.

wadoobaatig: A type of alder used for producing red dye.

wagidadin: (at/to the) top of the hill.

wanamani: An orange mashkiki that Anishinaabe people found in great abundance near Wanamani Zaa'igan Red Lake; it was also used for staining oars and for rock cliff paintings; red ochre.

Wanamani Zaa'igan: Red Lake.

wanangoosh(ag): Star(s).

wanii'igewin: Trapping.

Washkigwayaw: An Anishinaabe man who had a son (John), a daughter (Gikijii?) and a granddaughter, Mary Ann Bottle, who married Dedibaayaanimanook's cousin Shamaandi Kejick (Jiimis James Keesick's son) of Lac Seul.

wazhashk: Muskrat.

wazhashkowizh: A muskrat's dwelling during ziigwan.

wazhashkwedowensag: Dried apples.

waziswan: A nest, such as that of a bird, wasp, bee or other flying creature.

waziswanike: It makes a nest.

we'we(g): Snow goose (geese).

wemitigoozhi(wag): White man (men); Englishman (Englishmen); Euro-caucasian white man (men); English.

wemitigoozhiikwe: A white/English woman.

wemitigoozhiiwiziwin: Everything that is of the wemitigoozhiwag, including their customs, habits, ideas, beliefs, world views, institutions, systems, etc.

wiigobiin: Water grasses.

wiigwaas: Birch bark.

wiigwaasaatig(oog): (paper) birch(es).

wiigwaasijiimaan: Birch bark canoe.

wiijiiwaagan: Partner, spouse.

wiikenzh: Sweet flag; medicine derived from sweet flag rhizomes.

Wiikwedong: Thunder Bay.

wiinizis(an): Hair(s).

wiisaabikideng: Where the land has been recently cleared by a forest fire.

wiisaakodewikwe: A woman of mixed heritage (part Anishinaabe, part white/caucasian).

wiisaakodewinini: A man of mixed heritage (part Anishinaabe, part white/caucasian).

wiisagidakinookwe: How Dedibaayaanimanook's father expressed a cold, biting wind.

wiisigamin: The breeze is creating ripples on the lake; there is a gentle breeze blowing across the lake.

wiiyaasikewinini: Game warden; OMNR enforcement officer (literally, the man who takes care of wild meat).

wiiyaw: Body (that is left behind after death).

zaaga'igan (zaa'igan): Lake.

zaaga'iganiins(an): Small lake(s).

zaagiing: The mouth of a river.

Zaasibiman: James Angeconeb, Amanisookaan's brother.

zaaskwaaj: A mysterious, human-like being said to inhabit the deepest part of the woods.

zaa'weg: Perch.

zagakishinowag: The moose are resting to chew their cud. Anishinaabe hunters long noted that moose were scarcely seen for up to two weeks during the month of February when they remained quietly confined in one location to chew their cud. Whenever Dedibaayaanimanook's father noticed that there were no moose tracks at that time of year, he knew that they were resting.

zagataagan: Tinder.

zasakaabi: S/he is snow blind.

zegibanwôjiinzh: Cedar waxwing.

zesegan: Frozen rain.

zeseganaagon: Crystalized snow (it was used for making tea when travelling).

zhaabonigan(an): Needle.

zhaaboomin(ag): Gooseberry. Dedibaayaanimanook's cousins once came upon a clearing on a small island on Lac Seul Lake in which they found gigantic gooseberries.

Zhaaganaashii Nishôchiwag: The dance known as There Are Eight White Men.

zhaagigamiiwan: There is open water (i.e., break-up).

zhaashaagobiimagwaatig: Maple (said to be the moose's favorite food).

zhaashaawanibiisi(wag): Swallow(s).

zhaawaninoodin: A warm wind is blowing from the south.

zhagashkaandawe: Flying squirrel.

zhashagi: Pelican.

zhawenaniisi: Grackle.

zhigaag: Skunk.

zhiishiibanwiin: Shot gun shells; literally, duck bullets.

Zhiishiibishimowin: The Duck Dance (a dance introduced by wemitigoozhiwag in which participants were required to duck under each others' arms; however, Anishinaabe people preferred to think of the word as referring to the water bird).

zhiiwaagaminige: S/he add sweetener to her/his tea.

zhiiwaagamizigan: Syrup.

zhingibis(ag): Grebe ("hell divers," as Giigooyikewinini called them).

zhingobiig: Spruce boughs. In the days of Dedibaayaanimanook's mother's childhood, people use these for flooring and for matresses.

zhingosiwiminan: A type of berry.

zhingwaak(wag): White (Norway) pine(s).

Zhingwaako Minis: An island in Red Lake.

zhizhoobiigiiwin: Skin cream, lotion; ointment.

zhooniyaa ogimaa: Literally, the money boss; Indian agent.

zhoonzhaakwaa: Slippery surfaces have formed by water that has re-frozen during the night (a spring phenomenon).

zhoonzhagibii'an: There is (spring) slush on the ice. This stage precedes biinjskwajiwan that results in gichizigwaa.

zhôshkonibiikaa: It is slushy.

ziibiins: Creek.

ziigwan: It is early spring.

ziswesiminan: Chokecherries.

Asprey, David. <http://warsailors.com/forum/read. php?1,20594,20599#msg-20599,> July, 2005.

Coatsworth, Emerson S. The Indians Of Quetico. Toronto: University Of Toronto Press, 1957.

Digitalarkivet. 1900-Telling For 0301 Kristiania. RHD: 1900-Telling For 0301 Kristiania Digitalarkivet, June 11, 2005.

Haws, Duncan. Merchany Fleets, Vol. 34. Gateshead: Shield Publications, Ltd., 1998.

Helgason, Gudmundur. The U-Boats Of World War One, 1914-1918. <uboat.net>, September, 2005.

Hudson's Bay Company Archives (Winnipeg, MB), 1MA 34 B107/a/32, 33, 35.

Mancke, Elizabeth. A Company Of Businessmen: The Hudson's Bay Company And Long-Distance Trade, 1670-1730. Winnipeg: University of Manitoba, 19--.

Sjoforklaringer Over Kirgsforliste Norske Scibe i 1917. Sjøfartskontoret, Department Of Trade And Industry, Government Of Norway: Kristiania, 1917-1918, vol. 2, 124-130.

Smith, Gordon. Navies And Fleets, 1914-1918. naval-history.net, September 1, 2005.

Trout Lake Conservation Reserve Resource Management Plan, C2334. 2005.